What Is Good Academic Writing?

New Perspectives for English for Academic Purposes

Series editors: Alex Ding, Ian Bruce and Melinda Whong

This series sets the agenda for studies in English for Academic Purposes (EAP) by opening up research and scholarship to new domains, ideas and perspectives as well as giving a platform to emerging and established practitioners and researchers in the field.

The volumes in this series are innovative in that they broaden the scope of theoretical and practical interests in EAP by focusing on neglected or new areas of interest, to provide the EAP community with a deeper understanding of some of the key issues in teaching EAP across the world and in diverse contexts.

Forthcoming in the series
Pedagogies in English for Academic Purposes,
edited by Carole MacDiarmid and Jennifer MacDonald

What Is Good Academic Writing?

Insights into Discipline-Specific Student Writing

Edited by
Melinda Whong and Jeanne Godfrey

BLOOMSBURY ACADEMIC
LONDON • NEW YORK • OXFORD • NEW DELHI • SYDNEY

BLOOMSBURY ACADEMIC
Bloomsbury Publishing Plc
50 Bedford Square, London, WC1B 3DP, UK
1385 Broadway, New York, NY 10018, USA
29 Earlsfort Terrace, Dublin 2, Ireland

BLOOMSBURY, BLOOMSBURY ACADEMIC and the Diana logo are
trademarks of Bloomsbury Publishing Plc

First published in Great Britain 2021
Paperback edition published 2022

Cover design: Charlotte James
Cover image © Tuomas Lehtinen/ Getty Images

A catalogue record for this book is available from the British Library.

Library of Congress Cataloging-in-Publication Data
Names: Whong, Melinda, editor. | Godfrey, Jeanne, editor.
Title: What is good academic writing? : insights into discipline-specific student
writing / edited by Melinda Whong and Jeanne Godfrey.
Description: London ; New York : Bloomsbury Academic, 2021. | Series: New perspectives
for English for academic purposes | Includes bibliographical references and index.
Identifiers: LCCN 2020032078 (print) | LCCN 2020032079 (ebook) | ISBN 9781350110380
(hardback) | ISBN 9781350110397 (ebook) | ISBN 9781350110403 (epub)
Subjects: LCSH: Academic writing. | Language arts (Higher)–Correlation with content subjects.
Classification: LCC LB2369 .W438 2021 (print) | LCC LB2369 (ebook) | DDC 808.02–dc23
LC record available at https://lccn.loc.gov/2020032078
LC ebook record available at https://lccn.loc.gov/2020032079

ISBN: HB: 978-1-3501-1038-0
         PB: 978-1-3502-3504-5
         ePDF: 978-1-3501-1039-7
         eBook: 978-1-3501-1040-3

Series: New Perspectives for English for Academic Purposes

Typeset by Integra Software Services Pvt. Ltd.

To find out more about our authors and books visit www.bloomsbury.com
and sign up for our newsletters.

Contents

Notes on Contributors   vi

Foreword   ix

Introduction: The Good Writing Project   1
Melinda Whong and Jeanne Godfrey

1   A Collaborative Scholarship Model of EAP Research and Practice   9
    Jeanne Godfrey and Melinda Whong

2   The Written Discourse Genres of Digital Media Studies   31
    Simon Webster

3   Exploring Clarity in the Discipline of Design   57
    Clare Maxwell

4   Musicology and Its Others   83
    Karen Burland, Edward Venn and Scott McLaughlin

5   Good Academic Reflective Writing in Dentistry   111
    Marion Bowman

6   Dissertations in Fine Art   135
    Sara Montgomery

7   Good Writing in Linguistics   159
    Diane Nelson and Valentina Brunetto

Afterword   178
Ian Bruce

Index   191

Contributors

Marion Bowman is the International Tutor in the School of dentistry, University of Leeds, UK. Prior to working in EAP in Higher Education (HE), she taught biology at secondary schools in South Africa, and then TEFL (Teaching English as a Foreign Language) in Poland. She has an interest in supporting student writing within disciplines, and in how writing in the same genre differs in contrasting disciplinary contexts. She has experience of working within, and alongside, the curriculum in HE to enhance student academic writing in dentistry, computing, nursing, media studies and social work.

Valentina Brunetto is a Teaching Fellow in Linguistics at the University of Leeds. Her research interests are in the area of generative syntax and language acquisition. Her current research focuses on the processing of anaphoric relations and the interaction between complex syntactic structures and semantic interpretation. She teaches courses in linguistics as well as English for academic purposes.

Karen Burland is Professor of Applied Music Psychology at the University of Leeds, UK, and is currently Head of the School of Music. Karen has research interests in musical identities and their role in musical participation in a variety of contexts, including in music therapeutic settings. Karen is currently a University Student Education Fellow, and, in addition to her research on enterprise education, she is investigating the ways in which undergraduate and postgraduate students engage with, and perceive, employability activities during university and beyond. Her book *Coughing and Clapping: Investigating Audience Experience,* edited with Stephanie Pitts, was published in December 2014.

Ian Bruce is Senior Lecturer in Applied Linguistics at the University of Waikato in Hamilton, New Zealand. He has taught English and other languages in New Zealand and Japan. His research involves the application of genre theory to teaching academic writing. His theoretical approach is outlined in his book *Academic Writing and Genre* (2008), which has provided the basis for a number of published studies. His most recent book is *Expressing Critical Thinking through Disciplinary Text: Insights from Five Genre Studies* (Bloomsbury, 2020).

Jeanne Godfrey currently works at the University of Leeds Language Centre as a Teaching Fellow. She has been managing, teaching and writing in the fields of English language and English for academic purposes for over twenty-five years, and has held various posts in HE institutions, including BALEAP Chair, Head of Department, Principal Lecturer in Learning and Teaching, and Academic Writing Centre Director. Jeanne is also an author of student books. Recent titles include *How to Use Your Reading in Your Essays, Writing for University*, and *The Student Phrase Book* and *The Business Student's Phrase Book*.

Clare Maxwell is Lecturer in EAP in the Language Centre at the University of Leeds. She is currently seconded to the School of Design, where she is responsible for the design and delivery of bespoke in-sessional courses for taught postgraduate students. She has taught and co-led modules on the International Foundation Year programme and content-based pre-sessional programmes. Having previously taught for many years in Italy, she is author of EFL coursebooks widely adopted in Italian state schools. Her interests are in academic writing pedagogy, genre and disciplinary difference and specificity, with a particular interest in EAP in the Creative Arts.

Scott McLaughlin is a composer and Senior Lecturer at the University of Leeds. His research specializes in writing for the material indeterminacy of instruments; open-form music that explores the agential balance between instruments and humans in performance. Scott is Co-director of the Centre for Practice Research in the Arts (Leeds), and maintains an active interest in inter- and multi-disciplinary research and practice across the arts and sciences.

Sara Montgomery is a Teaching Fellow at the Language Centre, the University of Leeds. She started her EFL teaching career in Madrid, Spain, twelve years ago. Since 2011 she has worked in the UK, at the University of Southampton and at several private language schools, and in 2014 she joined the Leeds Language Centre. In this role her EAP and scholarship experience have developed due to involvement in the International Foundation Year and through module design, specifically for content-based pre-sessional modules. Her scholarship interests include multimodality and its links to EAP.

Diane Nelson is Senior Lecturer in Linguistics in the School of Languages, Cultures and Societies at the University of Leeds. A specialist in theoretical syntax and descriptive grammar, she has also taught academic writing and research methods to postgraduate students in linguistics for over twenty years.

Edward Venn is Associate Professor of Music at the University of Leeds. His pedagogical research focuses primarily on student engagement, particularly in digital and blended learning contexts. Between 2016 and 2019 he served as the Director of Student Education in the School of Music, and the Digital Education Academic Lead for the Faculty of Arts, Humanities and Cultures. He is Senior Fellow of the Higher Education Academy.

Simon Webster is Lecturer at the Language Centre at the University of Leeds, although he is partially seconded to the School of Media at the same institution. He has previously held posts as a language teacher and language teacher educator in a number of other European countries, in Asia and in the Middle East. His main research lies in the field of teacher cognition, where he has been principally engaged in teacher development studies. He also has a strong research interest in EAP disciplinarity and in the development of models of in-sessional EAP provision.

Melinda Whong is Associate Professor and Director of the Center for Language Education at Hong Kong University of Science and Technology. While she has taught in Asia, the Middle East and North America, her academic career includes over twenty years in the UK, most recently as Chair in Language Learning and Teaching at the University of Leeds. Originally trained in generative second-language acquisition, her career has been devoted to bridging the gap between linguistic theory and language teaching practice, most recently by promoting scholarship within EAP.

Foreword

Alex Ding, Ian Bruce and Melinda Whong, Series Editors

What Is Good Academic Writing: Insights into Discipline-Specific Student Writing is the first volume to be published in this series. In this foreword we would like, firstly, to briefly discuss some of the reasons for launching New Perspectives for English for Academic Purposes and then to locate how this volume fulfils the objectives we set for this series.

English for academic purposes (EAP) as a practice and discipline has developed significantly since its modest beginnings in the 1970s and we now have a full-fledged discipline with an ever-increasing body of research, publications, journals, associations, conferences and events. We know a great deal more now about the contexts and texts of EAP, using an array of established theories (genre theory, systemic functional linguistics, critical EAP and academic literacies) employing an ever more sophisticated range of methods and methodologies. However, there has been considerably less attention focused on other key areas and aspects of EAP, aspects such as (but not exclusively) the agency and identity of the practitioner, EAP pedagogies and the socio-economic contexts within which EAP occurs. This uneven development renders the knowledge-base of EAP somewhat unbalanced and partial, and a fuller, richer practitioner knowledge-base remains to be built.

The rationale for this series is to begin to redress this imbalance and begin to build to a richer knowledge-base by exploring aspects of EAP that we believe to be essential to EAP and essential to those researching and teaching in EAP but which, until now, have remained occulted, marginal or ignored. It's all too easy to assume that existing frameworks are the only frameworks when, in fact, there is no reason why other areas might not yield potentially useful insights, if explored more formally. The purpose of this series is to redefine and reorient EAP research and scholarship: to become the locus of cutting-edge EAP research in the coming years. This is why the three of us decided to launch this series.

What Is Good Academic Writing: Insights into Discipline-Specific Student Writing is the first volume to be published in this series, and we believe that this volume exemplifies many of the ambitions we hold for it. The chapters in this volume represent a local (University of Leeds) and collective endeavour by practitioners and content lecturers to understand better what is meant by 'good' student writing. This may seem a well-trodden path in EAP and this is perhaps partially true. However, this volume is significantly different in two important ways. Firstly, the questions, methods and approaches adopted by the authors reflect their concerns and interests in not only understanding student writing but importantly the motivation of all authors to improve and develop student education. The purpose of these authors is profoundly driven by concerns for the students they teach. It is the orientation of their work that is distinctive and this orientation is clear from the questions they ask and answer (which may or may not be the same questions and motivations of the EAP research community). Secondly, these projects and the subsequent writing up were undertaken alongside all their other professional activities, with only a small amount of time allocated to these projects. This is a positive example of what practitioners can individually and collectively contribute to knowledge with time and, most importantly, collegial support. We like to hope that this volume will inspire other universities and other language centres to believe that significant contributions to the EAP knowledge base can be achieved with adequate support and resources. Failure to support practitioners in their scholarship endeavours should be seen as an abdication of professionalism and limiting the knowledge that can usefully serve students and practitioners.

On a final note, we write this foreword in the midst of a global pandemic, and the outcome of this for EAP as a profession and for practitioners is unknown. What we can say is that EAP will undergo profound changes as a result, and we would hope that this volume contributes as a reminder of the values and value of EAP to the university community: to better understand students and practitioners and both their academic and educational needs, and to contribute to sharing our knowledge with them and our colleagues.

Introduction: The Good Writing Project

Melinda Whong and Jeanne Godfrey

This project is very much a product of time and place, in three different ways. To begin with, it reflects a trend within the academic discipline of English for academic purposes (EAP) towards a more discipline-specific orientation. As is desirable when there are developments in academic thinking, this trend has had a positive impact within institutional contexts. This is the second way in which this project is of its time and place, as it explores developments at one specific university in the north of England which took the ambitious step of moving all of its EAP provision to a discipline-specific orientation. While well grounded theoretically, revising the entirety of a curriculum was an ambitious endeavour, especially for a university as large as the comprehensive Russell Group institution in question. The concomitant requirement that all EAP practitioners would be expected, practically overnight, to deliver English for Specific Academic Purposes instead of English for General Academic Purposes provided a context in which there was much discussion and debate, and a strong need to work collaboratively both amongst EAP practitioners and with subject specialists. It is this context that brings us to the third feature which makes this project timely: the nature of EAP as a profession. To a large degree, casualization is still an unfortunate feature of an EAP career, especially at universities in English-speaking countries which rely heavily on international students for revenue. However, as EAP provision becomes recognized as valuable throughout a student's degree, more EAP practitioners are needed to provide EAP courses year-round. Year-round teaching means more stable full-time posts and even acceptance as members of the academic faculty – all of which leads to improvements for EAP as a profession. This level of development affords the opportunity for an environment in which EAP professionals can begin to work to their potential in terms of scholarly contribution within the academy. What is reported in this edited volume is a result of what is possible when a group of capable and committed practitioners are given a modest amount of support. What started out as a discussion amongst a small set of EAP practitioners evolved into what we hope will soon be much more the norm within EAP: a scholarship project about teaching and learning, for the benefit of student education which was conceived of, led and shaped by EAP practitioners in collaboration with subject specialists.

The idea for the 'Good Writing' project came about from a discussion which took place during a routine exercise of standardization amongst a group of EAP specialists with years of experience in teaching academic writing. What began as disagreement about what constituted good writing led to recognition of a gap of knowledge at a specific level in terms of what constitutes good writing in one discipline as opposed to another. It seemed to be a case of recognizing that the more you know, the more you realize just how much you don't know. For some time now, as the field of EAP has moved in the direction of discipline-specific specialism, EAP practitioners have needed to develop knowledge of practices, norms and expectations at the discipline-specific level. Yet development of such knowledge poses a challenge given the structural reality that EAP centres typically sit alongside academic disciplines. Conditions could hardly be more favourable than those within the institution which hosted this project: the EAP unit is respected as an academic unit, and an institution-wide approach of collaboration between EAP practitioner and subject specialist was brought in at university policy level. Yet as has been noted elsewhere, despite moves to embed programming within departments and access to discipline-specific practices (Wingate 2018), insider knowledge remains a challenge. A second motivation for this project was a desire to provide opportunity for EAP practitioners to exercise scholarly ambition. The reality is that many specialist teachers of EAP writing do not have the opportunity to engage in academic writing themselves. Taken together, these factors inspired the original idea for a project that would bring EAP and subject specialists together to explore what 'good writing' is at the subject level.

Participants in the project were identified based on a Call for Papers, sent out across the university. The initial plan was to match subject specialists with EAP specialists, forming pairs who would each co-author a chapter of an edited volume. In reality, it was naïve to think that academics who didn't know each other would be able to be paired up to conduct research. Instead, the volume includes some chapters authored by subject discipline specialists and some by EAP specialists. The shared motivation amongst all of the authors was a desire to develop better understanding of writing at the discipline level in order to be able to better articulate to students how to become successful writers themselves.

In order to ensure a level of coherence throughout the volume, a few parameters were established for each sub-project to adhere to. Each chapter was required to include analysis of student texts, with the suggestion of a focus at the level of postgraduate writing. In addition to contributing to a level of coherence, the thinking was that postgraduate level work would better exemplify discipline-specific differences than lower academic–level writing, which was assumed to embody more general academic features. Authors were also encouraged to explore the understanding of 'good writing' by lecturers in the discipline, based on the recognition that these are the people who ultimately differentiate between good and less-than-good writing when they mark their students' work.

The project from the beginning was conceived of as one of scholarship in the sense of Scholarship of Teaching and Learning (Fanghanel et al. 2015). In other words the research was devised wholly in the service of student education. As such, it required a level of commitment from each of the contributors which was to some degree 'above and beyond' required expectations. For the EAP practitioner contributors, a very modest amount of remit from teaching was given to allow time for the project. For the subject specialists, efforts had to come from time they would have otherwise given to research within their field. It remains to be seen whether the work done here would qualify as 'research' for the subject specialists. Indeed, it is hoped that one day, projects like this may no longer be seen as marginal activity within academia (Ding and Bruce 2017), but instead be fully respected and formally sanctioned.

While each chapter reports on a project conducted independently, regular communication with the Good Writing project contributors helped to ensure a level of coherence, and sought to provide any needed support. Contributors were invited to meet over 'working lunches' every six weeks or so, to compare notes and seek advice. This was also a place to identify areas where authors felt they could benefit from some specific training. We would like to thank Nigel Harwood for workshops that he generously delivered in support of the project, and Alex Ding for mentoring a number of the authors at the individual level. Working as a team of authors proved useful, especially for navigating the challenges of gaining access to appropriate examples of student writing and to securing permission for the use of student texts in a way that abided by ethical codes of practice. Regular communication also allowed us to debate some of the particulars of the project. In discussing the need for anonymity of student authors, for example, we quickly realized that it would be impossible to disguise the specific institution where this project was conducted, given that author information within this volume itself reveals institutional affiliation. Despite this, we agreed collectively to not name our institution, or to use specific department labels, because our findings and conclusions go beyond the local context. We also debated use of terminology. Because the points being made are not specific to the local context, efforts have been made to avoid institutional and/or national labels and practices, such as the choice of the word 'module' instead of 'course'. Where local or national practices are referred to, attempts have been made to define and/or clarify in order to ensure understanding. Other debates about terminology held wider significance. Whether to use the label of 'subject' or 'content' specialist, for example, is fraught with controversy. While trying to preserve a level of coherence, more often than not, we opted to allow each author to choose what seemed most appropriate within their specific project and the context of their particular discipline.

Another way in which coherence was achieved across projects was to require from the start a degree of coherence in terms of data and research method. Each of the chapters in this volume includes analysis of student texts; most also include considerations of the views of subject specialists who act as markers of student writing, thereby unwittingly defining what makes student writing 'good'. Each chapter is summarized below.

'A collaborative scholarship model of EAP research and practice' by Jeanne Godfrey and Melinda Whong

This first chapter of the volume situates the others by providing a general review of the EAP literature and mapping out the context in which the subsequent scholarship projects are situated. It also outlines pedagogic contexts and research frameworks that have informed research into student academic writing in the EAP field, particularly the ESP Genre Model paradigm. After summarizing ways in which these studies have generated important EAP pedagogy, Godfrey and Whong go on to discuss areas of research which they feel could be further developed both within and beyond the genre analysis framework. Turning to the question of student writing, the authors propose four specific areas of scholarship where they feel development is needed for better understanding what constitutes successful student writing. The authors promote an approach of collaborative scholarship between EAP practitioners and core-content tutors.

Key elements of the approach include the suggestion that the research agenda should be led by EAP practitioners, with analysis, discussion, implications and pedagogic application all being a collaborative effort between themselves and their core-content colleagues. In this way, the authors suggest, progress towards a fuller understanding of what constitutes good student writing could be made, with the aim of informing not only EAP practice but also how subject specialists articulate their concepts of successful writing to themselves and to their students.

'The written discourse genres of digital media studies' by Simon Webster

This chapter investigates academic writing in a relatively new discipline that stands apart from its social science relatives. It takes as a starting point the centrality of subject specialist perspectives in determining how 'quality' in student academic writing might be defined for the discipline. The chapter then describes a genre analysis methodology in which digital media studies subject specialists identify valued characteristics of a range of student academic writing discourse genres within the discipline. These genres span five separate genre families.

The chapter reports that a diverse range of academic writing characteristics were identified by the subject specialists as representing good academic writing during the research interviews. These features, however, could be seen to be specific to the individual discourse genres analysed and a patterning of desired characteristics identified for each. Furthermore, the work suggests that the discourse genres can be broadly grouped into either those that principally adhere to the academic conventions of the social sciences or those aligned to the professional conventions of the digital industries. The implications of these main findings are explored with the aim of providing the reader with an understanding of the academic writing skills required for the discipline and how these skills relate to the discipline's specific discourse genres.

'Exploring clarity in the discipline of design' by Clare Maxwell

This chapter focuses on a largely unfathomed and yet crucial aspect of student writing, that of clarity. Clarity is widely accepted as being crucial to good writing, and yet from an EAP perspective its subjectivity and multifaceted nature make it particularly difficult to explicate in a way that might help students enhance the clarity of their own writing. Through a small-scale exploratory study, the chapter examines the concept of clarity within the context of design. It draws on analysis of high-scoring dissertation-level assessments and interviews with subject specialists/assessors, in order to identify the different aspects of clarity considered to be key to good writing in the discipline, as well as features that are perceived to enhance or diminish written clarity. The study provides an interesting insight into subject specialists' perceptions of student writing, and what they value most highly. From this it considers the role that language plays in achieving written clarity, as perceived by those tasked with assessing students' work, in order to then consider implications for the teaching of EAP.

'Musicology and its others' by Karen Burland, Edward Venn and Scott McLaughlin

Music as a discipline is grouped within the arts and humanities, inheriting the writing practice and assumptions of that academic domain. Consequentially, good writing in music is centred on the argumentative essay and dissertation. However, since the late twentieth century there has been an increasing growth in music sub-disciplinary areas that draw on writing practices external to the arts and humanities. Thus electronic engineering, computer science, psychology, business and social sciences all offer significant source domains for music sub-disciplines commonly found across UK higher education, each bringing with them their own assumptions about good writing that intermingle with the dominant arts and humanities modality. This chapter uses semi-structured interviews to explore good writing in music from the perspectives of staff and taught postgraduate students across this range of music sub-disciplines. Discussion of the interviews centres on three areas that emerge as critical points across the sub-disciplines: criticality; developing a position, finding a voice; and teaching and learning argumentation. The interdisciplinary nature of a music degree – with students potentially studying across a range of sub-disciplines – leads to a fuzziness around writing genres that can be masked by the centrality of humanities modalities. Postgraduate study especially leans towards expectations that good writing engages with sub-disciplinary literature to enter the discourse of that community of practice.

'Good academic reflective writing in dentistry' by Marion Bowman

This chapter focuses on academic reflective writing (ARW), a new genre of student writing that is now widely used for the assessment of reflective practice in vocationally oriented higher education courses. As the author is based in a dental school, an insider's perspective of the student experience of ARW is presented. The hybrid nature of ARW is explored using high-scoring examples of two tasks from dentistry in combination with markers' insights. It is concluded that in order for student writers to successfully arrive at a transformed perspective of their clinical experiences, their writing must progress through a series of reflective levels. After selecting an appropriate case, the student writer must sketch the context, make personal links to the case, and analyse key features of the case either through reflective thinking or using literature, in order to arrive at a considered judgement with practical suggestions for future action. This complexity must be mastered within the constraints of what students feel it is permissible to say without falling foul of being judged as unprofessional against regulatory standards. In addition, the two tasks analysed here make contrasting demands on students which brings into question the notion of whether a coherent 'genre' is represented here.

'Dissertations in fine art' by Sara Montgomery

This chapter describes a small-scale study focusing on dissertations from a practice-based fine art master's (MA) course at a UK institution. The aims of the study were to gain insight into the purpose of the dissertation task, identify areas which may be challenging for the student writers and consider what are perceived to be good features of student writing according to subject specialists. The study included analysis of the task instructions as well as the assessment rubrics that were used to mark the work. The author conducted interviews with subject specialists who had contributed to marking the dissertations.

The dissertation task centres around the student writer considering their artistic practice in the context of contemporary culture and seeking inspiration, as well as aligning themselves with people undertaking similar work. Flexibility in planning is considered a good trait in construction of the dissertations; the content should remain loose enough to adapt to shifts in focus. Student writers devise their own research questions are encouraged to allow their research to be wide-reaching, perhaps cross-disciplinary. Well-developed research skills are necessary, particularly in selection of case studies. Features of good language are in how it is constructed, presenting clear arguments and having conviction.

'Good writing in linguistics' by Diane Nelson and Valentina Brunetto

Nelson and Brunetto focus on student writing in pure (or theoretical) linguistics, a discipline which, unlike the adjacent field of applied linguistics, has featured only rarely in the EAP literature. As an interdisciplinary field with a relatively young history, linguistics provides an interesting angle from which to observe the link between academic identities and epistemologies, and what is valued as good writing in the discipline. The authors argue that the unique nature of this field – which is at once 'hard' (drawing on the scientific method) and 'soft' (because of the evolving nature of its paradigms) – shapes features of writing such as the use of authorial voice and the use of evidence to support argumentation. Their analysis of student writing in MA and outstanding undergraduate dissertations shows that 'good' student writing in linguistics contains an awareness of these disciplinary conventions. Moreover, they show how a fine-grained analysis of student writing in the different sub-disciplines of theoretical and experimental linguistics can offer insights into the relation between methodological approaches in the discipline and student writing styles.

References

Ding, A., and Bruce, I. (2017). *The English for Academic Purposes Practitioner: Operating on the Edge of Academia.* Cham, Switzerland: Palgrave Macmillan.

Fanghanel, J., McGowan, S., Parker, P., McConnell, C., Potter, J., Locke, W., and Healey, M. (2015). *Literature Review. Defining and Supporting the Scholarship of Teaching and Learning (SoTL): A Sector-wide Study.* York: Higher Education Academy.

Wingate, U. (2018). 'Academic Literacy across the Curriculum: Towards a Collaborative Instructional Approach'. *Language Teaching* 51 (3): 349–64.

1

A Collaborative Scholarship Model of EAP Research and Practice

Jeanne Godfrey and Melinda Whong

Introduction

English for academic purposes (EAP) is a dynamic and growing field within English for specific purposes (ESP). EAP comprises two overlapping, yet distinguishable, centres of activity: pedagogy and research. There are EAP practitioners – academic professionals whose careers are primarily devoted to some form of teaching (many of whom also engage in academic scholarship to some degree), and there are also professional academics in the EAP field who engage in research while also sometimes practicing as teachers of EAP. In addition to these two overlapping profiles, there are also practitioners of the academic subjects that form the students' core course content, some of whom, for a range of reasons, find themselves teaching rhetorical conventions and associated lexico-grammatical features of English in the context of their discipline. In this chapter, we explore the potential for a collaborative approach to scholarship in which EAP and content specialists work jointly to explore academic practices.

In our exploration we focus on student academic writing. We begin by briefly setting the scene for EAP pedagogy and research respectively, before looking more closely at the relevant research on academic writing. As will become clear in our discussion, we have an orientation towards the context of UK higher education (HE) because this is where the research in this publication has been conducted. While this means use of local terminology at times, the concepts and argumentation are not bound by the UK context. Our exploration of academic writing highlights the fact that the ESP genre model is a predominant framework for EAP research and pedagogy, and our discussion of the literature leaves us arguing that while this approach is undeniably valuable, a more EAP practitioner-led scholarship agenda holds potential not only for nuancing our current understanding of academic genres, but for developing other areas of knowledge about student writing; moreover, we argue that such scholarship should involve both EAP and core subject practitioners. The second half of this chapter proposes four areas of scholarship that would benefit from such a collaborative approach. We begin, however, by giving a brief background to EAP, looking first at pedagogy and then at relevant research frameworks.

EAP pedagogic contexts

EAP as an area of pedagogy developed from the teaching of ESP in English-medium universities in the 1960s and 1970s, chiefly in Europe, North Africa and India. UK EAP expanded rapidly in the 1980s and 1990s, partly as a result of the drive of HE institutions to increase their intake of international students. The primary objective of EAP is generally agreed to be that of assisting students in achieving communicative competency in their academic community, with the underlying premise that it is possible to teach students the linguistic and para-linguistic features needed to operate successfully in their field of study.

In their summary of the development of ESP and EAP, Dudley Evans and St. John (1998) discuss the different levels of liaison between EAP and content tutors. They define co-operation as the first stage of EAP and content practitioner liaison, whereby the academic English teacher takes the initiative in acquiring knowledge of the conceptual and textual frameworks of their students' discipline(s). The next level of liaison is collaboration, where EAP and content tutor work together both inside and outside the classroom to design and prepare tasks and perhaps also team teach. An important approach to mention in this context is what is often referred to as 'embedded'. Examples of embedded provision are discussed by Dean and O'Neill (2011) in their 'Writing in the Disciplines' case studies. The book's contributing authors describe various forms of embeddedness, for example, that of academic writing tutors contributing to the redesigning of a first-year business studies degree module (Emmanuel et al. in Dean and O'Neill 2011). Wingate and others (Wingate 2015, Wingate, Tribble, Andon and Cogo 2011) have also helped to develop work in this area, for example, by conducting studies in which EAP-oriented tasks form part of the disciplinary course content, delivered either by the English language tutor or jointly between language and content tutor. The studies conducted by Wingate et al. have been influential in the growth of embedded provision in EAP, and Wingate has also looked at the benefits of 'collaborative-instructional' provision from an academic literacies perspective, demonstrating what she terms 'curriculum-integrated academic literacy instruction' (Wingate 2018). Developments in the embedding of EAP within the core disciplinary syllabus are based on two key premises; firstly, that developing EAP skills (and academic literacy skills in general) is important not just for students who use English as a second or foreign language but for all students; and secondly, that communication between EAP practitioners and content lecturers is fundamental for effective provision.

One result of the expansion and embedding of academic English teaching is that the EAP tutors find themselves developing an increasing amount of discipline-specific knowledge, together with the related challenge of trying to decide where the boundary is between teaching aspects of language and core content.[1] EAP tutors recognize that they are the linguistic experts, yet they often find themselves clarifying concepts and sometimes engaging in pedagogical activity which could be seen as teaching core content, for example, by giving a lecture on a subject in order to give their students listening practice.

The growth and development of UK EAP has occurred within the context of significant changes in UK HE. As noted by Murray and Sharpling (2019), the game-changing introduction of student fees has placed new levels of burden on academics, with students demanding higher levels of attention, and institutions being asked to demonstrate levels of teaching competence through, for example, the introduction of the Teaching Excellence Framework. There has also been a large increase in student numbers, particularly in the numbers of international students. These changes in the HE landscape have led to two specific outcomes. The first is that content academics are more likely to teach, and to teach language-related aspects of their discipline. One example of the latter might be a lecturer teaching an undergraduate degree in law giving her students a list of key phrases used in legal writing, or a revision of the style and structure required for a course 'Reflective Portfolio' assessment. The second (positive) outcome of the above changes in HE is an increase in the amount of resource and prestige for pedagogy and pedagogic research, with most universities now having centres for promoting teaching excellence. Related repercussions for EAP include a more fertile ground within academic departments for offers of joint working between core-content colleagues and those with expertise in academic English. Moreover, content tutors are more often engaging directly with their teaching in

---

[1] We recognize that the label 'content' as opposed to 'language' is problematic as the teaching of 'language' also entails content. We have settled for these labels in the absence of any other option that is any less problematic.

a way that allows for the development of expertise in academic literacy practices. Nesi and Gardner's (2006) interview-based research with content tutors reveals a strong feeling of responsibility for student rhetorical awareness, and an acknowledgement of the need to introduce students to the subject-specific conventions as part of their teaching remit. The net result of these trends can be seen as a coming together of EAP practitioners who are becoming more specialist in specific academic disciplines, and content tutors who are developing expertise in academic language.

In sum, progressive academic institutions and the EAP practitioners within them have increasingly recognized the need for an embedded approach to academic English and literacy provision within disciplines. Importantly, these offerings are increasingly accessible to all students as part of a positive process of academic development rather than as a remedial activity for non-native speakers of English. A generally agreed positive aspect of such provision is collaborative course design and teaching between EAP and core content practitioner.

EAP research frameworks

In this section we outline three key perspectives which have contributed to the orientation of research in EAP. The first and arguably most influential EAP research paradigm has been the ESP Genre Model. J.R. Martin and his colleagues were prominent in developing the concept of genre within ESP as a communicative event which is recursive, structured and staged and that exists to accomplish a particular social purpose (Martin 1985). As Wingate (2015) states, scholars such as Swales, Bazerman and Peck MacDonald have also helped to develop Halliday's concept of register in the context of specific academic genres, which members exploit to operate in their academic discourse communities. Swales, in particular, developed the idea of the 'moves' in scientific research papers needed to fulfil communicative purpose (Swales 1981, 1990). More recently, Bruce's dual genre perspective (Bruce 2008, 2009) looks at both the overall social purpose of the communicative event (the 'social genre') and at what he terms 'cognitive genre'; the way in which the text and language features are organized to fulfil an overall and/or individual cognitive purpose such as recounting, presenting an argument or explaining a process.

We need to note at this point that the complexity and fluidity of the concept of genre are recognized in the ESP Genre Model. Swales, for example, has over time reconceptualized the idea of communicative purpose as increasingly pluralistic and flexible, with genres able to be used by different participants for different purposes. He also notes that purposes evolve over time and across cultures (Askehave and Swales 2001; Swales 2004), and Bawarshi and Reiff (2010) similarly point out that the genres and lexico-grammatical choices through which they are manifested are continually changing. Examples of research findings that emphasize variation rather than conformity within genres include those of Biber, who notes that the degree of variation challenges our assumptions of what a genre typically contains (Biber 2002). Belcher and Hirvela (2005), looking at the qualitative dissertation, find that it is a 'fuzzy genre', and, more recently, Nathan's (2016) study establishes 'substantial variability' between the three different categories of thirty-six business-related case reports, noting that it would benefit tutors to be aware of such variation. We agree with Johns that 'genre as a research topic is nowhere near exhausted' (Johns 2013: 21).

A productive area of research within ESP genre studies is that of specificity. Contextualizing EAP within disciplines rather than across them has been increasingly acknowledged in the field as beneficial, and the work of Hyland and others has helped to promote general acceptance that there are meaningful differences to be found in the textual features of different disciplines (Hyland 2004a, 2004b, 2009a). As noted by Paltridge and Starfield (2013: 1050), Hyland's research demonstrates that the systematic structures within texts ensure a common understanding that is both context-specific and grounded in the intellectual community, but which poses significant challenges to students, who are likely to be focusing on content and epistemology rather than the conventionalized textual forms through which it is conveyed. Hyland and Shaw (2016) remind us that EAP students have their own particular purpose for studying and operating in English, namely to succeed in their chosen discipline, and that it is therefore appropriate for EAP practitioners and researchers to look at language patterns, conventions and features within specific academic disciplines and contexts rather than across them. North (2005) points out that we need to investigate which aspects of writing are generalizable and which are discipline-specific.

A second research framework that has significantly impacted EAP is that of critical theory and critical discourse analysis, through the work of scholars such as Lea, Street, Lillis, Turner, Wingate and Tribble. Lea and Street (1998, 2006) were seminal in using a critical perspective and the precept of language as social practice to examine the nature of the relationship between the institution and the student. Their Academic Literacies Model views this relationship as being primarily that of institutional exploitation of knowledge and power in order to maintain social control. In their seminal study, Lea and Street conclude that student writing 'problems' are in fact the result of tutors wrongly explaining academic writing in terms of surface features rather than as manifestations and representations of the theoretical, historical and ideological roots of their discipline. This surface approach incorrectly leads content tutors to conclude that 'poor' student writing can be 'fixed' by study skills practice and further socialization into the institutional academic culture (Lea and Street 1998).

Lea and Street, then, developed their model predominantly as a critical oppositional framework and tool for researchers rather than as a pedagogic approach (Lea 2004; Lea and Street 1998; Lillis 2003, 2006). Importantly, their framework addresses the context of whole institutions and all students rather than only the students with an L2 speaker profile who typically access EAP provision. Nevertheless, the questions and discussions generated by the academic literacies scholars have had a significant impact on EAP practitioners and researchers, and the academic literacies lens has been applied to aspects of pedagogy, as in, for example, Lillis' concept of student to tutor dialogue and student 'talkback' as opposed to feedback (Lillis 2003), and Wingate and Tribble's discussion of how principles from the fields of academic literacies and EAP can be shared to the benefit of both (Wingate and Tribble 2012).

There is one important, third thread in ESP and EAP research we would like to note here briefly. This is the ethnographic perspective, which provides a 'thick description' (Geertz 1973) of communicative events as an addition to textual analysis. Of direct relevance to our discussion further on in this chapter is the ethnographic perspective of research that incorporates the interviewing of staff and/or students as exemplified by, for example, Prior (1995), Tardy (2005), Gao (2012) and Krause (2001).

EAP research on academic writing: Through the lens of genre analysis

Let us return now to the research framework often used to analyse writing in EAP, that of the ESP Genre Model. In terms of professional academic writing, there have been many studies that look at sections of the published research journal article. Examples of such work include Brett (1994), Samraj (2002), Bruce (2008, 2009) and Basturkmen (2009, 2012). In addition to looking at sections of published papers, scholars have also investigated genre from the perspective of specific rhetorical functions. Notable here is the work of Ken Hyland, in, for example, his study of how authors express doubt and certainty (Hyland 1998), and his large-scale, cross-disciplinary study of authorial self-mention (Hyland 2001).

There is a cline between the two extremes of professional, published academic writing and that of student work, but distinctions between the two can be made. Studies focusing on student academic writing have, as with those looking at professional writing, often taken a genre analysis perspective, looking at how a genre's communicative purpose is manifested in features or aspects of language. They also often focus either on specific sections within a text (see for example Henry and Roseberry 1997; Samraj 2008) or on specific rhetorical functions throughout the whole text. Examples of the former include papers that examine dissertation acknowledgements (Hyland 2004c), and examples of the latter include studies which look at the language choices made by writers to convey engagement with the reader (Mei 2007) and authorial stance and voice (Hyland 2013). Hyland and Tse conduct a large corpus-based study to look at the differences in the metadiscourse of doctoral and master's dissertations between disciplines (Hyland 2004b; Hyland and Tse 2004).

An important third area of analysis of student writing is that of looking at how and to what extent these texts are situated within a particular genre. For example, Belcher and Hirvela (2005) look at qualitative dissertations, and Julia Huttner (2010) has compiled and used a corpora of fifty-five non-native speaker student essays to look at differences between student and expert genres. Bunton (1999) has conducted a genre analysis of the PhD thesis and higher-level metatext, and Moore and Morton (2005) have conducted a comparison of university student texts and International English Language Testing System (IELTS) writing. Finally, there are some interesting studies which look at the text types that surround student writing. There have been some large-scale studies that investigate disciplinary writing based on documents and information from lecturers, for example, Ganobscik-Williams (2004), Jackson et al. (2006), Melzer (2009) and Gillett and Hammond (2009). Hale et al. (1996) look at university tutor instructions for particular student writing tasks, and Paltridge (2002) compares the published advice on thesis and dissertation practices.

As shown above, an increasing number of genre analysis studies make use of corpora, enabling studies that use large data sets. Arguably one of the most influential of these has been that of Nesi and Gardner (2012), who compiled and analysed their British Academic Written English Corpus. This corpus consists of undergraduate and postgraduate student assignments which have all been awarded a mark of at least 60 per cent or equivalent, with 1,252 distinction-level and 1,402 merit-level texts.[2] Nesi and Gardner state that the overall aim of their study is 'to propose a system of describing and distinguishing between different types of tertiary-level writing tasks' (Nesi and Gardner 2012: 2), thereby enabling EAP practitioners to have a better understanding of the different types of writing students might need to produce.

To sum up, EAP genre-based research on student academic writing focuses on the communicative purpose of texts and on how these purposes are expressed at the level of organization and structure, and in turn how stages or moves are manifested at the level of sentence and phrase. Gardner and Nesi, for example, point out that they make use of systemic functional linguistic genre theory and its model of 'systematically relating the lexico-grammar through genre to assignment contexts' (Nesi and Gardner 2013: 27) in order to create their text categories. Examples they give of using language to identify genre are phrases such as '... will focus on ... ' or 'I will argue for ... ' found in essay introductions (Nesi and Gardner 2013: 34). As one reviewer of our chapter has pointed out, the focus on lexico-grammatical features in EAP pedagogy is gradually being replaced by an approach that develops students' genre awareness in terms of social and communicative purposes; nevertheless, the mapping of genre and text to the sentence and phrase remains a mainstay of EAP classroom practice.

EAP research on academic writing: Going beyond the genre lens

One concern we have about the predominance of a genre-based approach to the analysis of student texts is that it can lead to overgeneralized notions of conformity. Nesi and Gardner's study, for example, creates thirteen broad genre categories such as 'business', 'social sciences', 'humanities' or 'science'. Nesi and Gardner make clear that their categorization of different genres can only ever represent large genre families or prototypes within which there will be variation, and indeed, another important aim of their work is to generate more practitioner and also student awareness of the diversity of genres across disciplines. Nevertheless, the fact that they do present a nomenclature consisting of thirteen cross-discipline genre text-types (for example 'critique', 'proposal', 'literature survey') has been taken up and used by many EAP practitioners to

---

² In the UK system a 'merit' equates to 60–70 per cent while 'distinction' is any score above 70 per cent. Both are uncontroversially 'good', with any score above 75 per cent deemed exceptional.

fit the writing of their students into these categories. Indeed, Nesi and Gardner state their hope that 'readers [practitioners] can use these assignment types as templates or as stimulus for thought about the purpose and structure of the writing they expect their students to produce' and to 'serve as a reference for writing teachers to guide their students towards more appropriate stylistic and organizational choices' (Nesi and Gardner 2012: 2). Though it is probably not what Nesi and Gardner would want to promote, there is the danger that their findings can sometimes be taken by practitioners as definitive. While the value and usefulness of Nesi and Gardner's work and those of the other studies mentioned above are clearly evident from the amount of useful pedagogy and teaching materials they have generated, we feel that there would be benefit in being able to gain a more detailed understanding of, for example, 'the discursive essay' or 'writing in the social sciences'. We feel that investigations that can lead to a more nuanced understanding of writing practices would be beneficial for EAP teaching to students of all disciplines.

Another question we ask ourselves is how much genre-based studies really tell us about what constitutes 'good' student writing. Nesi and Gardner are careful to limit their analysis to merit and distinction level work, as are Woodward-Kron (2002), who uses twenty distinction-level essays to look at the role of descriptive writing in critical analysis, and Nathan (2016), who conducts a genre analysis of thirty-six business-related case reports marked as 60 per cent or above. However, such studies select top mark assignments using two assumptions; firstly that a high mark correlates with 'correct' or 'good' use of features of the genre, and secondly that this correlation is causal. We feel that it is worthwhile looking at the extent to which these assumptions are correct. There are a handful of studies we have so far found that explicitly include quality of work in their analysis. Petric (2007), for example, takes eight high- and eight low-grade MA theses written by ESL students, and Tribble and Wingate (2013) compare high- and low-scoring student texts. However, these studies use the same correlative assumptions as mentioned above.

One interesting study that does question the assumption of a causal link between accepted use of genre and writing being deemed 'good' is that of Tardy (2016), who looks at what student writing content tutors consider to be good even when it breaks with genre norms, and what types of genre flouting tutors mark down. Tardy reminds us of Bhatia's 'liberal' and 'conservative' genres (see Bhatia 2006), according to which some genres are more tolerant of innovation than others. Tardy interviews tutors and finds that creative content and evidence of logic, authority and awareness of situation and form can make a student text 'good' in the eyes of the tutor despite it being written in a way that steps far outside genre norms. She contrasts one genre-breaking 'good' student text with another that follows all the genre rules yet is considered 'poor' by the tutor. Importantly, the student who produced the good writing is not an expert writer consciously manipulating the genre, but one unconsciously making genre errors which are nevertheless more than compensated for by the text's interesting, sophisticated and creative content, thereby showing a good grasp of the subject matter. Tardy emphasizes that her work shows the need for understanding which genres can be played with, in which contexts and by whom.

Such discussions, combined with the aforementioned recognition of the fluidity of genre as a concept, have inspired us to question the nature of the link between the use of typical features of a particular genre and the production of 'good' student writing. We also take inspiration from scholars such as Freadman (2016), who, although coming from the perspective of new rhetoric studies rather than ESP, describes what she calls 'genre traps'. In her discussion Freadman identifies the problem of the constraining nature of genre as an issue in both rhetoric and ESP pedagogy, pointing out that genre analysis looks at recurrent and typified text, and that while useful, this does not tell us what is good or not good about these textual patterns. She argues that 'mastery of the genre may mean little more than the ability to avoid making egregious errors in controlled environments' (Freadman 2016: 8763). We also draw inspiration from another study by Nesi and Gardner (2006), in which they interview fifty-five content tutors from across a range of disciplines. Although the primary aim of this piece of research is to identify types of student writing by genre across different broad disciplinary categories, Nesi and Gardner also include questions which allow them to draw some very general conclusions about what tutors feel makes writing successful. Particular aspects mentioned by subject specialists are coherent structure, originality and creativity, critical analysis, argument development and clarity. What has yet to be determined, however, is how to capture these aspects in a way that can be taught to novice writers.

To summarize so far, we recognize that the existing ESP genre model used as the basis for much research and pedagogy in EAP has been fundamental in the development of both – indeed, it is the starting point of our own approach. Moreover, we appreciate the fact that the concept of genre in ESP and therefore EAP is complex and has benefitted from a range of critical perspectives, as outlined above. However, while we agree that student writing with a high mark can assumed to be 'good', the work of Tardy and others outlined here inspires us to question the extent to which the good mark does or does not correlate with normative features of text. What we propose here, therefore, is that the use of the ESP genre research framework to evaluate 'good' student academic writing is perhaps restrictive, with limitations arising from both the overgeneralization of genre categories and an assumption that what is typical in student writing is what makes it good. We note the need to investigate the following four questions: how much and in what ways 'typical' in terms of genre contribute to 'good' student texts; whether and in what ways non-typical genre moves contribute to 'good'; what other, non-genre aspects of typical texts might contribute to 'good' (for example reader engagement), and finally, what non-genre and non-typical aspects of language and text can constitute good writing.

Crucially in this chapter, we suggest that in order to investigate questions like these, much is to be gained when the people directly engaged in working with students on their writing explore the question. It is not a coincidence that our interest in the nature of the relationship between features of genres and evaluations of 'good' student writing has arisen from taking the perspective of the practitioner. We suggest that the addition of the EAP practitioner lens to the existing scholarship in the field holds much potential for going beyond the current genre model, and is key to progressing towards the ultimate aim of enabling a pedagogy that addresses what students understandably want: the ability to produce good, or better yet, 'excellent' academic writing.

Researching student writing: A way forward

Based on existing work in genre analysis in the field of EAP, there are a number of useful avenues down which a practitioner-led approach could lead us. In this section we identify four areas of scholarship that could benefit from practitioner attention, thereby developing both existing genre analysis research in the ways described above, and research that looks outside genre. Our aspiration is that, in time, these investigations will provide the missing pieces of the 'good writing' puzzle and ultimately provide an expanded basis for EAP pedagogy.

Firstly, there is scope for achieving a better understanding of existing findings from both within and outside the body of genre analysis studies, particularly with the needs of the EAP practitioner in mind. While the sound scholarship in academic writing to date has produced useful generalizations about this type of written discourse, the specific implications for teaching are less clear, because the findings have not yet shown us definitively how to help students achieve good writing. We see scope for systematic and in-depth exploration of these generalizations in order to explore the extent to which they are useful and effective, gaining further insight into which ones are most useful in helping our students write well. While such scholarship might be done in a number of ways, our suggestion of how to do this draws upon a type of methodology that does not tend to be associated with research in EAP, namely a more controlled experimental research method. One could, for example, manipulate texts to include or not include specific features in order to explore responses to specific generalizations (such as the choice to use quotation versus citation) and then give the texts to content tutors for marking. While one would not want to draw definitive conclusions from a single study done in this way, over time a robust body of experimental research could lead to useful understandings. This type of inquiry might provide evidence which allows us to better understand the causal relationship between features of text and judgements of quality, if any.

A second area of useful scholarship would be to get much more student writing data, and to do so through a practitioner lens. As shown in the chapters in this volume, practitioner analysis of student writing can lead to questions and perspectives which differ from those of established EAP research because the orientation of the analysis is different. Practitioners are strongly guided by the needs of their students, and if this orientation is also grounded in existing research and associated theory, practitioner analysis of student writing holds potential for a valuable additional angle on the complex endeavour to better understand the properties of text. Moreover, purely in terms of quantity, if a fraction of the large number of EAP practitioners began to engage in text analysis, this work could contribute to some of the gaps that still exist at the discipline-specific level. Studies looking at subjects that are under-reported in the literature and/ or are more fringe, emergent or inter-disciplinary would be particularly useful. Gathering more data in these subjects would be valuable not only because they would add to the overall amount of data, but also because as Paltridge et al. note, 'in new and emerging areas of study diversity is valued and there is less restriction on what a student can do in their writing' (Paltridge et al. 2016: 105). There is no limit to the amount of investigation needed to keep up with what is likely to be a never-ending requirement, given that disciplinary and cross-disciplinary practices are not static. Consideration of text through a practitioner lens could also contribute to developing a more nuanced understanding of broad generalizations that currently exist, such as the pedagogic assumption that 'complex ideas require complex sentence structure'. It would also be useful for the practitioner scholar to add to the current research that explores student writing in terms of educational context, for example, at the level of institution type, departmental culture or even individual content tutor.

A third area which could benefit from practitioner attention, particularly in relation to the marking of student writing, is a focus on the content tutor. Paul, Charney and Kendall (2001), for example, go beyond analysis of text to look at how texts are received as the measure of good writing, exploring how successful texts are in terms of audience impact. Tardy (2016) also calls for closer consideration of the role of the content tutor in perceptions of good writing. As already highlighted, in exploring the types of innovations in student writing that are valued by individual tutors, Tardy presents the case of a student text deemed good by the content tutor, despite its flouting of commonly accepted textual norms. This raises interesting questions about the relationship between features of text and the content tutor's priorities in evaluating student writing. We make the related observation that in looking at the links between tutor values and marking student writing, the critical perspective of the Academic Literacies Model outlined earlier would seem to be relevant, focusing as it does on the power relationships between tutor and student.

Murray and Sharpling (2019) have also considered the role of the content tutor, noting a need for further research to determine whether what is presented in EAP textbooks as good writing aligns with what content specialists say. They also discuss the role of the individual tutor in using assessment criteria, pointing out that different markers tend to notice and give value to different elements of the criteria, and stressing that it is the personal perception of the tutor that really counts in how student writing is measured against criteria. Nesi and Gardner's 2006 study also reveals that even when content practitioners use generic, institutionally imposed assessment criteria, they interpret them in a subject-specific way.

As noted earlier, tutors are able to articulate what makes writing good in general terms, but while useful as a starting point, this area would benefit from more in-depth research. In exploring content tutors' thoughts about student writing as part of an ethnographic approach, there is need for better understanding of their values, priorities and practices as they approach the task of marking. Hyland notes that content tutors' comments in feedback can convey 'implicit messages about the values and beliefs of the academic community' (Hyland 2009b: 132), and Huttner (2010) goes further and proposes the useful concept of the extended genre to capture the idea that considerations of genre need to take into account the marker and their values as 'secondary genre owners'. Echoing this sentiment but from a teacher perspective, Neumann (2001) notes the importance of individual academic's core beliefs in shaping disciplinary teaching, stating that diversity in practice is under-recognized, with research investigating this diversity being 'surprisingly embryonic'. By making the values of the content tutor the centre of research into writing, it may be possible to expand the EAP repertoire, offering another lens through which to understand EAP. Arguably, the EAP practitioner's remit to teach students to succeed in their academic study leaves them well placed to explore the perspective of the content tutor in relation to student writing. In sum, further research in this area holds potential to add to the thickness of description of student writing.

The fourth and final area in which we see scope for practitioner contribution is in the development of a meaningful metalanguage with which to understand, talk about and develop pedagogy related to academic writing, as both a process and a product. There is a small amount of pedagogical metalanguage in EAP that has been developed, including Wingate's 2012 essay writing framework and Davies' 2008 model for teaching inferential patterns. Generally, however, EAP relies heavily on the metalanguage developed by and for linguistic analysis, using concepts such as theme and rheme, rhetorical function and other discourse and lexico-grammatical markers that comprise meaning-making. We feel that there is potential for the development of a form of nomenclature, perhaps some type of 'assessment criteria language'. Such a metalanguage, oriented to both tutors and the students, would be useful not only for explaining to ourselves what we mean when we talk about 'good writing' within the EAP field, but also of agreeing on these explanations with content tutors. Importantly, a metalanguage may help to better explain to all parties the features that are more or less good than others. To illustrate, Nesi and Gardner (2006) note that content tutors value writing that is 'clear'. But what do they mean by this exactly? And do tutors from different disciplines (or even different tutors within one discipline in one institution) mean or expect different aspects or forms of writing which to them are 'clear'? Perhaps clarity has more to do with evidence of clear thinking than linguistic structures, and, if so, what is the relationship between clarity of thought and clarity of expression in writing? Opening the door to these kinds of questions could potentially lead to a rich set of agendas, all to the benefit of EAP in terms of both research and pedagogy.

In summary, we have suggested four areas which we see as ripe for further practitioner exploration: (i) a better and more practitioner-oriented understanding of existing findings; (ii) the gathering of more data and across a wider range of discipline areas, particularly in less reported, fringe, interdisciplinary and emergent fields; (iii) analysis of the values, understandings and practices of those academics who mark student writing; and (iv) the creation of a metalanguage to facilitate better understanding of the why and the how of good student writing. Fundamental to these is the suggestion of a practitioner-led orientation, leading us to the proposal of a model for how this research could be conducted.

A collaborative approach to scholarship: A model for research into student academic writing

Our argument for the *what* of research then, broadly speaking, involves going beyond a focus on typical features of standard text formats to see what other aspects of student writing content tutors consider to be 'good'. We feel that gaining this content tutor perspective is most powerfully arrived at via a collaborative scholarship approach between content tutor and EAP practitioner. This collaborative approach goes beyond the embedded EAP pedagogical approaches outlined earlier in this chapter, as it ventures into the realm of scholarly enquiry. We take encouragement from the work of Wingate and others in demonstrating the positive effects of collaborative design and planning of materials and interventions and also the mutual support that can develop between the writing and content practitioners. What we argue here is that both EAP pedagogy and its supporting theoretical perspectives would benefit from a further step. A collaborative scholarship approach would go beyond co-operation and collaborative task planning, design and delivery, to include working together to produce research perspectives and questions, and the conducting of investigations that address them. However, we also suggest that in such a partnership between content and EAP tutor, scholarship should be led by the EAP practitioner. It is the EAP practitioner who has the specialist knowledge of EAP – including knowledge of both what we know about academic writing, and what we still do not know, with access to this knowledge across disciplines. From this privileged position the EAP practitioner can potentially take the lead in developing the metalanguage for describing textual and linguistic features in student writing. This is not to suggest that the EAP practitioner is more important than the content specialist in the project. It is the content tutor who is able to guide the work in terms of the values and priorities within discipline, and who is likely to hold the key to gaining meaningful access to the relevant students, texts and fellow academics. Indeed, with content specialists having interest and knowledge in areas which have traditionally been the domain of EAP specialists, and with EAP specialists developing discipline-specific content knowledge through working within disciplines, the distinction between specialisms may blur somewhat in what might hopefully be explicit, examined and constructive ways. An important aspect of such blurring might be to help create opportunities for transformative relationships of legitimacy between student writer, content tutor and EAP practitioner as proposed in the academic literacies framework. Our vision sees a genuinely joint approach, with a healthy marriage of EAP and content tutor expertise.

The third and final part of this model is explicit recognition that the ultimate aim of the research is to improve upon classroom practice. It is this that classifies this type of research as scholarship. While also contributing to the growing body of knowledge in EAP, the end point should match the starting point, that is, student education. With this in mind, the final point in our model is to call for explicitly stated implications for teaching as a requirement for the research, echoing Cheng (2019). We recognize the limitations of research which, by nature, can sometimes be too theoretically removed to hold specific applicability. We do not see this as a problem per se. But our sense is that practitioner-led research as called for here is suitably 'near' enough to classroom practice that explicitly named implications for teaching should be possible.

The three core elements described above are the reason that we refer to our approach as a collaborative model for scholarship on student writing. Our proposed approach is a way of investigating student academic writing which is practitioner-led, while drawing on the strengths that both EAP and content specialists have to offer, and which is ultimately oriented to improving students' ability to write academic texts. A collaborative approach could include not only exploration of student writing, but also the conducting of joint research into curriculum design and pedagogy. It could also contribute to the repertoire of a meaningful metalanguage for understanding student writing in the full-range disciplines. Importantly, a rich collaborative model will see a range of methodologies used, so that we look not only at genre, but beyond it, to investigate what makes good – or even excellent – student writing.

Conclusion

We look forward to having a fuller understanding of what constitutes good student writing. Perhaps it is when the 'typified' is used in a way that seems invisible, letting the content, criticality and creativity shine through with minimum reader effort.

Perhaps clear content that aligns with reader expectations and values can sit above the structural features and patterns used to convey the content. Perhaps, in fact, the relationship between style and content is less clear than we think, especially in terms of the extent to which each contributes to the evaluation of writing. Our suggestion for a collaborative scholarship model is, we argue, one way to better understand this. It could also allow for a continuous and dynamic research dialogue between EAP and content practitioner within disciplines and sub-disciplines to the benefit of all. In short, we call for an opening up of scholarly exploration, urging practitioners to take the lead in working in collaboration with subject specialists.

References

Artemeva, N., and Freedman, A. (2016). *Genre Studies around the Globe: Beyond the Three Traditions*. Canada: Inkshed Trafford publishing.

Askehave, I., and Swales, J. M. (2001). 'Genre Identification and Communicative Purpose: A Problem and a Possible Solution'. *Applied linguistics* 22 (2): 195–212.

Basturkmen, H. (2009). 'Commenting on Results in Published Research Articles and Masters Dissertations in Language Teaching'. *Journal of English for Academic Purposes* 8 (4): 241–51.

Basturkmen, H. (2012). 'A Genre-based Investigation of Discussion Sections of Research Articles in Dentistry and Disciplinary Variation'. *Journal of English for Academic Purposes* 11 (2): 134–44.

Bawarshi, A. S., and Reiff, M. J. (2010). *Genre: An Introduction to History, Theory, Research, and Pedagogy*. West Lafayette, IN: Parlor Press.

Belcher, D., and Hirvela, A. (2005). 'Writing the Qualitative Dissertation: What Motivates and Sustains Commitment to a Fuzzy Genre?' *Journal of English for Academic Purposes* 4 (3): 187–205.

Bennett, N., Dunne, E., and Carré, C. (2000). *Skills Development in Higher Education and Employment*. US: Taylor & Francis.

Bhatia, V. K. (2006). 'Genres and Styles in the World'. In Kachru, B. B., Kachru, Y., and Nelson, C. L. (eds.), *The Handbook of World Englishes*, 446. Malden, MA: Blackwell.

Biber, D. (2002). 'On the Complexity of Discourse Complexity: A Multidimensional Analysis'. *Discourse Processes* 15: 133–63.

Brett, P. (1994). 'A Genre Analysis of the Results Section of Sociology Articles'. *English for Specific Purposes* 13 (1): 47–59.

Bruce, I. (2008). 'Cognitive Genre Structures in Methods Sections of Research Articles: A Corpus Study'. *Journal of English for Academic Purposes* 7 (1): 38–54.

Bruce, I. (2009). 'Results Sections in Sociology and Organic Chemistry Articles: A Genre Analysis'. *English for Specific Purposes* 28 (2): 105–24.

Bunton, D. (1999). 'The Use of Higher Level Metatext in Ph. D Theses'. *English for Specific Purposes* 18: S41–S56.

Cheng, A. (2019). 'Examining the "Applied Aspirations" in the ESP Genre Analysis of Published Journal Articles'. *Journal of English for Academic Purposes*, 38: 36–47.

Davies, M. W. (2008). '"Not Quite Right": Helping Students to Make Better Arguments'. *Teaching in Higher Education* 13 (3): 327–40.

Deane, M., and O'Neill, P. (2011). *Writing in the Disciplines*. Basingstoke, UK: Macmillan International Higher Education.

Dudley-Evans, T., St John, M. J., and Saint John, M. J. (1998). *Developments in English for Specific Purposes: A Multi-disciplinary Approach*. Cambridge: Cambridge university press.

Emmanuel, M., O'Neill, P., Holley, D., Johnson, L., and Sinfield, S. (2011). 'Taking Action in Business'. In Deane, M. and O'Neill, P. (eds.), *Writing in the Disciplines*. Basingstoke, UK: Macmillan International Higher Education.

Freadman, A. (2016). 'The Traps and Trappings of Genre Theory'. In Artemeva, N. and Freedman, A. (eds.), *Genre Studies around the Globe: Beyond the Three Traditions*. Canada: Inkshed Trafford publishing.

Ganobcsik-Williams, L. (2004). *A Report on the Teaching of Academic Writing in UK Higher Education*. London: Royal Literary Fund.

Gao, X. (2012). 'The Study of English in China as a Patriotic Enterprise'. *World Englishes* 31 (3): 351–65.

Gardner, S., and Nesi, H. (2013). 'A Classification of Genre Families in University Student Writing'. *Applied Linguistics* 34 (1): 25–52.

Geertz, C. (1973). *The Interpretation of Cultures* (Vol. 5019). New York, US: Basic books.

Gillett, A., and Hammond, A. (2009). 'Mapping the Maze of Assessment: An Investigation into Practice'. *Active Learning in Higher Education* 10 (2): 120–37.

Haas, S. S. (2018). 'Aargh! This Essay Makes Me Want to Poke Sticks in My Eyes!' Developing a Reader Engagement Framework to Help Emerging Writers Understand Why Readers Might (Not) Want to Read Texts'. *Journal of Academic Writing* 8 (2): 137–49.

Hale, G., Taylor, C., Bridgeman, B., Carson, J., Kroll, B., and Kantor, R. (1996). 'A Study of Writing Tasks Assigned in Academic Degree Program'. *TOEFL Research Reports* 44: RR–95.

Henry, A., and Roseberry, R. L. (1997). 'An Investigation of the Functions, Strategies and Linguistic Features of the Introductions and Conclusions of Essays'. *System* 25 (4): 479–95.

Hüttner, J. (2010). 'The Potential of Purpose-built Corpora in the Analysis of Student Academic Writing in English'. *Journal of Writing Research* 2 (2): 197–218.

Hyland, K. (1998). 'Boosting, Hedging and the Negotiation of Academic Knowledge'. *Text-Interdisciplinary Journal for the Study of Discourse* 18 (3): 349–82.

Hyland, K. (2001). 'Humble Servants of the Discipline? Self-mention in Research Articles'. *English for Specific Purposes* 20 (3): 207–26.

Hyland, K. (2004a). *Genre and Second Language Writing*. Michigan, US: University of Michigan Press.

Hyland, K. (2004b). *Disciplinary Discourses, Michigan Classics ed.: Social Interactions in Academic Writing*. Michigan, US: University of Michigan Press.

Hyland, K. (2004c). Graduates' Gratitude: The Generic Structure of Dissertation Acknowledgements. *English for Specific Purposes* 23 (3): 303–24.

Hyland, K. (2009a). 'Writing in the Disciplines: Research Evidence for Specificity'. *Taiwan International ESP Journal* 1 (1): 5–22.

Hyland, K. (2009b). *Academic Discourse: English in a Global Context*. A&C Black.

Hyland, K. (2013). 'Undergraduate Understandings: Stance and Voice in Undergraduate Reports'. In Hyland, K., and Guinda, S. (eds.), *Stance and Voice in Written Academic Genres*. Basingstoke, UK: Palgrave Macmillan.

Hyland, K., and Shaw, P. (eds.) (2016). *The Routledge Handbook of English for Academic Purposes*. Abingdon: Routledge.

Hyland, K., and Tse, P. (2004). 'Metadiscourse in Academic Writing: A Reappraisal'. *Applied Linguistics* 25 (2): 156–77.

Jackson, L., Meyer, W., and Parkinson, J. (2006). 'A Study of the Writing Tasks and Reading Assigned to Undergraduate Science Students at a South African University'. *English for Specific Purposes* 25 (3): 260–81.

Johns, A. M. (2013). 'The History of English for Specific Purposes Research'. In Paltridge, B., and Starfield (eds.), *The Handbook of English for Specific Purposes* (Vol. 592), 5–34. West-Sussex: Wiley-Blackwell.

Krause, K. L. (2001). 'The University Essay Writing Experience: A Pathway for Academic Integration during Transition'. *Higher Education Research and Development* 20 (2): 147–68.

Lea, M. R. (2004). 'Academic Literacies: A Pedagogy for Course Design'. *Studies in Higher Education* 29 (6): 739–56.

Lea, M. R., and Street, B. V. (1998). 'Student Writing in Higher Education: An Academic Literacies Approach'. *Studies in Higher Education* 23 (2): 157–72.

Lea, M. R., and Street, B. V. (2006). 'The "Academic Literacies" Model: Theory and Applications'. *Theory into Practice* 45 (4): 368–77.

Lillis, T. (2003). 'Student Writing as "Academic Literacies": Drawing on Bakhtin to Move from Critique to Design'. *Language and Education* 17 (3): 192–207.

Lillis, T. (2006). 'Moving towards an Academic Literacies Pedagogy: "Dialogues of Participation"'. In Ganobcsik-Williams, L. (ed.), *Academic Writing in Britain: Theories and Practices of an Emerging Field*. Basingstoke, Hampshire: Palgrave.

Martin, J. R. (1985). 'Process and Text: Two Aspects of Semiosis'. In Benson, J. D., and Greaves, W. S. (eds.), *Systemic Perspectives on Discourse* (Selected Theoretical Papers from the 9th International Systemic Workshop, Vol. 1), 248–74. Norwood, NJ: Ablex.

Mei, W. S. (2007). 'The Use of Engagement Resources in High-and Low-rated Undergraduate Geography Essays. *Journal of English for Academic Purposes* 6 (3): 254–71.

Melzer, D. (2009). 'Writing Assignments across the Curriculum: A National Study of College Writing'. *College Composition and Communication* 61 (2): W240.

Moore, T., and Morton, J. (2005). 'Dimensions of Difference: A Comparison of University Writing and IELTS Writing'. *Journal of English for Academic Purposes* 4 (1): 43–66.

Murray, N., and Sharpling, G. (2019). 'What Traits Do Academics Value in Student Writing? Insights from a Psychometric Approach'. *Assessment & Evaluation in Higher Education* 44 (3): 489–500.

Nathan, P. B. (2016). 'A Genre–based Study of Case Response Writing on an MBA Programme'. *Journal of Academic Writing* 6 (1): 122–33.

Nesi, H., and Gardner, S. (2006). 'Variation in Disciplinary Culture: University Tutors' views on Assessed Writing Tasks'. *British Studies in Applied Linguistics* 21: 99.

Nesi, H., and Gardner, S. (2012). *Genres across the Disciplines: Student Writing in Higher Education*. Cambridge, UK: Cambridge University Press.

Neumann, R. (2001). 'Disciplinary Differences and University Teaching'. *Studies in Higher Education* 26 (2): 135–46.

North, S. (2005). 'Disciplinary Variation in the Use of Theme in Undergraduate Essays'. *Applied Linguistics* 26 (3): 431–52.

Paltridge, B. (2002). 'Thesis and Dissertation Writing: An Examination of Published Advice and Actual Practice'. *English for Specific Purposes* 21 (2): 125–43.

Paltridge, B., and Starfield, S. (eds.) (2013). *The Handbook of English for Specific Purposes* (Vol. 592). West-Sussex: Wiley-Blackwell.

Paltridge, B., Starfield, S., and Tardy, C. M. (2016). *Ethnographic Perspectives on Academic Writing*. Oxford University Press.

Paul, D., Charney, D., and Kendall, A. (2001). 'Moving beyond the Moment: Reception Studies in the Rhetoric of Science'. *Journal of Business and Technical Communication* 15 (3): 372–99.

Petrić, B. (2007). 'Rhetorical Functions of Citations in High-and Low-rated master's Theses'. *Journal of English for Academic Purposes* 6 (3): 238–53.

Prior, P. (1995). 'Redefining the Task: An Ethnographic Examination of Writing and Response in Graduate Seminars'. *Academic Writing in a Second Language: Essays on Research and Pedagogy*, 47–82.

Russell, D. R. (1991). *Writing in the Academic Disciplines, 1870–1990*. Carbondale: Southern Illinois University Press.

Samraj, B. (2002). Introductions in Research Articles: Variations across Disciplines. *English for Specific Purposes*, 21 (1): 1–17.

Samraj, B. (2008). 'A Discourse Analysis of Master's Theses across Disciplines with a Focus on Introductions'. *Journal of English for Academic Purposes* 7 (1): 55–67.

Swales, J. (1981). *Aspects of Article Introductions*. Michigan, US: University of Michigan Press.

Swales, J. (1990). *Genre Analysis: English in Academic and Research Settings*. Cambridge University Press.

Swales, J. (2004). *Research Genres: Explorations and Applications*. Cambridge: Cambridge University Press.

Tardy, C. M. (2005). 'Expressions of Disciplinarity and Individuality in a Multimodal Genre'. *Computers and Composition* 22 (3): 319–36.

Tardy, C. M. (2011). ESP and Multi-method Approaches to Genre Analysis'. *New Directions in English for Specific Purposes Research*, 145–73.

Tardy, C. M. (2016) 'Bending Genres, or When Is a Deviation an Innovation?' In Artemeva, N., and Freedman, A. (eds.), *Genre Studies Around the Globe: Beyond the Three Traditions*. Canada: Inkshed Trafford publishing.

Tribble, C., and Wingate, U. (2013). 'From Text to Corpus–A Genre-based Approach to Academic Literacy Instruction. *System* 41 (2): 307–21.

Wingate, U. (2012). '"Argument!" Helping Students Understand What Essay Writing Is About'. *Journal of English for Academic Purposes* 11 (2): 145–54.

Wingate, U. (2015). *Academic Literacy and Student Diversity: The Case for Inclusive Practice*. Bristol, UK: Multilingual matters.

Wingate, U. (2018). 'Academic Literacy across the Curriculum: Towards a Collaborative Instructional Approach'. *Language Teaching* 51 (3): 349–64.

Wingate, U., and Tribble, C. (2012). 'The Best of Both Worlds? Towards an English for Academic Purposes/Academic Literacies Writing Pedagogy'. *Studies in Higher Education* 37 (4): 481–95.

Wingate, U., Andon, N., and Cogo, A. (2011). 'Embedding Academic Writing Instruction into Subject Teaching: A Case Study'. *Active Learning in Higher Education* 12 (1): 69–81.

Woodward-Kron, R. (2002). 'Critical Analysis versus Description? Examining the Relationship in Successful Student Writing'. *Journal of English for Academic Purposes* 1 (2): 121–43.

2

The Written Discourse Genres of Digital Media Studies

Simon Webster

Introduction

Digital media studies is a relatively new, burgeoning and fast-evolving discipline (Flew 2014). The strong demand for digital media studies programmes in higher education institutions internationally and the rapid consolidation of digital media studies as a distinct field of study are perhaps unsurprising in light of the digital turn (Westera 2013). However, although students are generally required to produce academic writing on these programmes, there is a dearth of literature which identifies digital media studies discourse genres and which explores issues of quality in this writing. Given the importance of discipline-specificity for academic writing development and instruction (Hyland 2000), such a lack of empirical research presents a problem for both the digital media studies student and the EAP practitioner alike.

This chapter reports on EAP practitioner research that was conducted in response to this need for greater understanding of academic writing for digital media studies. Set in a UK higher education context, the research explores subject specialists' understandings of the discourse genres that the students are required to produce at undergraduate (UG) and postgraduate (PG) levels of study. It therefore forms part of an EAP tradition of aiming to better understand the written products expected of students outside the classroom (Hardy and Friginal 2016; Sharpling 2002) so that conceptions of disciplinary academic discourse norms do not rely on 'intuition or folk beliefs' (Harwood 2005: 150). Such genre insights can then be adopted by EAP practitioners to help students become 'academic insiders' (Olwyn, Argent and Spencer 2008) through their knowledge of relevant disciplinary genres.

Literature review

Academic writing genres

A genre can be considered 'a distinctive category of discourse of any type, spoken or written' (Swales 1990: 3). Although there is strong interest in genre study more broadly (see, for example, Miller and Devitt 2019), in the context of student academic writing, genres would include, for example, laboratory reports, research proposals and essays (Nesi and Gardner 2012). The concept of genre has been fundamental in the study of second-language writing in ESP (Johns 1997; Hyland 2007; Tardy 2009). On the basis that student academic writing will be most successful when it adheres to the conventions expected by the academic community (Hyland 2008), genre studies have sought to identify predictable features of written academic discourse genres. Well-established research into such genre features has resulted in considerable understanding of rhetorical text functions that feature in written discourse genres (e.g. Swales 2004; Samraj 2005; Swales 2004). As well as identifying the diversity within genre groups, the degree of 'openness' of individual discourse genres (i.e. the degree to which they demonstrate bound characteristics) has also been explored in this research (see, for example, Swales 1990; Bhatia 2004).

The notion of genre is also important as a basis for EAP programme design and classroom pedagogy (Flowerdew 2000). Understanding of genre establishes the kinds of texts that are expected in the target context, their structure and the disciplinary paradigm underpinning why they are written as they are (Hyland 2007). For students, the explicit needs analysis that disciplinary genres provide often results in a positive response to genre-oriented tasks in academic writing materials (Jou 2017). Indeed, EAP practitioners have exploited such insights into academic discourse genres for pedagogic purposes through, for example, the use of genre exemplars in the EAP classroom (see, for example, Cheng 2008; Hardy, Römer and Robertson 2015) since an exemplar provides 'a textual instance which is required for the realisation of a specific written genre' (Tribble 2017: 31).

Writing within specific disciplines

Recognition of differences in disciplinary academic writing is central to ESP and EAP practices (Hyland 2000) with genre research closely associating disciplines with specific genres (Cheng 2008). Although text genres reflect the broad values of the community in which they are produced (Miller 1984), academic text genre research has also highlighted the significant disciplinary differences that exist within genres (see, for example, Hyland and Shaw 2016). These variations, it can be seen, reflect the respective academic traditions and conventions of the individual disciplines. Such an understanding calls into question the value of generalizing academic writing practices across disciplines and genres (see, for example, Hyland and Tse 2009). Indeed, as Nesi and Gardner (2012: 2) point out, 'successful assignments are those which achieve the intended purpose of the writing task, with due acknowledgement of disciplinary norms and expectations.' Students therefore need to develop specific academic literacies (Lea 2004; Lea and Street 2000) associated with their field of study, and the quality of academic genre writing will depend on its appropriateness and ability to '[consider] particular settings or social circumstances' (Roe and den Ouden 2018: 3). It is also worth noting that these local settings result in considerable diversity within the disciplines themselves (Trowler and Wareham 2008; Kuteeva and Negretti 2016).

This recognition of disciplinarity in discourse genres has long had implications for the teaching of academic writing and, indeed, there have been attempts to make such disciplinary differences in writing explicit for academic writing instruction (e.g. Hardy and Friginal 2016). Whilst EAP practitioners are increasingly seeking greater disciplinary-specificity in their EAP teaching (De Chazal 2014), however, there are challenges to identifying what this disciplinary specificity constitutes. One approach to achieving a better understanding of written discourse genres has been to analyse the writing tasks set by subject specialists (see, for example, Moore and Morton 2005; Carter 2007). As Melzer (2009) argues, in advocating such an approach, 'instructors' writing assignments say a great deal about their goals and values, as well as the goals and values of their discipline' (Melzer 2009: 240). However, such information is normally implicit and the assignments themselves often lack the detailed rationales that would facilitate a deeper understanding of subject specialists' expectations (Haggis 2006). This suggests the need for an evidence-based pedagogy (Tribble 2017) and that subject specialists' explanations of the discourse genre requirements for their assignments would be a useful development. According to genre-based EAP pedagogy, students can then be sensitized to identify genre structures through a process of 'rhetorical consciousness-raising' (Hyland 2007: 13) in which genre knowledge is made more explicit (Tardy 2009).

Digital media studies

Both 'new media studies' and 'digital media studies' have been applied as labels to academic courses related to digital practices. The shift away from the term 'new media' can, in part, be explained by the fact that media technologies which are now considered to be old were themselves once considered to be new (Flew 2014). However, 'new media', rather than focusing primarily on specific technologies, could also be understood to explore 'the contemporary cultural concepts and contexts of media practices' (Dewdney and Ride 2006: 20). The present study adopts the term 'digital media' throughout to reflect its established dominance both in academic programme nomenclature and as a preferred term in academic literature in the field.

If we apply Belcher's (1989) classic classification of disciplines based on their epistemological characteristics, digital media studies' relatively unspecified theoretical structure and its relationship with real-world issues would situate it alongside other social sciences as a soft, applied discipline. The study of digital media, however, can be approached from a range of disciplinary paradigms, including sociology, computer science, social psychology, the creative arts and applied humanities (Livingstone 2005). It is important, therefore, to clarify that this study explores digital media studies within the institutional context of a school of media and communication. In addition, whereas many media programmes contain elements of digital media (television studies or digital photography courses, for example), digital media studies as a field can be viewed as encompassing both the production of digital artefacts and a critical consideration of the affordances and implications of digital practices (Reyna, Hanham and Meier 2018).

Academic writing in digital media studies

There is a lack of published disciplinary-specific EAP writing materials available for students and EAP practitioners with only a limited range of subject areas, such as business (e.g. Bailey 2015) and electrical engineering (e.g. Smith 2014), represented. EAP writing course books tend to focus on the development of general academic writing skills and, even where a recognition of genre differences exists, the genres included tend to be very limited (e.g. case studies, literature reviews and reports in Day 2018) and discipline-free. Within the field of digital media studies, this lack of disciplinarity in academic writing materials is also very evident. The literature is instead limited to professional text writing for digital platforms such as multi-media products and the Web (see, for example, Garrand 2006; Kuehn and Lingwall 2018). There is also a literature, though not relevant to the scope of this present study, on digital media writing where this refers to instances of digital writing with images and digital audio files as opposed to text (see, for example, DeVoss et al. 2005). For academic writing purposes, therefore, digital media studies has tended to be subsumed under the broader category of social science writing, where there has been considerable research into genre characteristics of argumentative essays (see, for example, Hyland 1990; Wingate 2012; Bruce 2018).

Methodology

Methodological rationale

This research is predicated on the understanding that subject specialists are the ultimate arbiters of what constitutes quality in students' academic writing since it is they who assign assignment grades in accordance with the literacy values of the academic community to which the students are aspiring (Wingate 2016). The current study consequently adopts an emic approach (Silverman 2016) to capture a fine grain, contextualized understanding of subject specialists' expectations regarding student academic writing, including their understandings of specific tasks and the programme-wide and institutional contexts in which student academic writing is produced. The research fully acknowledges the subjective nature of the perspectives accessed as even individual subject specialists within the same faculty may have different interpretations of what constitutes good writing (Thaiss and Zawacki 2006). However, such qualitative research offers the potential for themes to emerge which will provide insight into the subject of the research (Cohen, Manion and Morrison 2007) and where differences in data generated can be as significant as the commonalities (Stake 2010).

Research question

This research aims to answer the question: What do higher education digital media subject specialists believe represents good student academic writing in the field?

Research setting and the participants

The research was conducted in a large, established school of media in a UK higher education setting. Email invitations to participate in the study were sent to the six subject specialists identified as delivering core modules on digital media programmes at UG and/or PG levels. Of these six potential participants, five responded positively and one of the subject specialists declined to respond. Informed consent was obtained for each of the five final participants.

Research methods

Semi-structured interviews (Kvale 1996) of approximately one hour were conducted with each of the five participants. This interview format was designed to facilitate clarification and probing of participants' responses to take place (Kvale and Brinkmann 2009) and for interviews to flow naturally whilst exploring predetermined core areas of interest for the research (Drever 2003). In advance of the interviews, the participants were each asked to provide two pieces of distinction-level student academic writing that they had personally assessed for assignments on core digital media modules. These assignments (with accompanying task description, task guidance, assessment criteria and formal assessment feedback) formed the basis of the interviews, with participants asked to explain their understanding of the tasks and the student academic writing exemplars. The 'talk around texts' (Lillis 2008: 355) therefore served to access 'insider community understandings of [their] rhetorical effectiveness' (Hyland 2005: 178).

The interviews were structured to first explore the subject specialists' beliefs regarding the field of digital media studies and the implications of this framing for students' written academic assignments. The second stage involved an interviewer-guided in-depth analysis of the academic writing practices in the selected assignments. During this stage, elements of the formal assignment feedback were introduced for the participant to discuss with reference to the respective assignment. In the third stage, the participants were invited to comment on any additional aspects of the student work that they believed to constitute good academic writing practice. The interviews were all audio-recorded.

Student academic writing was chosen for the study because 'expert performances' (Bazerman 1994: 131) such as textbooks and research articles are not representative of the assessed genres which students have to write (Tribble and Wingate 2013), and it is unrealistic to expect students to write like professionals (Hardy and Friginal 2016). The apprentice exemplars chosen therefore 'constitute a more realistic target performance than professional genres' (Flowerdew 2000: 37). Each participant chose exemplars from two different assignment tasks and the selection of these tasks was negotiated between the researcher and the individual subject specialists to include a range of assessment tasks from across the school's two digital media degree programmes (one UG and the other PG).

It is worth noting that the L1 status of the authors of the exemplars was not a consideration in this selection process since, as Tribble (2017) argues, what is most important is how representative exemplars are of agreed practices.

Data analysis

The interview audio-recordings were professionally transcribed and the transcripts checked for accuracy by the researcher. Relevant sections of the transcriptions were then cross-referenced to the sections of the student academic writing referred to in the interviews. After initial readings to familiarize myself with the content and identify emerging themes (Cohen, Manion and Morrison 2007), data was then coded using commercially available software according to themes which emerged through a largely inductive process (Kennedy 2018) but which were also guided by broad *a priori* categories central to the main research question. The emerging themes were then revisited and refined through a cyclical coding process (Miles and Huberman 1994).

Research ethics

Institutional ethical approval was granted for this research project, and informed consent (Murphy and Dingwall 2001) was obtained from all of the research participants. All data was held securely in an anonymized form, and participants were guaranteed confidentiality and anonymity in the published findings. As I was a colleague of the participants, it is necessary to recognize the ethical issues surrounding this relationship (Kimmel 1998) and the potential pressure for subject lecturers to participate. However, I exercised no institutional authority over the participants and they appeared to engage with the research as a collaborative undertaking to explore disciplinary academic writing to the benefit of the students.

Findings

Findings introduction

In total, ten distinction-level written academic assignments were analysed during the five interviews. This sample represented eight separate assessment tasks as two of the subject specialists selected student work from the same

Table 2.1 Discourse genres by genre family.

Genre family	Discourse genre
Report	Internet policy report (UG) Mobile media report (UG) Interface design evaluation report (UG)
Research proposal	Research proposal (UG)
Argumentative essay	Mobile media essay (UG) Critical essay (PG) Critical essay (PG)
Reflection	Critical reflection (PG) Critical reflection (PG)
Research project	Dissertation (PG)

assessment tasks. The discourse genres of the student academic writing analysed are grouped by genre family and listed in Table 2.1. The discourse genres, which are listed in the right-hand column, are additionally labelled as being at either a UG or a PG level of study.

The presentation of findings that follows is structured by genre family. Within each of the genre family sections, subject specialists' understandings of individual pieces of student academic writing are reported in turn. The five subject specialist participants appear anonymized as participants A–E. The section begins with the findings for subject specialists' analysis of the written reports produced by the digital media studies students.

Digital media studies reports

Report One (Participant A)

The first written report was a UG assignment for which the students were required to produce a report in which the most important Internet policy challenges relevant to the workings of a chosen platform were explained. The subject specialist interviewee, participant A, explained that the assignment guidance included a template for the structure of the report and that the student assignment selected for analysis had adopted this structure effectively:

> When you look at the kinds of documents that you get in policy studies and policy reports, it's all headers and sub-headers according to various arguments and evidence that make up the documents […] This student has shown insight in the choice of platform and been very systematic in applying legal concepts and developing the content in each section.

The participant also highlighted the importance of evidence and explanation for the report:

> This is unlike a standard discursive essay in that it requires a high degree of evidence and explanation, which reflects the nature of policy studies. It's not like an argument essay. It just needs good evidence.

He identified the following written report extract as exemplifying this desired use of evidence:

> According to the [Chinese] regulations, all registered users must release their personal information including ID numbers or other indirect identifiers to service providers for government verification.

The language of such reports, according to the participant, should be 'impersonal' and 'informational' in line with industry norms in report writing. The inclusion of language such as 'chilling effect' and 'Chinese citizens have figured out a way', which appeared elsewhere in the student's text, was therefore regarded as inappropriate, whereas the following sentence was cited as being more indicative of the required informational language:

> [Sina Weibo] has seen a decline in the competitiveness since 2013 partly due to the excessive government manipulation of its services and WeChat, a social media platform offering a semi-public communication environment.

Report Two (Participant B)

The second report analysed was a UG assignment in which students were required to design a digital media product in response to an identified current need or opportunity. The assignment task description was as follows:

> Produce a specification report, detailing exactly how your system should be implemented, containing items such as a site map or process map, designs and screenshots or storyboards showing the user journey through a system. [The report] should also include a risk assessment/mitigation brief and predicted budget and timescale.

The subject specialist, participant B, provided the following explanation of the task:

> For this task, the students have to develop a new system to solve a problem which they have identified through their analysis of mobile media literature. They need to develop an informed and argued rationale for the proposed system and then to produce the appropriate accompanying documentation with a competitor analysis, fee breakdown, risk assessment and concept work, etc. Students will be used to seeing these documents and usually follow the standard industry format

we show them. The academic writing here requires very clear, simple language in an accessible report format. It's that skill you often see with text on professionally-produced websites with good integration of concise text and graphics.

For the participant, a particular strength of the selected student assignment was that it adopted an industry-standard structure:

> So, you can see that the report is structured as we might expect. So, how the new system works, the timeline, the risks involved, problems and suggested solutions for the product design ... It also follows industry conventions in the production of specification documentation for the system design and structure.

He also valued the clarity of the student's report writing and chose the following extract from the report as an example of text which 'is direct, concise and unambiguous':

> Solution: Programme a push-notification to appear in the case of missing nutritional or recipe information to let the user know that the information they are requesting is not yet available.

The skilled integration of text and graphics also required for the task was identified in the following extract:

> Tap the button to segue to a View Controller with the recipe of the photographed dish.
>
>   (with an arrow indicating corresponding graphics)

In addition, clear rationales for the product design that appeared in the student's report writing were positively rated. The participant provided the following example as demonstrating 'a clear case for [the student's] product design based on previous research':

> A study by Vaterlaus et al. (2014) finds that recipes on social media are very appealing and recipe apps widely downloaded because individuals are genuinely interested in discovering new and palatable recipes in a convenient way. The emphasis on convenience suggests that this app should be designed.

Report Three (Participant E)

The third written report task was a UG website evaluation. The interviewed subject specialist, participant E, explained that the task was designed to reflect digital media professional processes:

> We ask the students to write an evaluation of a website to inform their own practical work, which is industry standard practice.

For the participant, the report requires the effective application of industry-recognized criteria and he identified an instance of this feature of good report writing in the following extract:

> The website lacks clearly defined areas, as most pages have a lot of information with few distinctive areas or logical links with information, making the site cluttered and difficult to scan – which was a criticism from the focus group (Appendix One). To improve this, the content can be organised into clearly defined areas using boxes, and dividers can indicate that information belongs to a section.

He goes on to state that the standard assessment criteria adopted across the digital media programme do not fit such written reports:

> So, that is not a formal academic piece of research as such. It's a written piece, but we shouldn't be applying written criteria like referencing and depth of knowledge and understanding and things in something that is a more commercially oriented piece of writing [...] I create new criteria to fit the specific tasks.

This distinction that is made between the report and other assignment tasks also becomes evident in the degree of formality expected. Owing to the practical nature of the assignment, the subject specialist states the following:

> This is somewhere in between something where we can say, 'Don't worry about how this is written'. It's not like the design blogs where we say, 'This is just you reflecting and thinking about colour or typography' or something. But it's also not at the other end of the spectrum. It's not their final dissertation or something.

Thus, the participant regarded the use of the personal pronoun 'we' as being acceptable in 'We produced an online survey, which was shared on Facebook' whilst he also commented positively on the more formal tone created by the use of the passive voice in the relative clause. He also highlighted the need for students to substantiate their arguments in the reports:

> Quite often, we get the first years coming in and stating something that either is or sounds like their own personal opinion and I have to say, 'This is not the place for this. Obviously, you can have an opinion but that opinion needs to be substantiated in some sort of way, or some sort of evidence in line with the argument of another scholar or something'.

The following sentence from the chosen report provides an instance where this desired substantiation was identified as lacking:

> However, there were some disadvantages, such as the reactive effects of the face-to-face interactions, but this was reduced as participants were comfortable enough to speak freely.

Digital media studies research proposal

Proposal One (Participant A)

This section presents the findings for the UG written research proposal assignment that was included in the study. The task description was as follows:

> You will produce an essay-length research proposal which describes an independent study that could be feasibly carried out in the future. You will not actually carry out the research, but you will explain how the study would be conducted.

A template for the proposal with headings and sub-headings was provided in the assignment guidelines. The subject specialist, participant A, explained that this template was to encourage the same content organization required for grant applications:

> The way I sort of prepared them for that was I gave them some examples of essentially funded research proposals like AHRC, which have clear kind of boxes you have to complete, usually online, on things like impact, ethics, the methods you're going to apply. […] The subheadings are the same in these assignments.

The student research proposal analysed was regarded by the participant as having not only adopted the required structure but having shown 'clear thought and argument'. The following extract was identified as an example of good argumentation as it provides a conclusion arrived at through the systematic introduction of appropriate support:

> Twitter could therefore be seen as a key platform to raise awareness for causes that exist outside mainstream politics, especially movements that criticise the status quo.

The participant also identified language in the student assignment which reflected that featured in the formal documents studied on the course. In the methodology section, for example, these included: 'A potential flaw in the research is … ' and 'The research has thus been designed to minimise subjective analysis.'

Digital media studies argumentative essay

Essay One (Participant B)

The first student essay task required UG students to identify a specific development in mobile media and critically analyse its relationship to society. The subject specialist, participant B, explained that students could choose the content and structure they felt most appropriate for the essay and that critical argumentation was the priority:

> There's no set way for students to do this but they need to develop a critical argument and avoid just being descriptive. We assess this work according to the school criteria for undergraduate work so that's knowledge and understanding, intellectual skills and then presentation [and referencing].

He identified strong paragraphing as being 'essential' for good academic essay writing and provided the following commentary on a paragraph from the student essay analysed:

> If we look at this section – 'With Snap Maps represented as a cartoon map where 'avatar' friends travel round the map like a game board, Snap Maps can be likened to the idea of 'gamification' – it gives a clear focus to the paragraph and then the student goes on to develop that concept of gamification in the rest of the paragraph before moving onto a separate idea.

He also highlighted the strong writing stance in the student's discursive writing as being highly significant in his positive evaluation of the work. The following extract provides an instance of this stance from the student's essay:

> Snap Inc. argues Snap Maps is the next big way of meeting up with and engaging with friends nearby (Snap Inc., 2017). This essay will argue the contrary, that it is a privacy and surveillance concern, with possible detrimental effects on its users and wider society.

Additionally, the participant noted examples of formal written style that he regarded as being appropriate for such an argumentative essay. He commented, for example, on the fact that the use of the phrase 'a user may choose not to share their location with any of his or her friends' successfully avoids the use of the personal pronoun 'you', which he associated with weaker writing. He also stated that his expectations of such features of a student's academic writing increased in tandem with the student's stage of study:

> The undergraduate students, especially first years, may not have done much formal essay writing beforehand so I make allowances and provide more guidance. Clearly, by the time we get to MA dissertations, we're expecting them to be show a much stronger understanding of academic style.

For the participant, conciseness and precision also contributed to the quality of the academic writing as in the following extract:

> Snapchat is an image sharing mobile app, popular for the ability to send self-deleting timed photos, videos and chats.

Essay Two (Participant C)

The second essay analysed was in response to a PG assignment task with the following title:

> What are the strengths and limitations of approaching digital media as [data/narrative/code/sensory]? What does such an approach reveal and mask? What does this suggest to you about methods?

The subject specialist, participant C, regarded the task as 'a standard discursive essay', adding that 'it was explicitly structured around engaging critically with one or more of the methods that they'd been practising and trying out in the practical sessions'. She identified the paragraph below as an example of the critical thinking required for such an essay:

> There is a group called spammers or organised posters who use this platform to seek profit [...] When the researchers collect the data from the social media platforms to visualise, the posts of spammers are included in their raw data. Researchers use data cleaning to mask them and then visualised the cleaned data, which leads data to an incomplete state in data visualisation.

In addition to highlighting the successful questioning of the reliability of data in this extract, the participant also added a comment in the formal feedback that provides further insight into the critical thinking she sought in the essay:

> If you could add an extra sentence in which you say that this calls into question the very idea of being able to get truthful data, you would have nailed it.

Whilst critical thinking and its development through strong paragraphing were central to the participant's focus, she also placed value on the formal style of the students' academic writing and the use of disciplinary lexis:

> The sentence 'Data visualisation can be employed to reveal the relationship among data, which is greatly different to simply enumerating data' creates the right kind of tone. All of these expressions like 'social network communities' and 'targeted blog posts' create concise and precise meanings that we use as a matter of course but that students have to pick up very quickly.

The participant was also conscious of her own preferences in students' academic writing. Her comments on students' written conclusions are included below as an example:

> By the time we get to the end, I know what the students have said and don't want to read it all again repeated in a long summary of their earlier points. I know they have been taught to do that but it doesn't help to show the quality of their understanding.

These comments are particularly revealing as they contrast with the personal preferences of participant D in the following section.

Essay Three (Participant D)

The third essay was a separate student response to the same PG task as in the section immediately above. Participant D's beliefs about the essay conclusion, however, can be seen to contrast those of the other subject specialist:

> She summarises the main points systematically and this brings everything together and helps you to get a good sense of the overall arguments that have been made. I think an essay needs this kind of completeness and sometimes the conclusions are a bit cursory.

The quality of the argumentation remained one of the strongest indicators of quality in essay writing for the participant, however. He identified the following extract as identifying strong argumentation:

> According to the website, its subscribed museums update its information daily. Although it collects ten most popular museums based on Facebook page likes, we do not know whether the statistics are reliable or updated regularly. What's more, it tends to equate the most 'liked' museum on Facebook with the most popular one in reality, which is totally not the case. And the top ten list becomes quite different if based on Twitter followers […] For those museums with amazing exhibitions, for instance, that are very likely not to get the public attention they deserve if they fail to create a buzz on any social media platform.

The interviewee explains how this section demonstrates good quality essay writing as follows:

> You can see the second point that he or she makes here about the fact that the top 10 museums on Facebook is radically different from the number of museums who get good ratings on Twitter or have even got Twitter followers. So again, you know, you choose your social media platform and you'll get radically different results out of those. It's a good, original point to make.

Digital media studies reflection

Reflection One (Participant C)

The first written reflection was a PG assignment in which students were required to reflect on practical digital projects in which they had developed promotional campaigns in groups. The subject specialist, participant C, explained the task as follows:

Most of the students will go on to work in creative industries organisations where team working will be the norm so the projects aim to simulate that work environment within the course. The reflective critique asks them to look back at that process from a critical perspective and to consider any limitations.

The participant explained that the reflective task allows a degree of informality in the students' writing:

> But what I'm keen on getting students to do is reflect on their own learning process. I'll tell the students that their language can be more informal here, that they can use the first person, they can include some bullet points and so on and so on. The piece is asking for a personal response so it's not a traditional essay and students can adopt the format and style that works best for them.

Consequently, the participant found the tone of the opening sentence of the student reflection analysed (below) to be perfectly appropriate:

> More than once I have had a voice in my head: 'Why we need a group when I believe I can complete this task on my own more easily and effectively?'

The participant, however, did point out the importance of strong argumentation with support from the literature for digital media studies at PG level. She regarded these qualities as being present in the following extract:

> I am more of a listener than a speaker and felt worried about my performance as a group leader. Studies show that quietness is one of three major grounds for a disqualified leader.

Reflection Two (Participant D)

The second written reflection was for the same PG reflective task as in the section immediately above. The subject specialist, participant D, similarly highlighted that teamwork was integral to the digital media studies programme:

> We as a team are keen to get them to practice and learn about working in teams. So, yeah, I mean the module in a way at that point was set up in some ways like an emulation of a working environment, or simulation of a work environment.

The participant also felt that the task permitted 'a more subjective tone' owing to the 'lived experience' of the students that the task asked them to explore. The use of the first person and the emotive tone of 'panicking' in the extract below was therefore viewed as perfectly permissible:

> Because this was at the beginning of the project, I was panicking about how to complete the whole project like this.

Although the participant stated that he 'would normally advise students not to include bullet points in a discursive essay', the flexible format for the reflections, he argued, allowed their use as in the reflection extract below:

> We then divided the task for the following week:
> - We would all try to find more (vegetarian) participants
> - The research leads would try to write a report on the research we'd done so far
> - Student X and I would try to out some letter designs in PS/Illustrator
> - Student Y would draw/make a set up/layout for the website.

Indeed, the participant viewed adoption of bullet points in this context as 'effective' since, as he states, 'it is essentially a list of points and in this format the information is very accessible without trying to put it all into a paragraph.'

Digital media studies research project

Research Project One (Participant E)

The research project analysed was a PG dissertation task, which the subject specialist, participant E, noted, 'allows digital media students the scope to choose topics within media and communications broadly'. He stated that the structure of the chosen student academic writing was 'logical' and that it 'follow[ed] a standard formula that most communications students adopt':

> It's possibly a bit formulaic but they are taught 'Here is my abstract, here is my introduction, here is my literature review' and she shows that she can apply an appropriate research method and present her research appropriately.

Effective signposting was a characteristic of the research writing which the participant valued in the dissertation:

> She guides the reader though the work, not just saying, 'First, I'm going to do this and then I'm going to do that' in the introduction but she also links the sections and reminds the reader how a section relates to earlier and later content.

A strength of the work overall was seen as being its objectivity. A perceived lapse in this objectivity, however, led the participant to criticize the use of personal perspective as follows:

> So, she says, 'What interests me about this' or 'What fascinates me most about this finding'. I just felt I had to point out to the student at these points that, really, what you think is interesting is not relevant to an MA level dissertation. What is the contribution to the field?

Table 2.2 Academic writing characteristics valued by subject specialists.

Genre family	Academic writing characteristics
Report	• The structure and organization should follow industry norms. • There should be a strong focus on evidence and explanation. • Language should be largely formal and impersonal. • Self-referencing should be limited to reporting students' own research.
Research proposal	• The structure and organization should follow a standard format. • Clear argumentation should be evident. • Lexis and syntax common to research documents should be adopted.
Argumentative essay	• The structure and organization can take different forms. • There should be effective paragraphing which develops argumentation. • There should be strong critical thinking and writer stance. • The language should be formal and impersonal. • Disciplinary lexis should be adopted.
Reflection	• The structure and organization can take different forms. • Informal language can be introduced. • Personal referencing can be employed.
Research project	• The structure and organization can take different forms. • The writing should be objective. • There should be effective signposting. • Language should be formal.

This section has presented selected findings for each of the examples of discourse genre analysed. Table 2.2 summarizes the desired features identified in the findings for each genre family and the discussion section which follows explores the implications of these findings.

Discussion

Diversity of written discourse genres

The research identifies Diversity of written discourse genres that span five separate genre families. Although the study makes no claim to provide an exhaustive list of possible written discourse genres for the discipline, this genre diversity remains highly significant. Moreover, the findings indicate that these discourse genres can be broadly categorized as either those which principally adhere to the academic conventions of the social sciences or those aligned to professional conventions of the digital industries. The 'imagined reader' (Thaiss and Zawacki 2006) for digital media studies assignments can therefore be conceived as representing both the academic and the professional community. This academic-professional focus emerges in the findings as a prime factor in distinguishing the academic writing requirements for digital media studies from those of its social science relatives. Indeed, in essence, it reflects the inseparability within the discipline of the digital technologies themselves and their cultural and expressive practices (Dewdney and Ride 2006).

The academic grouping of written discourse genres comprises the essays, the research proposal, the research project and the reflections. Such genres do not aim to model real-life writing contexts (Olwyn, Argent and Spencer 2008) but instead provide a means for students to demonstrate subject understanding and skills relating to academia (see Nesi and Gardner 2012). The subject specialists' expectations of these genres therefore broadly adhered to established social science academic assessment criteria for written academic work. The written reports in the study, however, represent professional dimensions of digital media studies, and students were expected to demonstrate an ability to produce documents which conformed to industry standards. The Internet policy report, for example, is aligned with the structure of legal policy documents and can be seen to reflect the increased prominence of issues of law, policy and governance with the rise of the Internet (Flew 2014). The distinct nature of each of these discourse genres (such as the digital product design report and the website evaluation report) also highlights this discipline-specificity and the limitations of generalizing the academic writing knowledge and skills required by students across genre families.

Variables in the quality of students' academic writing

The findings strongly suggest that subject specialists' understandings of quality in student academic writing are fundamentally linked to the discourse genres in question. This genre-bound conception of quality is most evident in the distinct grouping of desirable academic writing features for each of the discourse genres included in the study. The significant differences which exist can therefore be attributed to the communicative purpose of the discourse genres (Johns 1997; Miller 1984). Particularly noteworthy was evidence of a spectrum of discourse genre openness (Bhatia 2004) ranging from conservative genres, in which text structure and language conventions were more fixed (e.g. an internet policy report which describes, explains and evidences), to the more liberal genres which permit flexibility of structure and language use (e.g. a reflection which seeks to evaluate experience). The constraining power of genres (Hyland 2007) therefore varies considerably across the diverse examples related to digital media studies.

The study explored subject specialists' individual understandings of the quality of students' academic writing. The divergence of personal preferences of these participants is perhaps most evident in the views of participants C and D regarding the role of essay conclusions. However, these two participants acknowledged the range of possible approaches that might be adopted for this liberal discourse genre, which is not easily reducible to a fixed set of genre characteristics (Dudley-Evans 2002). As a result, they did not appear to penalize student work that did not conform closely to their own preferences. There was also evidence that assessment criteria for written work were at times either interpreted flexibly or genre-specific alternatives were produced. These subject specialist practices can be attributed to the limitations of standardized criteria developed for written academic work across a broad range of media-related academic programmes. Participant B, for example, describes the need to rework institution-wide criteria designed for argumentative essays to make them suitable for professional discourse genres such as an industry-standard website evaluation. This professional dilemma further highlights the distinctiveness of the academic writing discourse genres required of digital media studies students.

Pedagogic implications of the findings

The findings identify a patterning of desirable and permissible academic writing characteristics for each of the individual digital media studies discourse genres. The distinctiveness of each of the groupings provides a clear indication that academic writing in the discipline is not limited to a single set of characteristic but instead requires the development of skill in producing academic writing for a range of digital media studies discourse genres. EAP practitioners will therefore need to prepare students to produce academic writing using discourse genres from up to five genre families: reports, research proposals, argumentative essays, reflections and research projects.

Given this range of disciplinary discourse genres, it would be useful for digital media studies students to be introduced to the concept of genre itself (see Swales 2004). Student awareness of the relationship between genre purpose and form can potentially not only develop their tolerance for the range of genres they may be asked to produce but also provide the basis for a deeper understanding of *why* certain academic writing characteristics are associated with a specific genre. In addition, when genre-awareness includes 'the job [genres] have to do' (Tribble 2010: 161), students should be better prepared to select the appropriate writing strategies for their own specific assignment tasks (see, for example, Negretti and Kuteeva 2011, on genre awareness and meta-strategies).

The findings indicate the academic writing characteristics that could usefully be introduced by the EAP practitioner for each genre family (see Table 2.2). For example, subject specialists valued written reports that conformed to industry conventions in terms of the organization, the use of evidence and the formality and clarity of language use. I have argued that these are most usefully taught in the context of the genre purpose (which, of course, includes the degree of academic or professional orientation of the genre). The listed characteristics, however, do also in themselves provide a reference list for digital media studies academic writing course design.

A significant finding in the research was the spectrum of flexibility of the digital media studies discourse genres. Thus, although Flowerdew rightly warns us against considering all genre exemplars' 'rigid and prescriptive models for students to emulate blindly' (Flowerdew 2000: 370), alongside open genres such as the essay and the reflection there were a number of very closed discourse genres. The report genre family, for example, requires that students follow the structure and organization of professional documentation within the digital media industries very closely. As a result of this prescriptiveness, industry models (and research grant applications) can be adopted by EAP practitioners as exemplars for classroom analysis and adapted replication. For those genres that the research identifies as being more open (reflections and essays), exemplar analysis, where employed, will need to take a different form. Instruction should instead focus on examples of specific desired characteristics, such as critical thinking and strong argumentation, in order to provide contextualized examples to aid student understanding of how the features contribute to the genre purpose.

Conclusion

Summary

This research identifies and explores a number of academic writing genres in the field of digital media studies, providing subject specialists' understandings of quality for each of the discourse genres included. Particularly noteworthy in the study is the breadth of genres associated with the discipline. Furthermore, the genres can be broadly categorized as having either a predominantly academic or a professional orientation, with the latter category reflecting digital media professional requirements in the outside world. This range of discourse genres which students are required to produce can be seen to distinguish the discipline from many of its social science relatives, which typically lack such a pronounced professional leaning.

There are several implications of the research for the teaching and learning of academic writing for digital media studies. Firstly, the discrete academic writing requirements that emerged for each of the analysed discourse genres are presented as a reference for academic writing course design or individual study. This research therefore provides an empirical basis for the selection of genre-related academic writing skills to be developed for digital media studies. However, the research also clearly indicates varying degrees of prescriptiveness in these characteristics as a result of the openness of some discourse genres. As a result, learners need to develop a strong understanding of how the different genres relate to their overall discipline and the ways in which the genre purpose determines both its linguistic features and the flexibility with which the academic writing task can be undertaken.

Limitations of the research

Disciplines are context-dependent (Trowler 2014), and this research will clearly reflect the academic programming of the institution in which it was conducted as well as the values and priorities of individual subject specialists. EAP practitioner research into disciplinary genre, though strongly advocated within the field (see, for example, Bruce 2008), also tends to be small-scale with limited data generated as in this study, which adopted one-off interviews with a small sample of subject specialists. The study acknowledges these constraints and makes no claim as to the generalizability of the findings. However, the study does offer potentially valuable insights into academic writing in this discipline, providing as it does insider disciplinary genre knowledge. This can be of benefit to those outside the discipline's 'expert' community (see Shaw 2016), such as EAP practitioners and the students themselves, but could also potentially facilitate the development of pedagogical content knowledge (Shulman 1987), which is of value for the community of subject specialists itself (Hedgcock and Lee 2017).

References

Bailey, S. (2015). *Academic Writing for International Students of Business.* Abingdon: Routledge.

Bazerman, C. (1994). *Constructing Experience.* Carbondale, IL: Southern Illinois University Press.

Becher, T. (1989). *Academic Tribes and Territories: Intellectual Enquiry and the Cultures of Disciplines.* Milton Keynes: Open University Press.

Bhatia, V. K. (2004). *Worlds of Written Discourse: A Genre-based View.* London: Bloomsbury Publishing.

Bruce, I. (2008). *Academic Writing and Genre: A Systematic Analysis.* London: Continuum.

Bruce, I. (2018). 'The Textual Expression of Critical Thinking in PhD Discussions in Applied Linguistics'. *ESP Today* 6 (1): 2–24.

Carter, M. (2007). 'Ways of Knowing, Doing and Writing in the Disciplines'. College Composition and Communication 58 (3): 385–418.

Cheng, A. (2008). 'Analyzing Genre Exemplars in Preparation for Writing: The Case of an L2 Graduate Student in the ESP Genre-based Instructional Framework of Academic Literacy'. *Applied Linguistics* 29 (1): 50–71.

Cohen, M., Manion, L., and Morrison, K. (2007). *Research Methods in Education.* New York: Routledge.

Day, T. (2018). *Success in Academic Writing.* Basingstoke, Hampshire: Palgrave Macmillan.

De Chazal, E. (2014). *English for Academic Purposes.* Oxford: Oxford University Press.

DeVoss, D. N., Cushman, E., and Grabill, J. T. (2005). 'Infrastructure and Composing: The When of New-media Writing'. *College Composition and Communication* 57 (1): 14–44.

Dewdney, A. and Ride, P. (2006). 'New Media as a Subject'. In Dewdney, A., and Ride, P. (eds.), *The New Media Handbook,* 20–8. Abingdon: Routledge.

Drever, E. (2003). Using Semi-structured Interviews. Glasgow: SCRE, University of Glasgow.

Dudley-Evans, T. (2002). 'The Teaching of the Academic Essay; is a Genre Approach Possible?' in Johns, A. M. (ed.), *Genre in the Classroom: Multiple Perspectives,* 225–36. Mahwah, NJ: Lawrence Erlbaum Associates.

Flew, T. (2014). *New Media.* South Melbourne: Oxford University Press.

Flowerdew, L. (2000). 'Using a Genre-based Framework to Teach Organizational Structure in Academic Writing'. *English Language Teaching Journal* 54 (4): 369–78.

Garrand, T. (2006). *Writing for Multimedia and the Web.* Oxford: Elsevier.

Haggis, T. (2006). 'Pedagogies for Diversity: Retaining Critical Challenge amidst Fears of 'Dumbing Down'. *Studies in Higher Education* 31 (5): 521–35.

Hardy, J. A., and Friginal, E. (2016). 'Genre Variation in Student Writing: A Multi-Dimensional Analysis'. *Journal of English for Academic Purposes* 22: 119–31.

Hardy, J. A., Römer, U., and Roberson, A. (2015). 'The Power of Relevant Models: Using a Corpus of Student Writing to Introduce Disciplinary Practices in a First Year Composition Course'. *Across the Disciplines* 12 (1): 1–20.

Harwood, N. J. (2005) 'What Do We Want EAP Teaching Materials For?' *Journal of English for Academic Purposes* 4 (2): 149–61.

Hedgcock, J. S., and Lee, H. (2017). 'An Exploratory Study of Academic Literacy Socialization: Building Genre Awareness in a Teacher Education Program'. *Journal of English for Academic Purposes* 26: 17–28.

Hyland, K. (1990). 'A Genre Description of the Argumentative Essay'. *RELC Journal* 21 (1): 66–78.

Hyland, K. (2000). *Disciplinary Discourses: Social Interactions in Academic Writing.* London: Longman.

Hyland, K. (2005). 'Stance and Engagement: A Model of Interaction in Academic Discourse'. *Discourse Studies* 7 (2): 173–92.

Hyland, K. (2007). 'Genre Pedagogy: Language, Literacy and L2 Writing Instruction'. *Journal of Second Language Writing* 16 (3): 148–64.

Hyland, K. (2008). 'Genre and Academic Writing in the Disciplines'. *Language Teaching* 41 (4): 543–62.

Hyland, K., and Shaw, P. (2016). *The Routledge Handbook of English for Academic Purposes.* Abingdon: Routledge.

Hyland, K., and Tse, P. (2009). 'Academic Lexis and Disciplinary Practice: Corpus Evidence for Specificity'. *International Journal of English Studies* 9 (2): 111–29.

Johns, A. M. (1997). *Text, Role and Context: Developing Academic Literacies.* Cambridge: Cambridge University Press.

Jou, Y. J. (2017). 'Hidden Challenges of Tasks in an EAP Writing Textbook: EAL Graduate Students' Perceptions and Textbook Authors' Responses'. *Journal of English for Academic Purposes* 30: 13–25.

Kennedy, B. (2018). 'Deduction, Induction and Abduction'. In Uwe, F. (ed.), *The SAGE Handbook of Qualitative Data Collection*, 49–64. London: SAGE.

Kimmel, A. (1998). *Ethics and Values in Applied Social Research.* London: SAGE.

Kuehn, S. A. and Lingwall, A. (2018). *The Basics of Media Writing: A Strategic Approach.* London: SAGE.

Kuteeva, M., and Negretti, R. (2016). 'Graduate Students' Genre Knowledge and Perceived Disciplinary Practices: Creating a Research Space across Disciplines'. *English For Specific Purposes* 41: 36–49.

Kvale, S. (1996). *Inter Views: An Introduction to Qualitative Research Interviewing.* Thousand Oaks, CA: SAGE.

Kvale, S., and Brinkmann, S. (2009). *Interviews: Learning the Craft of Qualitative Research Interviewing.* Los Angeles, SAGE.

Lea, M. (2004). 'Academic Literacies: A Pedagogy for Course Design'. *Studies in Higher Education* 29 (6): 739–56.

Lea, M., and Street, B. (2000). Student Writing and Staff Feedback in Higher Education'. In Lea, M., and Stierer, B. (eds.), *Student Writing in Higher Education: New Contexts*, 32–46. Buckingham: The Society for Research into Higher Education and Open University Press.

Lillis, T. M. (2008) 'Ethnography as Method, Methodology, and 'Deep Theorizing'. Closing the gap between text and context in academic writing research'. *Written Communication* 25 (3): 353–88.

Livingstone, S. (2005). 'Critical Debates in Internet Studies: Reflections on an Emerging Field'. In Curran, J., and Gurevitch, M. (eds.), *Mass Media and Society*, 9–28. London: Hodder Arnold.

Melzer, D. (2009). 'Writing Assignments across the Curriculum: A National Study of College Writing'. *College Composition and Communication* 61 (2): 240–61.

Miles, M. and Huberman, M. (1994). *Qualitative Data Analysis: An Expanded Sourcebook*. London: SAGE.

Miller, C. (1984). 'Genre as Social Action'. *Quarterly Journal of Speech* 70 (2): 151–67.

Miller, C. R., and Devitt, A. J. (2019). *Landmark Essays on Rhetorical Genre Studies*. Abingdon: Routledge.

Moore, T., and Morton, J. (2005). 'Dimensions of Difference: A Comparison of University Writing and IELTS Writing'. *Journal of English for Academic Purposes* 4 (1): 43–66.

Murphy, E., and Dingwall, R. (2001). 'The Ethics of Ethnography'. In Atkinson, P., Coffey, A., Delamont, S., Lofland, J., and Lofland, L. (eds.), *Handbook of Ethnography*, 339–51. London: SAGE.

Negretti, R., and Kuteeva, M. (2011). 'Fostering Metacognitive Genre Awareness in L2 Academic Reading and Writing: A Case Study of Pre-service English teachers'. *Journal of Second Language Writing* 20 (2): 95–110.

Nesi, H., and Gardner, S. (2012). *Genres across the Disciplines: Student Writing in Higher Education*. Cambridge: Cambridge University Press.

Olwyn, A., Argent, S., and Spencer, J. (2008). *EAP Essentials: A Teacher's Guide to Principles and Practice*. Reading: Garnet Publishing.

Reyna, J., Hanham, J., and Meier, P. C. (2018). 'A Framework for Digital Media Literacies for Teaching and Learning in Higher Education'. *E-Learning and Digital Media* 15 (4): 176–90.

Roe, S. C., and den Ouden, P. H. (2018). *Academic Writing: The Complete Guide* (3rd ed). Toronto: Canadian Scholars.

Samraj, B. (2005). 'An Exploration of a Genre Set: Research Article Abstracts and Introductions in Two Disciplines'. *English for Specific Purposes* 24 (2): 141–56.

Sharpling, G. (2002). 'Learning to Teach English for Academic Purposes: Some Current Training and Development Issues'. *English Language Teacher Education and Development* 6 (1): 82–94.

Shaw, P. (2016). 'Genre Analysis'. In Hyland, K., and Shaw, P. *The Routledge Handbook of English for Academic Purposes*, 243–55. Abingdon: Routledge.

Shulman, L. (1987). 'Knowledge and Teaching: Foundations of the New Reform'. *Harvard Educational Review* 57 (1): 1–22.

Silverman, D. (2016). *Qualitative Research* London: SAGE.

Smith, R. (2014). *English for Electrical Engineering in Higher Education Studies*. Reading: Garnet Publishing.

Stake, R. (2010). *Qualitative Research: Studying How Things Work*. New York: The Guilford Press.

Swales, J. (1990). *Genre Analysis: English in Academic and Research Settings*. Cambridge, Cambridge University Press.

Swales, J. (2004). *Research Genres: Explorations and Applications*. Cambridge: Cambridge University Press.

Tardy, C. M. (2009). *Building Genre Knowledge*. West Lafayette, Indiana: Parlor Press.

Thaiss, C., and Zawacki, T. M. (2006). *Engaged Writers and Dynamic Disciplines: Research on the Academic Writing Life*. Portsmouth, NH: Boynton, Cook Publishers.

Tribble, C. (2010). 'A Genre-based Approach to Developing Materials for Writing'. In Harwood, N. (ed.), *English Language Teaching Materials: Theory and Practice*, 157–78. Cambridge: Cambridge University Press.

Tribble, C. (2017). 'ELFA vs. Genre: A New Paradigm War in EAP Writing Instruction?' *Journal of English for Academic Purposes* 25: 30–44.

Tribble, C., and Wingate, U. (2013). 'From Text to Corpus–A Genre-based Approach to Academic Literacy Instruction'. *System* 41 (2): 307–21.

Trowler, P. (2014). 'Depicting and Researching Disciplines: Strong and Moderate Essentialist Approaches'. *Studies in Higher Education* 39 (10): 1720–31.

Trowler, P., and Wareham, T. (2008). 'Tribes, Territories, Research and Teaching'. New York: The Higher Education Academy.

Westera, W. (2013). *The Digital Turn: How the Internet Transforms Our Existence*. Bloomington, IN: AuthorHouse.

Wingate, U. (2012). 'Using Academic Literacies and Genre-based Models for Academic Writing Instruction: A "Literacy" Journey'. *Journal of English for Academic Purposes* 11 (1): 26–37.

Wingate, U. (2016). 'Academic Literacy across the Curriculum: Towards a Collaborative Instructional Approach'. *Language Teaching*: 1–16.

3

Exploring Clarity in the Discipline of Design

Clare Maxwell

Introduction

On setting out to explore what constitutes 'good' student writing from the point of view of the subject specialists tasked with assessing that writing, it was perhaps inevitable that the question of 'clarity' would emerge as a key area of focus. Clarity is broadly acknowledged to be an essential and desired quality of academic writing: 'crucial to student writing success' (Nesi and Gardner 2006: 102), 'an imperative of effective student writing' (Barnard 2010: 434) and 'highly prized' within the academy (Turner 2011: 7). Indeed, early on in this exploratory study, which focuses on student writing in the discipline of design, the recurrent emergence of clarity as something that is key to good student writing ultimately led to the feeling that it warranted more in-depth investigation.

While the need for clarity is widely viewed as a 'given' in good academic writing, it is by no means 'clear' in itself. More than half a century ago, Polanyi (1966, cited in Turner 2011) identified clarity as an example of 'tacit knowledge': widely required and valued by subject tutors, who are yet often unable to explain its meaning. Lea and Street (2000) confirmed this view of clarity as something that subject tutors often appear unable to explicate, and Barnard (2010: 436) is critical of the apparent lack of attempts to rectify this:

there is no discussion of what clarity means or how one knows if something is clear or not. When invoked, clarity's desirability is almost always taken for granted, and clarity is almost always spoken of as if its meaning were obvious.

The inability to define or, at least, explicate clarity is problematic of course, since an inability to articulate the nature of such an important, apparently 'crucial', aspect of academic writing will inevitably make the task of ensuring clarity in their writing particularly difficult for student writers. From an EAP perspective, the problem is compounded. The BALEAP (British Association of Lecturers in English for Academic Purposes) competency framework states that it is the role of the EAP practitioner to 'help students find their way into the writing and speaking practices of their disciplines and institutions' and 'raise students' awareness of discourse features of texts in their disciplines' (BALEAP 2008). The subjective nature of clarity therefore is particularly problematic, since the EAP practitioner's understanding of what constitutes clarity in academic writing may be different from that of the subject tutor, and yet s/he is tasked with helping students improve their writing in such a way as to satisfy the expectations and requirements of subject tutors and markers.

In an attempt to address the ambiguity surrounding the concept of clarity, this study seeks to examine 'clarity' in academic writing in more detail, firstly by looking at how it has been theorized in the literature, and subsequently by exploring perceptions and manifestations of clarity in student academic writing in one university setting. The initial aim of the study was to understand to what extent clarity is a key feature of good writing produced by taught postgraduate students in the discipline of design. From this, the following questions emerged:

- What *is* clarity in this context? What makes writing 'clear'?
- Which aspects of clarity are particularly highly valued?
- What are the implications of this on EAP and, more specifically, on teaching academic writing?

The context of design

Design is a creative, vocational and practice-based discipline (Melles and Lockheart 2012), with its own peculiarities and challenges in terms of the type of writing and genres that students both encounter and are required to produce. It can be described as a soft applied discipline (Biglan, 1973, in Becher 2006), largely concerned with the application and use of knowledge to both create and prepare for a career (Nesi and Gardner 2006). However, as a relatively recent addition to the academy it might still be considered an 'emerging' discipline (Baynham 2000), with a perceived need to assert its status within the academy (Candlin 2000; Lea and Stierer 2000; Melles and Lockheart 2012). This is perhaps evident in its adoption of many traditional academic conventions, resulting in traditional assessment genres (such as the dissertation, and literature review), existing alongside more 'creative' (Borg 2012) and 'professional' genres, such as reflective reports and portfolios (Baynham, 2000; Candlin 2000; Lea and

Stierer 2000; Nesi and Gardner 2006; Melles and Lockheart 2012), which appear to 'support acquisition and consolidation of professional knowledge' (Lea and Stierer 2000: 9).

While there exists notable research into design pedagogies and writing in design (for example, Borg 2012; Bhagat and O'Neill, 2009; Orr and Shreve 2018), design is a relatively under-represented discipline in the EAP literature. It is, for example, noticeably absent from many of the studies exploring disciplinary difference and genre, and often from corpora of student writing (such as the BAWE corpus). While the disciplinary context of this study was primarily the result of circumstances allowing relatively easy access to primary data and interview subjects, a study exploring student writing in design from an EAP perspective will surely provide some welcome insight into the practices of a lesser-explored discipline.

The nature of clarity

A crude online dictionary search is enough to highlight the complexity of the concept of 'clarity'. A single dictionary entry already encompasses various aspects: 'the quality of being **coherent and intelligible** ... of being **certain or definite** ... of **transparency or purity** ... of being **easy to see or hear**' (Oxford University Press 2019) (my emphasis). It is not difficult to see how these aspects of clarity could apply to writing, and indeed references to clarity in the literature in many ways reflect these dictionary definitions, however crude. 'Intelligibility and cohesion', for example, might relate to 'clarity of expression', that is, how language is used to communicate the writer's message. Lillis and Turner (2001: 20) note the traditional view that language should be 'clear and concise and not get in the way of the message', and Turner (2018: 9) later adds that writing should be 'free from linguistic or conceptual obstacles'. These views appear to reflect the historical, largely Western, 'conduit' model, in which language was considered simply a means for transmitting and communicating knowledge and reason (Turner 2011, 2018). In this way, language and knowledge came to be considered 'separate', or at least, 'separable'. Value was placed on the assumed 'transparency' of language and that, in order to not distract from the message, the language should be somehow 'invisible' (Lillis and Turner 2001).

Clarity of expression, however, may not always result in clarity of message. Barnard (2010) argues that language clarity does not necessarily equate to transparency: sophisticated use of 'clear' language can be cleverly used to 'hide' the truth. In addition, he points out that specialized language and jargon can be used to deliberately 'obfuscate' a message: ostensibly to exert power, hide truth, or cover a lack of substance (Barnard 2010). Language, then, can be 'clear', but the message may not be, suggesting that while clarity of expression may play a role in achieving clarity, it cannot be the only factor. Important questions also remain as to how clarity of expression is achieved, which aspects of language impact on it and how language can be rendered 'invisible'.

Turner (2011) points out that subject tutors want students to show understanding of their subject, including key terms, and to avoid 'vagueness'. Students need to clearly articulate their understanding of the subject by achieving an appropriate level of fluency in the discourse and through accurate use of appropriate and well-explained terminology. The challenge this might present in relation to clarity is highlighted in Barnard's (2010) view that 'jargon' in professional academic writing is often both overused and misused, sometimes deliberately, with the effect of reducing clarity and creating a barrier to entry into the discourse community: to 'fix students' places as students' (Barnard 2010: 444). Students thus need to master the terminology to such a level as to ensure that clarity and precision are not negatively impacted through either inaccurate or excessive use.

Explicitness, in a written context, might equate to the crude dictionary definition of 'being easy to see', and has also been indicated by subject tutors as a desirable feature of student writing (Lillis 2001). Couture (1986: 71) suggested that at its highest level, explicitness requires 'features that make meaning clear with the least possibility of conflicting interpretation'. Evidently this could save the reader effort, by contributing to ease of reading; however, this too is an ambiguous concept: Lillis (2001) showed it to encompass a number of broad features, including linking, stating relevance, avoiding vagueness, ensuring cohesion and showing understanding. Turner (2018), on the other hand, equates ease of reading to what she neatly labels the 'smooth read, [...] free from linguistic or conceptual obstacles' (p9), presumably therefore accurate but also coherent.

The literature suggests then that clarity is considered an essential feature of good student writing widely valued amongst subject tutors. Attempts to explore and explicate clarity have highlighted both its ambiguity and subjectivity, while providing a glimpse of its multifaceted nature. Turner (2011: 20) suggests that it may be a value that 'cuts across disciplines'; however, there appears to have been little attempt to explore how it is manifested in practice, what impacts on it and how this might differ between disciplines. This exploratory study, while not pretending to provide definitive answers, is a tentative first step towards understanding the role and nature of clarity in one disciplinary context.

The study

Context

This small exploratory study was carried out within the School of Design of a Russell Group university in the North of England. It aims to create a snapshot impression of the perceived nature and value of clarity amongst subject lecturers, and how clarity is manifested in samples of 'good' student writing in this context.

The School offers one MSc and five MA programmes. The MA programmes vary from the more design practitioner-focused to those incorporating an entrepreneurial, business or retail angle. The latter include modules offered by the university's Business School. Due to the widely acknowledged differences between disciplines (Hyland 2004), this study focuses solely on modules offered by the School of Design.

Procedure

The study combined semi-structured interviews of subject lecturers with analysis of samples of master's dissertation–level student writing. Documentation relating to the samples and their respective master's programmes was also examined, including feedback sheets, marking criteria, assignment briefs and programme handbooks. Ethical approval for the study was sought and granted by the University's Research Ethics Committee,[1] and consent was gained from all interviewees, as well as from the students whose work is used in the study.

Sample data set

The data set (Table 3.1) consisted of five scripts from two MA programmes (henceforth Programme A and Programme B). Dissertation-level samples were selected, as these were considered to be comprehensive of the type of writing that students produce throughout their master's programme: indeed, on the programmes in question, earlier assessment tasks are often designed to be developmental for the final projects. The Dissertation (Programme B) very much corresponds to a standard dissertation in form and structure. The Reflective Report (Programme A) is, to all intents and purposes, equivalent to a dissertation; however, it might be considered something of a 'hybrid genre'. While it includes many features of a traditional dissertation (abstract, literature

---

[1] Ethical approval received 28th March 2018, reference LTSLCS-083.

Table 3.1 Sample data set.

	Type	Programme	Grade
Sample 1	Reflective Report	Programme A	75
Sample 2	Reflective Report	Programme A	72
Sample 3	Reflective Report	Programme A	72
Sample 4	Dissertation	Programme B	80
Sample 5	Dissertation	Programme B	70

review, methodology, findings etc.), it also incorporates additional sections focusing on design development and outcomes, reflection and evaluation.

Scripts were chosen based on the high grades awarded: all at Distinction level in the range of 70 to 80. This followed the assumption that an exceptional grade indicates good writing from an assessment perspective. All scripts were by students whose dominant language is not English.

Semi-structured interviews

Semi-structured interviews were held with three subject lecturers, all of whom teach and assess on the two programmes and are experienced markers of dissertation-level projects. These included both programme leaders and one module leader (from programme B). The programme leaders were interviewed twice, and the module leader once. All were interviewed individually.

The aim of the first interview was to gain insight into the subject lecturers' general thoughts about 'good' student writing in the discipline. Time was taken to explore the themes that emerged, and to identify priorities in terms of what is important in student writing. The value of clarity, or traits linked to clarity, emerged early in the interviews, and was a recurrent theme throughout. From here the focus on clarity took shape, to be explored in more depth in the second interviews.

The second interviews explored the nature of clarity through semi-structured questions and examination of the written scripts. The subject lecturers were asked to identify examples of good (or poor) clarity in the scripts prior to meeting. During the interview the subject lecturers were invited to explain their perceptions of the clarity of each example. Unsolicited documentation relating to the examples of clarity was supplied by the programme leaders, both of whom had highlighted and annotated the scripts. This proved useful for cross-referencing between the interview transcripts and the scripts, and subsequent analysis.

Analysis of programme documents

The following documents relating to the two academic programmes, the assessment tasks and the samples were also examined:

- Programme and module handbooks
- Assignment briefs
- Assignment marking criteria
- Individual assignment feedback

An initial study of these documents was carried out to identify broad themes, features and aspects of writing that emerged as valued features of 'good writing'. Following the first interviews, as the theme of clarity emerged, the documents were examined more closely for references to clarity, in order to understand the perceived 'nature' of clarity within the context of the discipline, programmes, modules and assignments.

Findings

The importance of clarity

The words 'clarity', 'clear' and 'clearly' all appear, to a greater or lesser extent, in all programme documents. Clarity is referred to prescriptively in the module handbooks, assignment briefs and assessment criteria, and formatively in assessment feedback. Reminiscent of Barnard's (2010) observations, the multifaceted and ambiguous nature of 'clarity' is evident, particularly due to the differing contexts in which it is used, leaving it open to interpretation. The Dissertation task brief, for example, requires '*clear aims and objectives*', and that the dissertation be written '*with clarity*', while the marking criteria rewards '*clearly cited*' references, a '*clear conclusion*', and a demonstration that benefits and limitations of the methodology are '*clearly understood*'. It is not clear what would constitute 'clarity' in these cases, each hinting at different aspects which could potentially be interpreted as: explicitness, lack of ambiguity, transparency or even accuracy.

The word 'clarity' and its related forms are often accompanied by other words that appear to add nuance and possibly hint at meaning. The Dissertation task brief, for example, requires students to '*produce a written dissertation which reports **clearly and concisely** on their investigation*' and '*write with **accuracy and clarity***', while the marking criteria requires '***clear and specific** objectives*' and a '*clearly and unambiguously described* problem' (my emphasis). Although not certain, the references to *conciseness, accuracy, specificity* and *lack of ambiguity* could perhaps be interpreted to indicate intended meaning, further emphasizing the varying aspects of clarity. The potential challenges students face in interpreting the concept of clarity are highlighted by inevitable variations in the language used, particularly when differentiating between bands in marking criteria (my emphasis):

> *Band 80–100: The problem identified is clearly and **unambiguously** described.*
> *Band 70–79: The problem identified is **explicitly** described.*
> *Extract from Dissertation marking criteria (Programme B)*

During the first interviews, clarity was confirmed as an important, even essential, feature of good student writing by all interviewees, and became a recurrent theme. Reflective of the ambiguous nature of clarity, frames of reference varied, and an equally varied picture emerged of what the subject lecturers perceive to be 'clear', and how this is achieved.

Even when referring directly to the sample scripts, the difficulty of explicating clarity (Lazer and Barnaby 2015; Lea and Street 2000; Lillis 2001; Turner 2011) was very much apparent. One attempt to explain what made a particular paragraph clear ultimately resulted in the subject lecturer reading the paragraph aloud and preceding each sentence with 'first she says … then she says … ', with no real explanation of what made it clear. It may also be significant that another lecturer identified more examples of 'poor' clarity than good, suggesting that it is perhaps easier to identify and explain 'poor' examples. Even so, it was possible to identify some key themes in the subject lecturers' perceptions of clarity.

Ease of reading and language accuracy

All three of the subject lecturers indicated ease of reading as an important feature of good student writing, and closely linked to clarity. Subject Lecturer 1 (SL1) described good student writing as '*clear, legible, and easy to understand and comprehend*' and Subject Lecturer 2 (SL2) as '*when you read it you feel comfortable reading it in the way that they've expressed it*'. During the first interviews, the subject lecturers attributed 'ease of reading' to language accuracy, recalling Turner's (2018: 8) 'smooth read ideology' which, from the perspective of the subject lecturers, indeed appears to refer to the lack of 'linguistic obstacles'. The perceived impact of these obstacles on ease of reading was felt by default to impact on ease of marking:

Often their writing is clumsy, it's badly structured, has poor spelling, poor grammar.
And it makes it very difficult to read, to teach and to assess.

(SL1)

The predominant focus on language accuracy was interesting, since *clarity of expression* (a catch-all phrase often used in programme documents and by the subject lecturers to encompass language use, including accuracy and academic style) does not appear in the marking criteria for the assignment tasks used for this study. Indeed, it rarely appears in any of the assessment criteria used at master's level within the School, and, when present, carries relatively little weight (generally 5–10 per cent).

In line with the marking criteria, all subject lecturers interviewed stated unequivocally that students are not penalized for language errors, largely due to the university's inclusive marking policy, which states that:

Where spelling, grammar and punctuation do not form part of the assessment criteria, and the intended meaning of the coursework is clear and presented coherently, marks should not be deducted for inaccuracies in the use of English language.

(University of Leeds 2016)

Tutors confirmed that they will only penalize for language inaccuracy if they are unable to understand what the student is trying to say, and indeed this is reflected in the high grades awarded to the samples in this study, which are by no means error-free. Table 3.2 shows the results of a snapshot error analysis carried out on a single page of each sample script. The same page (from the Literature Review) of each script was selected to ensure consistency of comparison, and language errors on the page were counted and categorized by type. The results show significant differences in quantity and nature of language errors between scripts.

This simple analysis does not intend to correlate language accuracy with grade, or indeed with 'good' writing. However, the almost total lack of errors in the highest scoring sample (Sample 4) is noticeable, as is the presence of considerably more errors in Sample 3. The latter has in any case received a distinction, demonstrating that language accuracy is not a barrier to receiving a high grade, and presumably that the impact on comprehension has not been great.

While tolerance of language inaccuracies is not necessarily an indicator of written clarity, it does appear to confirm the markers' ability to 'see past' the language (Carter and Nash 1990, cited in Turner 2018; Bond 2018), and to mark purely on the merit of content. In fact, although there were 'grumbles' relating

Table 3.2 Snapshot language error analysis of one page per sample.

	Grade	Errors	Nature of errors
Sample 1 p7	75	11	Vocabulary choice (6); sentence structure (1); articles (1); punctuation (1); question forms (1); construction of noun phrases (1)
Sample 2 p7	72	8	Prepositions (3); verb forms (2); vocabulary choice (1); articles (1); plurals (1)
Sample 3 p7	72	32	Verb forms (9); vocabulary choice (including collocations) (6); use of articles (4); prepositions (3); word forms (2); possessives (2); plurals (2); spelling (1); punctuation (1); verb tenses (1); construction of noun phrases (1)
Sample 4 p7	80	2	Plurals (1); pronouns (1)
Sample 5 p7	70	17	Articles (9); vocabulary choice (including collocations) (4); punctuation (2); prepositions (1); pronouns (1)

to issues of poor grammar, spelling and structure, overall the subject lecturers demonstrated a high level of tolerance of language errors, and, despite some frustration, there was evidence that they make considerable effort to decipher students' writing where errors are present (Lillis 2001; Turner 2001):

> You have to try and be fair, and try to see beyond clumsy writing style. And try and get a sense that the student has understood … but it's challenging … and really, good writing shouldn't be making the reader do that sort of work.
>
> (SL1)

There was also a suggestion that markers acquire an ability to recognize the patterns of writing, and thus errors, of certain L1 writers:

> It's quite a similar writing pattern and […] they'll miss the word 'the' out, things like that and that's a pattern with a lot of Chinese students. And I think you know that as a tutor.
>
> (SL1)

This ability, similar perhaps to learning a form of linguistic variation, appears to help the subject lecturers to understand the content, and see 'beyond' the errors. It seems then that, to an extent, these subject lecturers are adopting a 'more flexible interpretative stance' as advocated by Turner (2018: 13).

What is not evident from these observations is which language inaccuracies might impact clarity enough to impede successful communication. It is reasonable to assume that the types of error seen in Sample 3 did not create great difficulties, or, at least, not enough to significantly impact the grade. Further investigation, beyond the scope of this study, would be necessary to understand if this was due to the nature of the errors or the individual ability of the marker to see past them, or a combination of both.

Language complexity

It seems fair to assume that certain language issues will result in a more substantial loss of clarity than others, leading to more severe difficulties of comprehension. In this case the use of 'over-complicated' language was perceived to be a greater barrier to ease of reading than language inaccuracy. Two of the subject lecturers expressed frustration that students, in their attempts to adopt a more formal, academic register, often seem to '*try too hard*', resulting in writing that is '*very, very wordy*' and '*repetitive*':

> Sometimes, they've got to write in a way that appears to be convoluted and overly clever, but it doesn't work.
>
> (SL1)

SL3 neatly labelled the desired, less complex language style as '*clean*' academic language, achieved by avoiding the use of '*expensive*' words to try and sound academic:

> I say to them, just be to the point. Tell me what it is, instead of going around, what was the finding? Sometimes they go around and around and I cannot understand.
>
> (SL3)

This use of over-complex language appears in this case to create the kind of 'linguistic obstacles' (Turner 2018) that interfere with ease of reading, creating what Turner refers to as a 'rougher ride through the text' (Turner 2018: 13). Vardi (2000) found this to be an issue that counters an expectation and desire for writers to use 'plain English' (Barnard 2010; Turner 2018). In this case the subject lecturers expressed this desire for students to write in a more 'simple' but 'coherent' way, concentrating on making their point clear rather than on using over-elaborate language: '*If it's short, say it's short!*' (SL3)

The idea that students may be 'trying too hard' is significant, as it suggests a gap in expectations between the students and subject lecturers relating to the conventions of academic writing. Logically, writing in 'plain English' should be easier, raising the question as to why students would deliberately make things harder for themselves. Despite the subject lecturers' view that the students should express their ideas in a 'simple' way, it is of course widely acknowledged that academic writing in English is complex (Barnard 2010; Biber and Gray 2010; Coxhead and Byrd 2007) and that this can affect clarity (Barnard 2010). The difficulties students have in understanding and adopting these conventions are equally well documented (Lea and Street 2000; Lillis and Turner 2001; Vardi 2000).

In addition, the question arises as to whether subject lecturers really do favour simplicity in students' writing. As is common at postgraduate level (Nesi and Gardner 2006), both programme leaders encourage their students to model their writing on published journal articles, in some cases with a view to potential publication. The complexity generally seen in journal articles (Barnard 2010) is somewhat at odds with the expressed preference for simplicity, and on examination of the scripts themselves, it is noticeable that all offer frequent examples of relatively complex language:

> Meanwhile, the shape curvature, color saturation and the shape-color congruency of the package would influence the consumer expectation for the subsequent taste experiences. (Sample 3)
>
> Self-achievement and possession in Indian culture was not defined as single individual's success but rather a success of the entire family which collectively secures a higher social position in the society. (Sample 5)
>
> emotional marketing has seen a new marketing shift towards making emotional links and long-term attachment between the company and consumers stronger. (Sample 4)

Despite some (admittedly relatively minor) language errors, these student writers demonstrate a good ability to produce many of the linguistic features identified by Coxhead and Byrd (2007) as typical of academic prose, including effective and accurate use of 'long nouns' and 'big words' (p134) as well as lengthy, well-constructed noun phrases incorporated into compressed sentences (Biber and Gray 2010; Coxhead and Byrd 2007). These examples suggest therefore that it is not language complexity *per se* that creates a problem, but the ability of students to manage and produce that complexity.

While the highest scoring of the scripts, Sample 4, consistently makes highly effective use of complex language, the others are less consistent. Sample 2, for example, often uses shorter, simpler sentences, albeit to express less complex ideas:

White is also a popular colour in typographic design. According to Na and Suk (2014), white is a very suitable background colour in reading materials.

(Sample 2)

In this example sentence structure is comparatively simple, but with some basic terminology the student is able to demonstrate good understanding of design principles. Students struggling to use complex language, then, could perhaps be encouraged to use a simpler style rather than risk compromising on clarity. It is to be seen, however, the impact this might have on the students' ability to express more complex ideas. Barnard (2010) suggests that prioritizing clarity over complexity is to limit students' ability to express more complex ideas, and advocates allowing the inevitable errors and loss of clarity in favour of helping students explore those ideas. The subject lecturers themselves, however, appear to believe that adopting a simpler writing style would not create such a barrier: '*It is possible to express complex ideas with simple words*' (SL1). Further investigation would be needed to test the veracity of this claim.

Clarity of understanding

It was noticeable that during the second interviews, with the sample scripts providing context, much less attention was paid to language and form, and other aspects relating to clarity came to the fore. Language issues, when raised, were indicated in relation to more complex aspects of clarity. This appears to reflect Murray and Sharpling's (2018) findings that subject lecturers tend not to focus unduly on 'individual elements of language accuracy' (p9). Although it should be considered, of course, this reduced attention to language may also have been due to the relatively high levels of language accuracy in the chosen samples, and the resulting 'invisibility' of the language (Turner 2011).

It is understood that, unlike writing by experts, which is expected to 'transform and create knowledge' (Vardi 2008), a key purpose of student writing is to demonstrate understanding of new skills and knowledge (Gardner and Nesi 2013; Vardi 2000). The two programme leaders in this study confirmed that the main purpose of these dissertation-level assignments is to show understanding of what has been learnt, and to demonstrate an ability to apply this to a design project and/or research. It is perhaps unsurprising then that when exploring the samples, discussions more frequently focused on the student writers' ability to clearly articulate their understanding:

As long as they understand the field, they use the right terms, they know what they're saying, they understand [...] that is where clarity comes from in terms of [...] writing about design.

(SL3)

This observation suggests that understanding is fundamental to written clarity: that clarity in writing requires clarity of thought and understanding, and, without the latter, it will be difficult to achieve the former. This view was shared by SL2, who observed the link between understanding and clarity:

It only affects the grade if, because they don't understand the language, they don't understand what they're reading. So, if they've not understood what they're reading then they're clearly not going to [...] be able to express what they've understood.

(SL2)

SL3 noted that it is often when students attempt to present their own stance that they have difficulty expressing themselves clearly, highlighting the link between written clarity and clarity of thought. The following was indicated as an example in which, even with expert knowledge providing a schema, or 'conventional knowledge framework' (Ricoeur, 1983, cited in Couture 1986: 72) for deciphering meaning, the marker was unable to make sense of the second part of the sentence:

Maintaining a consistent visual identity is important, while multiplicity is not the enemy of the designers.

(Sample 2)

On the surface, the issue might appear to be one of language, yet it is difficult to pinpoint what the language issue could be (poor vocabulary choice?, inappropriate and/or ineffective use of metaphor?, mistaken inclusion of the word 'not'?). Comprehension is certainly lost, and in this case the subject lecturer highlighted the dilemma, when marking, of not knowing whether the issue is one of language ability, that is, the student simply not using the right *language* to articulate their point, or of the student having failed to understand a key concept. Clearly this dilemma is significant, due to the potential impact of the latter on the student's grade.

   Seemingly minor language errors were, in effect, seen to become an issue only if they had an impact on how clearly the student demonstrated understanding. SL3, for example, expressed frustration at the indiscriminate and repetitive use of cohesive devices in Sample 3, namely the overuse (and misuse) of 'meanwhile' and 'therefore'. This contributed to an impression that the literature review was *'patched'*: as if *'dropping statements from the literature [...] almost like bullet points'* (SL3) which, although connected by theme, had no clear thread between them. The weak use of connectives appeared not to have an impact on the reader's ability to understand the points made; however, the fact that SL3 *noticed* the language illustrates not only how language can become visible when it is a problem, but that it is indeed made visible by the presence of other, more significant issues which create a mismatch with the 'expectations of what academic writing should be' (Lillis and Turner 2001: 65):

> I'm not sure she understands, that's what I'm saying. Did she understand? And that's when I start to not understand what [...] trying to say. Is it because of the language? Or is it because they don't understand what they are trying to say? Or what the paper was about?
>
> (SL3)

In this case the real issue was the perceived 'patching' of the literature review, highlighted by the perceived language issue, which in turn created doubts in the marker's mind as to whether the student had understood.

Use of terminology

A noticeable quality of all five of the scripts is the competent use of discipline-specific and technical terminology. All include a wide range of technical terms, and successfully use appropriate and well-constructed noun phrases and collocations. The importance, highlighted by SL3, of using 'the right terms', is reminiscent of one of the notions of 'explicitness' indicated in a study by Lillis (2001), that requires students to demonstrate understanding of 'key terms' (p57). Due to the interdisciplinary nature of design, this often requires students to gain a good command not only of the language of the multiple areas of design, and of research methods, but also of a range of areas well beyond their usual field of study. Sample 3, for example, which although identified as the least grammatically accurate, demonstrates competence in the use of terms relating not only to aspects of design (*'color saturation', 'shape-color congruency'*) but also food and nutrition (*'dietary habits', 'energy-dense food intake', 'healthy portion control', 'recommended serving size'*), healthcare (*'co-morbidities', 'healthcare expenditure'*) and marketing (*'consumer behaviour', 'purchase intention'*).

Although the accurate and fluent use of the terminology demonstrates understanding, it is interesting that clarity of understanding can, again, be impacted by even small errors:

> The colour match of flat style logos are always very simple, generally no more than three colours. (Sample 2)
>   Children are obsessed with obesity. (Sample 3)

In both of these examples the subject lecturer pointed out that the incorrect technical term used in the first example ('colour match' should be 'colour combination'), and the poor verb–noun collocation used in the second, while not a major barrier to comprehension, again create doubt for the marker as to whether the student has understood. The ability to use terminology fluently and accurately appears therefore to be an important factor in clearly demonstrating understanding of, and ability to apply, newly accumulated knowledge.

Explicitness of links

A recurring feature of many of the examples of 'good' clarity highlighted during the second interviews was the explicitness of links. This paragraph from the literature review of Sample 1 was highlighted by SL3:

> Gagne et al. (2015) also list some pragmatic 'events of instruction' for different aims about instructional design which are significant reminders for design my motion graphics. For example, establishing proper expectancies for learners by informing them frequently of the learning tasks; reminding them of previous content for effectively long-term memory retrieval. Ensuring the stimuli are received by learners with carefully stimulation. Also appropriate semantic encoding is needed for guiding in learning process. Finally, encouraging learners to make responses can also enhance long-term memory. For more deep strategies, Morrison et al. (2013: 103) further suggest: 1) integration, which enables learners to understand new things in their own words. 2) organisation, so that learners are able to understand how new ideas related to existing ones. 3) elaboration, that reinforces their learning outcome by adding their own ideas to the new information. They are details not only designers but also educators need to be aware of while designing educational materials.

From an EAP practitioner's perspective, the clarity of this paragraph may not be particularly striking: there are evident issues of grammar, structure and cohesion that impact ease of reading. However, what *is* clear in this paragraph is the relevance of the literature to the student's project, which is explicitly (if rather inexpertly) stated both early in the paragraph: *'which are significant reminders for design my motion graphics',* and in the concluding sentence. In this case, explicitly indicating the links between every aspect of the research and the project aims is considered key, and evidently trumps the clarity of expression compromised by less accurate use of language:

> She was very good at understanding what she read and then clearly explaining what she understood, and **how that would inform her future design development**.
>
> (SL3)

Similarly, Sample 3 uses effective cohesive devices to refer both forward and back and, again, explicitly states the relevance of her points to her research:

> **The above research** introduced the background and the causes of children obesity, which explain the importance of controlling the children obesity.' **It is also the motivation of the project.**
>
> (Sample 3)

This form of explicit indication of links between the literature and the students' research, and between the research and project aims, was frequently identified by both programme leaders as an example of good clarity, reflecting the notions of what it means to 'be explicit' identified by Lillis (2001): the importance of making links between claim and evidence, between sections, and between content and research question.

Clarity of purpose

Closely linked to the desired explicitness of links seen above, both subject lecturers identified further examples in the scripts of clarity at text and paragraph level that were noticeably enhanced by effective use of meta-discourse in the form of explicit statements of intention:

> The review first focuses on consumer behaviour, then workings of sharing economy followed by the explanation of rental apparel behaviour. (Sample 5)
> In the subsequent sections, the different types of marketing strategies associated with experience psychology are presented [etc] (Sample 4)
> The literature review mainly covers the following 4 themes. (Sample 3)

This was a recurrent theme, and indeed, it was the explicitness of the students' statements of intent that the lecturers seemed to particularly value: *'the student sums up what she is going to present, then presents it'* (SL2).

This preference was expressed by all three of the subject lecturers in relation to setting out clear aims and objectives. On examination of the sample scripts it was noticeable that all five approached this in the same way: with a brief statement outlining the aims (between one and three sentences), followed by the objectives in 'list-like' form, that is, as a list but with full sentences (Leedham 2015). There was variation in the format of the latter including the use of sub-headings: '*Objective 1, Objective 2 ...* ' (Sample 4), bullet points (Sample 3) and numbers (Samples 1, 2 and 5). It is perhaps significant that the Reflective Reports (samples 1, 2 and 3) all expressed the aims in a single sentence, suggesting that specific instruction may have been given.

From a language perspective, it was also noticeable that a common feature of the examples of good clarity identified by the subject lecturers within the samples was the effective use of discourse markers. The examples varied; however, all made effective use of clear discourse markers indicating intent at section or paragraph level. These include the more formulaic move-markers, as seen in one of the abstracts: '*The purpose of the research project is to ...*'; '*The aim is to ...*'; '*The key findings indicate that ...*'; '*This research concludes that ...*'; '*The study suggests that ...*' (Sample 5). Even when expressed somewhat clumsily: '*due to these reasons*' (Sample 5), or informally: '*in the end*' (Sample 3) the clarity of intent remains, creating flow and enhancing ease of reading by directing the reader through the text.

Discussion

The findings confirm that clarity is complex, multifaceted and subjective, and show how its meaning and manifestation can vary according to context. From an academic literacies perspective, this apparent complexity and subjectivity suggests that clarity is not something that can be 'defined' as such: as to do so would be to adopt a monologic view of language as static and transparent (Lillis 2003). The nature of clarity is by no means static or fixed, and hence it would be neither productive nor accurate to try and label it under a single definition.

For this study to be useful in the context of EAP practice, however, this complexity needs to be unpicked in order to understand the implications for teaching academic writing. Breaking clarity down into its various aspects, in turn linked to linguistic features that are seen to affect it in certain contexts, might help EAP practitioners, academic writing tutors and even subject lecturers or students themselves, to interrogate and explore the role and perception of

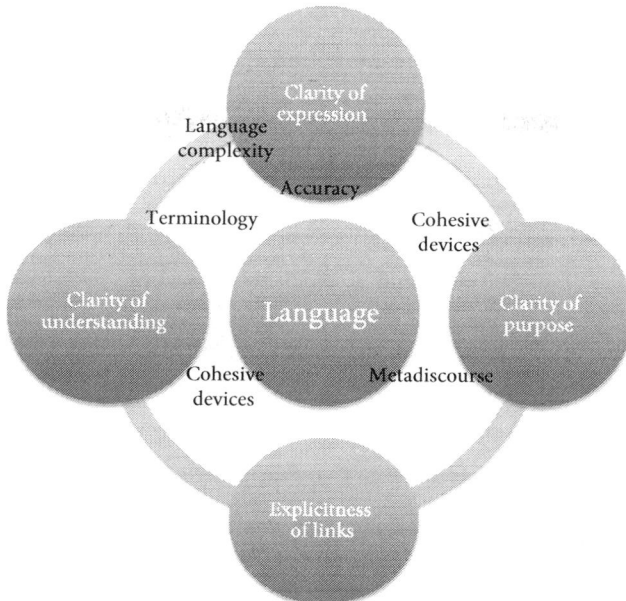

Figure 3.1 *Mapping clarity in design.*

clarity in their own context, helping them to understand and identify priorities for enhancing written clarity.

The diagram in Figure 3.1 is an attempt to map the broad themes identified in the findings that emerged from this study. It is intended to help 'demystify' and understand the perception of clarity ostensibly in the context of this study, but might also be seen as a heuristic that could be used to explore and gain a greater understanding of clarity in writing and how it can be manifested in other contexts.

Sub-categories of clarity

In the context of this study, four broad areas of clarity were identified: clarity of expression, clarity of purpose, explicitness of links and clarity of understanding. Based as they are on a study of limited scope, the identified categories are inevitably both context-driven and subjective. All the same, they provide useful sub-categories, and a starting point from which to identify features that impact clarity, whether within the context of this study or beyond. It is of note that the categories emerging from the study generally correspond to aspects of clarity previously seen in the literature, suggesting their potential applicability to other contexts. From that perspective this study confirms the importance of those aspects of clarity in practice and has seen what they can 'look like' on the page in one specific context.

The four sub-categories of clarity identified are represented as being linked (Figure 1). This is significant since, as the study progressed, it became increasingly apparent that they cannot be 'separated' completely: they appear to interact to create an overall sense of clarity. Clarity of understanding, for example, is seen to be affected by clarity of expression, and can be enhanced by explicit expressions of purpose, all of which can combine to create the 'smooth read' (Turner 2018) favoured by the subject lecturers and markers.

Language

It might be tempting to understate the role of language in achieving clarity, due to the apparent ability of subject lecturers to 'see past' the language, the demonstrated tolerance of language errors and the insistence that language is not a key determiner of grade. In the context of this study, *clarity of student understanding* arguably emerged as the most important sub-category in terms of impact on grade: indeed, while subject lecturers appeared more open to giving students the benefit of the doubt in terms of issues relating to language accuracy, questions relating to clarity of understanding created greater difficulties due to the need for rigour in assessment. This parallels the findings of Murray and Sharpling (2018: 8) who found that markers:

> were not obviously preoccupied with more formal aspects of language such as accuracy and range of vocabulary, grammar and syntax, but instead were often more attentive [...] to other dimensions of student writing.

Throughout the study it became increasingly evident, however, that clarity in the sub-categories does depend on the successful use of a series of linguistic features. This reaffirms the central role of language in achieving clarity (hence its position in the centre of the map in Figure 1). The emergence of aspects of language use as key to clearly demonstrating understanding appears to confirm that language, used as it is to articulate ideas, is central to both building understanding and the process of meaning-making (Turner 2018), and that arguably language and content cannot be separated.

Linguistic features impacting written clarity

Linked to this, the findings show that the various aspects of clarity can be manifested in different ways, encompassing various linguistic features, which may have a greater or lesser impact on the clarity of the piece from the perspective of the reader. The following features were seen to enhance (or diminish) clarity within the sub-categories:

- Accurate and appropriate use of specialist terminology from relevant fields
- Appropriate use of cohesive devices and discourse markers
- Effective use of meta-discourse
- Well-controlled language complexity
- Language accuracy

These features are seen to have a varying impact on clarity, and, as with the sub-categories, may intersect. For this reason they are represented as 'floating' between language and the sub-categories (Figure 1). This reflects the link between language and clarity but can also highlight the greater or lesser 'closeness' to one or the other. In the context of this study, the use of technical terminology is seen as a key factor in expressing clarity of understanding; however, it also lies close to language accuracy since it was observed that even minor inaccuracies in the use of the terminology raised doubts relating to understanding. Similarly, effective meta-discourse can be used to both clearly state intention and explicitly indicate links between ideas, sections and theory and practice, hence its position between the two.

Both the sub-categories and the linguistic features represented in Figure 1 are, of course, specific to the context of design within this study. They illustrate not only their impact on clarity, but highlight the value placed on certain features of writing by specialists in this subject area. It is likely that beyond this context they will be subject to disciplinary variation. While use of meta-language to express purpose emerged as key within this context of design, for example, Lea and Street (2000) note that for some, in other disciplines, this is neither needed nor appreciated. The diagram in Figure 1, therefore, represents a mapping exercise that would likely look very different according to the discipline, context or even specific assignment being studied: features and aspects of clarity might be moved, removed or added depending on the picture that builds within the specific discipline or context.

Implications and conclusions

The value placed on clarity in student writing will be of little surprise to those involved in teaching or assessing student academic writing. There is an implicit assumption that students should express their message clearly, and yet this quest for clarity, so evident in the rubrics of marking criteria and assignment feedback, has remained an ambiguous and relatively unfathomed aspect of student writing. This snapshot study has taken a tentative first step towards identifying, on a practical level, some of the ways in which clarity can be achieved, and how it can impact the student's ability to achieve the key purpose of assessed work.

From an EAP perspective, the evident complexity of clarity, and its subjectivity dependent on the context in which it is required, suggest a need for both students and those teaching academic writing to understand and reflect on what constitutes clarity in their own context, and how it is manifested within the discipline in which they are operating. An increased awareness and understanding of clarity on the part of the EAP practitioner could in turn be transferred to the students through a more explicit focus in academic writing classes, more careful wording of feedback and attentive analysis of assignment guidelines and task briefs. A mapping process such as that shown could aid EAP practitioners in pinpointing which aspects of their students' writing might cause issues and why, and how these might be addressed.

While this study has identified language as central to achieving greater written clarity, as with other important written features such as 'argument' and 'structure' (Lea and Street 2000), the achievement of clarity may also be linked to the tacit disciplinary conventions of meaning-making and knowledge-creation of the discipline. Lea and Street (2000: 39) point out that:

> What makes a piece of student writing 'appropriate' has more to do with issues of epistemology than with the surface features of form to which staff often have recourse when describing their student's writing.

If this is the case, then clarity needs exploring beyond the linguistic features that manifest it. In the context of a creative, applied discipline such as design, for example, the ability to clearly and explicitly express how theory has informed the research and/or design, requires critical thought as well as understanding. Mastering the appropriate language to achieve the former will not be enough to achieve the latter. Murray and Sharpling (2018: 9) suggest that EAP courses 'should perhaps focus less on language *per se* and more on other aspects of writing such as students' understanding of subject-specific content and their critical engagement with it', and this seems key with regard to improving written clarity. The importance of developing criticality, as well as honing academic reading skills, for the purpose of improving clarity should not be underestimated. As pointed out by the subject lecturers, if students have not understood what they have read they will struggle to express the rationale of their project or argument clearly. Clarity relates both to language and content: they cannot be separated. Achieving written clarity will require clarity of thought and understanding coupled with the most effective language to articulate that thought. At a practical level, students need to be encouraged to take an analytical approach to clarity itself, in order to identify what is valued and constitutes clarity in their own discipline. Encouraging students, as readers themselves, to analyse, question and evaluate the clarity of both professional writing within their discipline, and their own writing and that of their peers might help them to identify the multiple facets of clarity themselves, and gain an awareness of its subjectivity.

It would be reductive to base the value of clarity purely on assessment; nonetheless, students need to understand that the potential impact of clarity on their grade goes well beyond basic language errors, for which it seems subject lecturers show good levels of tolerance. However, it is also important to point out that the sub-categories and linguistic features pertaining to clarity identified here may differ not only according to discipline, but also according to purpose and audience of the written text. As seen previously, students are commonly encouraged to model their writing on journal articles (Nesi and Gardner 2006), and yet the purpose of such texts is very different: the importance of 'clarity of understanding' in a journal article, for example, would surely be less important, since (a) the student would be writing for an expert audience assumed to already have some knowledge of the subject, and (b) acceptance for publication would presumably in itself be acknowledgement of the student's (albeit recently acquired) 'expert status' and hence understanding. Language accuracy, on the other hand, might become a higher priority in the context of writing for publication, with expert readers showing less tolerance of inaccuracy. Increasing students' awareness of these differences could thus help students improve their writing beyond the immediate needs of their assignments and towards future professional needs.

Inevitably, the scope of a small-scale exploratory study of this type is limited and thus presents numerous opportunities for further research in a variety of directions. While the aim of this study was specifically to explore perceptions of clarity from the perspective of the reader/subject specialist/marker, the socially situated nature of student writing points to the value of extending the study of clarity to encompass the perspective of the student writer. This might then allow an additional focus on potential cultural differences in the perception of clarity. From a linguistic perspective there will likely be additional linguistic, stylistic and textual features that impact clarity, which did not emerge from this small-scale study. Such features might include structure, argumentation, layout and use of visuals: all of which would merit investigation. There is also, of course, scope for more in-depth linguistic research into the very specific features of language identified in this study in order to evaluate their real impact on clarity from the perspective of the reader. It would be interesting, for example, to explore which language inaccuracies have a greater impact on clarity, as well as the potential impact of sentence structure, sentence length, paragraph structure or paragraph length. In addition, further, similar exploratory studies in other disciplines would help build a broader picture of clarity and test the hypothesis of differences between disciplines, which would in turn help to create an increased understanding of clarity and its complexities across the academy.

References

Allison, D. (2004). 'Creativity, Students' Academic Writing, and EAP: Exploring Comments on Writing in an English Language Degree Programme'. *Journal of English for Academic Purposes* 3: 191–209.

Baghat, D., and O'Neill, P. (2009). '*Writing Design:* A Collaboration between the *Write Now* CETL and The Sir John Cass Department of Art, Media and Design'. *Art Design & Communication in Higher Education* 8 (2): 177–82.

BALEAP. (2008). *Competency Framework for Teachers of English for Academic Purposes.* https://www.baleap.org/wp-content/uploads/2016/04/teap-competency-framework.pdf.

Barnard, I. (2010). 'The Ruse of Clarity'. *National Council of Teachers of English (NCTE)* 61 (3): 434–51.

Baynham, M. (2000). 'Academic Writing in New and Emergent Discipline Areas'. In Lea, M. R., and Stierer, B. (eds.), *Student Writing in Higher Education.* Ch. 1. Buckingham: Open University Press.

Becher, T. (2006). 'The Significance of Disciplinary Differences'. *Studies in Higher Education* 19 (2): 151–61.

Biber, D., and Gray, B. (2010). 'Challenging Stereotypes about Academic Writing: Complexity, Elaboration, Explicitness'. *Journal of English for Academic Purposes* 9: 2–20

Bond, B. (2018). *Understanding the Intersection of Language, Disciplinary Knowledge Communication and Identity. Project Report.* Leeds: Leeds Institute for Teaching Excellence.

Borg, E. (2012). 'Writing Differently in Art and Design: Innovative Approaches to Writing Tasks'. In Clughen, C., and Hardy, C. (eds.), *WiD: Building Supportive Cultures for Student Writing in UK Higher Education*. Bingley: Emerald Group Publishing.

Candlin, F. (2000). 'Practice-Based Doctorates and Questions of Academic Legitimacy'. *International Journal of Art and Design Education* 19 (1): 96–101.

Carter, R. and Nash, W. (1990). *Seeing through Language*. Oxford: Blackwell.

Couture, B. (1986). 'Effective Ideation in Written Text: A Functional Approach to Clarity and Exigence'. In Couture, B. (ed.), *Functional Approaches to Writing: Research Perspectives*, 69–92. London: Frances Pinter.

Coxhead, A., and Byrd, P. (2007). 'Preparing Writing Teachers to Teach the Vocabulary and Grammar of Academic Prose'. *Journal of Second Language Writing* 16: 129–47.

Gardner, S., and Nesi, H. (2013). 'A Classification of Genre Families in University Student Writing'. *Applied Linguistics* 34 (1): 25–52.

Hyland, K. (2004). *Disciplinary Discourses. Social Interactions in Academic Writing*. Michigan: The University of Michigan Press.

Lazer, G., and Barnaby, B. (2015). 'Working with Grammar as a Tool for Making Meaning'. In Lillis T. et al. (eds.), *Working with Academic Literacies. Case Studies towards Transformative Practice*. Ch. 21. Colorado: The WAC Clearing House.

Lea, M. R., and Stierer, B. (2000). 'Editor's Introduction'. In Lea, M. R., and Stierer, B. (eds.), *Student Writing in Higher Education*, 1–13. Buckingham: Open University Press.

Lea, M. R., and Street, B. V. (2000). 'Student Writing and Staff Feedback in Higher Education: An Academic Literacies Approach'. In Lea, M. R., and Stierer, B. (eds.), *Student Writing in Higher Education*. Ch. 2. Buckingham: Open University Press.

Leedham, M. (2015). 'Learning from Lecturers: What Disciplinary :Practice can Teach us about 'good' Student Writing'. In Lillis, T. et al. (eds.), *Working with Academic Literacies. Case Studies towards Transformative Practice*. Ch. 12. Colorado: The WAC Clearing House.

Lillis, T. (2001). *Student Writing. Access, Regulation, Desire*. London: Routledge.

Lillis, T. (2003). 'Student Writing as "Academic Literacies": Drawing on Bakhtin to move from Critique to Design'. *Language and Education* 17 (3): 192–207.

Lillis, T., and Turner, J. (2001). 'Student Writing in Higher Education: Contemporary Confusion, Traditional Concerns'. *Teaching in Higher Education* 6 (1): 57–8.

Melles, G., and Lockheart, J. (2012). 'Writing Purposefully in Art and Design. Responding to Converging and Diverging New Academic Literacies'. *Arts and Humanities in Higher Education* 11 (4): 346–62.

Murray, N., and Sharpling, G. (2018). 'What Traits Do Academics Value in Student Writing? Insights from a Psychometric Approach'. *Assessment & Evaluation in Higher Education* 44 (3): 489–500.

Nesi, H., and Gardner, S. (2006). 'Variation in Disciplinary Culture: University Tutors' views on Assessed Writing Tasks'. In Kiely, R. et al. (eds.), *Language, Culture and Identity in Applied Linguistics*. Ch. 6. London: Equinox Publishing.

Orr, S., and Shreve, A. (2018). *Art and Design Pedagogy in Higher Education: Knowledge, Values, and Ambiguity in the Creative Curriculum.* Abingdon: Routledge.

Oxford University Press. [Online]. (2019). s.v. Clarity. Available from: https://www.lexico.com/definition/clarity (Accessed 6 January 2020).

Turner, J. (2011). *Language in the Academy. Cultural Reflexivity and Intercultural Dynamics.* Bristol: Multilingual Matters.

Turner, J. (2018). *On Writtenness. The Cultural Politics of Academic Writing.* London: Bloomsbury.

University of Leeds Taught Student Education Board. (2016). *Policy on Inclusive Coursework Marking.* [Circular]. Leeds: University of Leeds.

Vardi, I. (2000). What Lecturers Want: An Investigation of Lecturers' Expectations in First Year Essay Writing Tasks. *Pacific Rim First Year Experience Conference.*

4

Musicology and Its Others

Karen Burland, Edward Venn and Scott McLaughlin

Approaching the concept of good writing within music is no easy matter. As with any disciplinary area within higher education, music's boundaries are 'never stable nor objects of study fixed in stone' (Hyland 2015: 34). To compensate for this mutability, Ken Hyland suggests that 'the distinctive existence of disciplines can be informed by study of their rhetorical practices' (2015: 34). But the rhetorical practices of music are largely absent from the EAP (English for Academic Purposes) literature,[1] often subsumed and hidden within broader disciplinary groupings. One might argue that the significant role afforded to the argumentative essay within the arts and humanities, into which music is often grouped, is thus also true for music, and can inform notions of what good writing might constitute in this area (Gardner and Nesi 2013; Mei 2006; Wingate 2012). On the other hand, many music students will be exposed within their studies to modules and writing genres that derive from the social sciences or STEM subjects, problematizing the neat parcelling of music's disciplinary (rhetorical) practices into a single, mutually exclusive category (Cooper and Bikowski 2007). In this chapter we examine and critique the ways in which categorical groupings around disciplinary organization and writing genres are understood in the context of music in higher education from the perspectives of taught postgraduate (PGT) students and academic staff. By better understanding the issues underpinning good writing within music, this chapter offers the basis for further study in this area.

---

[1] EAP is described by Ding and Bruce as a 'specialist branch of English-language teaching concerned with preparing students to undertake university study [... and] cope with the writing requirements of higher education' (2017: 1–2). EAP necessarily covers a broad range of topics, including curriculum design and pedagogy across different academic genres, but also extending into rhetoric, systemic functional linguistics and academic literacies.

Music(ology) and its others

One of the most immediate challenges facing music students as they approach tasks centred upon writing is the diversity to be found within the subject area. Different national organizations responsible for the accreditation of music programmes draw attention to the various specializations that can be found within such programmes: sub-disciplinary areas such as performance, music history, music theory, music psychology/therapy, composition, pedagogy, jazz/popular music studies and music technology are commonly encountered, as are, increasingly, emerging areas such as music business and music and well-being (see, for instance, Quality Assurance Agency 2016; Australian Tertiary Education Quality and Standards Agency 2017; National Association of Schools of Music 2018). As this rudimentary list demonstrates, these sub-disciplines embrace approaches to the study of music that sit within traditional arts and humanities programmes (e.g. music history or, more broadly, musicology) as well as those that link to other meta-disciplinary groupings (musicology's 'others', such as psychology, pedagogy, technology, and business). As a result of these meta-disciplinary overlaps, one of the key challenges students face when grappling with the diverse expectations of, and demands within, each of the sub-disciplinary areas, is how to write in an appropriate manner. However, teaching practices around EAP are rarely made explicit by staff. The learning of good writing in music is frequently assumed rather than stated, delivered tacitly through exposure to texts – typically published research articles (Gardner and Nesi 2013) – rather than through studied reflection of their characteristics. To understand good writing in music, therefore, is to confront not only the increasing diversity of writing styles and genres required by its many sub-disciplines, but to reflect upon the implicit hierarchies and assumptions about writing within and across these sub-disciplines.

There has been growth in the number of attempts to capture the breadth of music as an area of academic study. Cook (2000) presents a critical examination of how one might think about music with obvious value for pedagogues as a text for discussion, but there is no attempt to situate the ideas within an educational framework. A more student-focused critical introduction to music studies can be found in Harper-Scott and Samson (2009). Each individual chapter is devoted to one of the sub-disciplinary areas commonly found in undergraduate music curricula (including, and extending beyond, the list above). The focus of the collection, however, is on introducing and stimulating thought within each of the areas (much in the spirit of Cook); there is no attempt at defining ways of writing appropriate to these sub-disciplines, other than for Harper-Scott to note in the introduction that, whilst at university, 'you will learn, of course, to hone your writing and oral skills to a range of particular applications' (Harper-Scott 2009: 2).

Both of these examples (and a more recent third, Heile et al. 2018, aimed primarily at practitioners rather than students) emerge from UK academia, reflecting in part the relatively consistent core of sub-disciplinary content within a UK music degree. Despite these origins, their intended market is global, as part of what might be considered an international trend towards a critical, reflective stance towards the subject matter (see Sarath 2014; and the international contributors to Burnard and Haddon 2015, and to Rink, Gaunt and Williamon 2017). Nor is such a shift restricted to Anglophone academic communities (for an overview of disciplinary rethinking in German-speaking countries, see for instance Calella and Urbanek 2013; Gardner and Springfeld 2014; Hentschel 2018). However, in all of these instances the target audience is academic, and the impact of such disciplinary rethinking on writing practices is barely recognized. The implication remains that educators will absorb – or have already absorbed – and then transmit good writing practices to their students that are consistent with the rhetorical demands of the (sub)discipline.

Eva Moreda Rodríguez (2018) offers a rare disciplinary reflection on the act of writing itself. Noting that while thinking and writing about music are 'inextricably linked', she recognizes the desire for students to 'consider, and maybe practice, how each of the genres and styles [of writing about music] differ' (2018: 126), and that the 'extended undergraduate essay' is taken as the quintessential undergraduate genre (2018: 128). Here, the underlying assumption seems to be that the traditional musicological subjects (primarily music history) form the point of departure. This can be contrasted with alternative modes of writing, including those afforded by new media (such as blogs, reflective commentaries and hypertexts (2018: 129)). Moreda Rodríguez acknowledges that such writing genres may not necessarily aspire to the same levels of accuracy of grammar and spelling as the traditional essay (p. 130), encourage the adoption of a more subjective, personal style (2018: 131), or have the quality of a work-in-progress (2018: 132). Nevertheless, this focus on style falls short of identifying what good writing in such genres might look like; rather, Moreda Rodríguez simply observes that such modes of writing need not match that found in other genres.

The 'rhetorical practices' that function to define music as a discipline (Hyland 2015: 34) cannot therefore be reduced to the genre of the argumentative essay that characterizes traditional musicological writing, given the presence in the curriculum of its others (which is to say, alternative writing tasks including those originating within other broad disciplinary groupings such as social sciences). Nor, on the other hand, can we discount the foundational role of the argumentative essay in the way that academic staff conceive of good writing. (It is notable that the most common forms of writing that emerge in the interviews for our study are the argumentative essay and the report, but that within these forms the genre of writing is diverse due to differing expectations of sub-disciplines.) The precise definition of writing genres within music runs the same risk of semantic slippage and fuzziness of boundaries that marks discourse around disciplinary areas (Cooper and Bikowski 2007; Lea and Street 1998). Nevertheless, the adoption of stable categories of genre families (such as those found in Gardner and Nesi 2013) offers a starting point for approaching music-specific rhetorical practices, if only to highlight the permeability of these categories and the play that takes place within them in more local disciplinary and sub-disciplinary contexts.

This chapter therefore aims to answer two primary research questions:

1. Given the diversity of sub-disciplinary approaches and writing genres within music curricula, how do music students and academic staff conceive of good writing?
2. What are the pedagogical implications of these student and staff perspectives?

Methodology

In order to understand rhetorical practices around good writing in music, we employed a social-constructivist approach using semi-structured interviews to explore the commonalities and points of divergence across the sub-disciplines of music, from the perspectives of five staff members and four PGT students (including two international participants – one staff member (Arthur) and one student (Layla)). Staff members were selected to represent the range of subject areas represented in the school. The four PGT students were selected to ensure a spread of disciplines, and were recommended by the staff participants as high-achieving students who would be well situated to answer the interview questions to an appropriate level of depth. In terms of background, all the students completed undergraduate studies at UK universities, with two of them being continuing students from Leeds: see Appendix One for a table of interviewee information. The use of semi-structured interviews reflects prior studies in the field (Lea and Street 1998; Nesi and Gardner 2006). Interview questions explored the characteristics of good (and poor) writing and its perceived impact on the quality of the work, the ways in which good writing is taught and acquired, and the challenges faced by students in developing their writing (as well as the strategies used by staff to help students in this aspect of their work) (see Appendix Two for a full list of questions). The interviews were conducted by Burland (n=7) and Venn (n=2) who worked from the same interview schedule and discussed the interviews during the period of data collection to ensure consistency. The interviews were transcribed verbatim and then analysed by Burland using thematic analysis (Braun and Clarke 2006). Thematic analysis is a useful technique for understanding individuals' personal perceptions and experiences of phenomena whilst also facilitating the identification of more general trends and comparisons within the data. Burland carried out the initial coding, which revealed six main themes (each consisting of a small number of sub-themes). These were discussed by all authors, and the themes were revised and consolidated to create three final themes (criticality, developing a voice, and teaching and learning argumentation). These three themes provide the structure for the discussion of the results below. Ethical approval was obtained from the Arts, Humanities and Cultures Faculty Research Ethics Committee (LTMUSC-090). Participants were provided with full information about the study when they were invited to attend an interview, and they each provided consent before the interviews commenced. Participants are referred to with pseudonyms and their sub-discipline and role (staff or student) are also indicated after quotations (e.g. Charlotte, music psychology, staff).

Context and sample

The study focuses on PGT writing in the School of Music, University of Leeds, UK: we chose this focus because PGT students possess an appropriate level of experience and objectivity to discuss their own writing in relation to their varied experience at UG level and on their current programme. To provide some more local context for our discussion, it is worth outlining the breadth of programmes taught within the School of Music. At undergraduate level the School offers five single-honours programmes in music, and although three of these engage explicitly with disciplinary conventions from outside of the arts and humanities (business, psychology, electronic engineering), all students have the potential to take modules (and thus encounter writing genres) from a variety of subject areas. Conversely, all students are delivered academic skills training in their first year that underpin the writing of extended argumentative essays, and the majority go on to develop these skills further in later years of study. At PGT level, the School offers master's-level programmes in applied psychology of music, performance, composition, electronic and computer music, music and management, and musicology. Although these programmes offer a greater degree of specialization in particular musical sub-disciplinary areas, there is, on the one hand, optionality within programmes that potentially exposes students to other sub-disciplinary practices and, on the other, a limited range of writing genres that cut across the programmes (albeit inflected, in certain cases, in response to the demands of each sub-discipline). Students and staff alike are thus required, to varying extents, to be familiar with differing norms and expectations of a number of sub-disciplinary areas – a practice Lea and Street describe as 'course switching', analogous to code switching (1998: 161). Only a small percentage of PGT students at Leeds have also completed UG music programmes at Leeds, but both anecdotal evidence and the research of Harper-Scott and Heile et al. indicate that the UG experience around academic skills and writing is largely similar across the UK.[2]

Table 4.1 demonstrates the *compulsory* written assignments encountered by PGT students enrolled on the master's programmes in the School of Music, mapped onto the writing genre families outlined by Gardner and Nesi (2013). The purpose here is not to reduce the differences between these assignments and thereby highlight commonalities between programmes (although such commonalities exist) but to establish a baseline vocabulary that enables the fluidity of thinking within and between genres to become more apparent. At the time of the study, all students took an academic skills module that required them to complete a literature survey; essays both argumentative (emphasizing critical thinking) and discursive (which includes programme notes for performance modules) cut across all programmes. It can be observed from Table 4.1 that: first, the majority of students will still be required to complete at least one argumentative essay within their study; second, argumentative essays will count for a significant proportion of the credit-bearing assessments; third, students in programmes such as Music and Management would likely take optional modules requiring argumentative essays; and finally, that given the students' typical undergraduate background, notions of the argumentative essay would likely form a central component of student understanding of what constitutes good writing.

---

[2]   With only two international representatives in the sample, it is inevitable that writing practices within UK higher education became the focus of this study. In fact, the approaches and perspectives offered by all staff and students, regardless of background, were remarkably coherent, suggesting that the practices described in this chapter can be taking as representative of EAP more widely.

Table 4.1 Compulsory Written Assignments in the PGT programmes (School of Music).

Genre/Programme	Musicology	Electronic and Computer Music	Music Psychology	Music and management	Composition	Performance
Case study			X	X		
Critique			X			
Essay (argumentative)	X	X	X	X	X	
Essay (discussion)			X	X		X
Exercise				X		
Literature survey	X	X	X	X	X	X
Narrative recount				X		
Research report		X	X	X	X	

Despite the argumentative essay – and, by extension, argumentation within other genre types – being so central to the academic experience, Ursula Wingate has noted that 'many academic teachers and students have fuzzy concepts of argumentation, which may be linked to a fuzzy understanding of what the genre "essay" entails' (2012: 146). In order to examine this understanding, interview participants comprised five academic staff (representing the sub-disciplines of composition, musicology (both historical and aesthetics), music psychology and music management), and four PGT students (representing composition, musicology, music psychology and music management). The small sample size acts as a natural constraint on the depth of insight that can be achieved, and whilst generalizations are impossible to draw (either for the School in-itself, or music as a discipline), the study can provide questions and probe theoretical ideas for future research.

Results and discussion

The diversity of sub-disciplinary areas within music represented in the sample meant that a range of writing genres (using Gardner and Nesi's 2013 categorization) were mentioned by academic tutors and students in response to the (non-specific) interview questions, but also that (notionally) the same type of genre was discussed in relation to multiple subject areas. Thematic analysis of the interviews revealed a fuzziness of thinking about genre that corresponds to Cooper and Bikowski's identification of the 'difficulty in classifying writing assignments into neat, mutually exclusive categories' (2007: 218). This is conceivably a reflection of the productive tensions between the musicological argumentative essay (as a benchmark for thinking about writing in music) and trans-disciplinary affordances from the social sciences and STEM subjects that inflect understanding of different genre families and writing practices within other musical sub-disciplinary groups. In particular, this tension gives rise in the data to a blurring of distinctions between genre families on the one hand and competing understandings of what particular categories (most notably 'essay') might mean in practice.

More broadly, thematic analysis revealed two principal themes that the participants' perceived as characteristic of good writing, and a third that relates to teaching and learning:

1. Criticality
2. Developing a position, finding a voice
3. Teaching and learning argumentation

The fuzziness of thinking about genre is reflected – inevitably, and to varying extents – in discussions within these thematic groupings, and points to the complexity of thinking about good writing in music. As a result, the data allow for an exploration and problematization of good writing in music against the background of genre as an orienting concept.

Criticality

To be able to position your work in relation to others and acknowledge what's come before and how this work builds up on that.

(Jack, composition/technology, staff)

Given that critical thinking is central to conceptions of higher education (Johnston et al. 2011; Woodward-Kron 2002), it is of no surprise that all participants discussed aspects of criticality in relation to good writing. The importance of critical thinking within the music undergraduate experience is embodied by the centrality of the musicological essay (the 'quintessential undergraduate genre' (Moreda Rodriguez 2018: 128)), and the lessons learned here continue into PGT programmes. Similarly, Gardner and Nesi note the essay as the genre in which students are intended 'to demonstrate/develop the ability to construct a coherent argument and employ critical thinking skills' (2013: 38). This definition, then, gives clues to what might comprise good essay writing – namely *critical thinking* and *constructing a coherent argument*. There is evidence within our data that these elements are important for conceptions of good writing in music in general, although the way in which this works in practice, and in different sub-disciplines, is perhaps more complex.

At a superficial level, there were differences in the ways that criticality was described by those working and studying within the different sub-disciplines and these aligned with the focus of the writing: writing about creative or professional practice (e.g. composition, technology, management, performance) required integration of theory and practice, alongside providing a rationale for, and critical reflection of, that practice. Writing in other sub-disciplines (psychology, musicology, aesthetics) focused mainly on developing an argument through 'the analysis and evaluation of content knowledge' (Wingate 2012: 146). The genres which are most typical of these two general sub-disciplinary 'camps' could be aligned with aspects of, in turn, the Essay and the Research Report (see Table 4.1), which may suggest that good writing in these contexts might be expected to be different. However, the data we collected suggest that this is not the case, and that the ways in which these writing genres are understood (and applied) in music are different from their description in the literature, which has implications for how good writing is understood.

Criticality and the (musicological) essay

Students working in musicology, aesthetics and psychology will typically write essays (including extended dissertations) which require them to demonstrate an understanding of their knowledge, to engage critically with the literature, or to develop a particular argument. Within this particular grouping of sub-disciplinary areas, the focus is on working with the literature to build a critically informed argument:

> Engagement with relevant literature is obviously very important ... Doing so in a way that's integrated into the argument and the stages the argument needs to go through rather than just sort of as some sort of division into ... 'writers x,y, and z have looked at the topic, allowed me to do a little literature review, [laughs] and then present my own argument' ... having a bit of a flow and managing to sort of build in looking at what other people have said in conjunction with making your own argument. I think is something that characterizes strong students.
>
> (Sam, aesthetics, staff)

Students seemed to share this understanding, discussing the need to integrate the literature carefully within their writing in order to justify a particular approach, as well as to present a clear argument.

> If you don't explain completely where your point has come from then it's open to the criticism of, and it's open to wrongful misinterpretation as well. Because if you've not fully explained why you're saying something it's very easy for someone to criticize it and be like 'well here are the five things you probably mean!'
>
> (Ellie, musicology, student)

How does this shared understanding emerge? Students uniformly identified practice and trial and error as the source of this learning, as described below:

> People judge writing in different ways and good writing is different for everybody, so I think getting different people's opinions on a piece of work is really valuable because that kind of represents what, what we've said about there being different viewpoints on a piece of work and I think the more opinions you can get – so whether that's like, discussing in class about, like, particular piece of work and going through it, like, methodically, I think that could be quite good.
>
> (Seren, music psychology, student)

Seren's comments are typical of the other student participants, who identified the value of testing their writing through gathering feedback on work-in-progress from staff and peers, and through practice. The implication here is that students tacitly absorb critical principles through discussion with academics and peers. The sense that there is no 'right' answer further complicates this process, pointing to the need for those working in music to go further in clarifying the expectations and principles of good writing. The assessment criteria – which students are pointed to both in general teaching and via feedback – do address ideas of good writing, but as explained in the introduction these are often tacit understandings. It is perhaps revealing that the students did not mention assessment criteria, despite the fact that they were all clearly discussing written assignments within the interviews, and this perhaps further emphasizes the tacit nature of good writing in music.

Moving beyond the demonstration of critical engagement with literature, staff discussed how good writing could also emerge from a *creative criticality* (Cooper 2018) through which students work with the literature in order to generate new ideas and perspectives.

> The things I tend to like are where someone has suggested a new interpretation of a piece of music … you say to students 'well how is this going to change my life?' … and actually these [the essays he was discussing at this point] have because you read that and you think 'yes … I hadn't thought of seeing the work like that' or 'by invoking that context … you really have created a new interpretation of that piece of music'. So … it's the sources he's found in a sense but it's also the way he's applied those and created this new reading of the piece of music.
>
> (Lennie, musicology, staff)

Charlotte echoes Lennie's comments, stating her preference for psychology dissertations to 'draw on stuff outside of psychology, so interdisciplinary. That shows me a bit of creativity in trying to think outside the discipline to get some wider perspectives on the topic' (psychology, staff). Although framed in slightly different terms, students concurred. Seren (a music psychology student) described her approach to critical writing as a creative process in which she was 'trying to problem find … and balance that to show you've thought about it in light of relevant literature'.

The data suggest that – at least within the genre of the essay – critical engagement with literature provides a context for *original* interpretations or arguments to be proposed. This goes beyond Gardner and Nesi's (2013) definition of genre, but may be explained by the fact that the staff and students here are generally only discussing work at master's level.³ Whilst not specifically stated in the UK Quality Assurance Agency's 'Characteristics Statement' for a master's degree, originality is an implicit criteria for higher-achieving research projects (2015). For music sub-disciplinary areas in which the extended essay (i.e. dissertation) is the main credit-bearing component of the programme, the association of originality and good writing is perhaps inevitable.⁴ It is worth noting that the assessment criteria refer to originality in the first-class grade bands only. However, while the above discussion may suggest that criticality is applicable only within the context of the essay, other examples suggest that it is equally important within other sub-disciplines and genres.

Criticality within the research report

Students working across a number of sub-disciplinary areas at master's level in music will be required to complete at least one Research Report (see Table 4.1). The purpose of such tasks (in Gardner and Nesi's terms) is:

> To demonstrate/develop ability to undertake a complete piece of research including research design, and an appreciation of its significance in the field. Includes student's research aim/question, investigation, links and relevance to other research in the field.
>
> (2013: 40)

This definition suggests that good writing in this genre might include evaluating the literature, addressing a research question and justifying the chosen research design. In the specific cases of composition and music technology modules (compulsory for students on these programmes), students are required to develop portfolios of practice and write accompanying narratives to contextualize their work and justify their decision process. Our data suggest that these elements were used as markers of good writing within this context, though the sub-disciplines of composition and technology required an additional level of critical thinking than Gardner and Nesi's definition would allow for. As Jack describes below, these sub-disciplines require students to explicate their practice through

---

³ Nesi and Gardner (2006) do discuss originality, although it is conflated with creativity as 'the most frequently stated desirable quality' after the quality of coherent structure (p. 113). They also mention originality as something expected from final-year students, less so from students in lower years.

⁴ The sense that critical engagement with literature helps the writer to develop authorial positioning (cf. Wingate 2012) in addition to originality is discussed further in the next section, and highlights the way in which different elements interweave to constitute disciplinary concepts of good writing.

a regular cycle of self-critique and evaluation in relation to a contextual frame (such as influences and peers).

Jack teaches composition and technology, and reported that a large number of students struggle to know how to explicate their practice in writing:

> It's when students try things that don't work and they say 'It didn't work so I didn't put it in the report'. And I'm like, 'I know you've done so much work and there's nothing in this report that's two pages long' because something has not worked. They'd learned loads from it but they hadn't been able to reflect on that … I think that's the biggest mistake that we see every year. People make a mistake and they just leave it out as though it's not part of the process that they do, or that's not work that they did because it didn't lead towards the final thing.

Criticality within the context of technology and composition requires the student to write critically about the process of developing their practice, taking into account where ideas come from, how they are implemented and considering their various successes and failures as a process leading to the final submitted work. Criticality here is at least partly about objective reporting of the process, but also (ideally) in allowing analysis to emerge from reportage. There is a tension here between the expectations of writing within the Research Report genre (this discussion will be continued below) and Jack's requirement for criticality. Whilst this may appear to be a different conceptualization of criticality than discussed above, it could be argued that the only distinction is *what* is being evaluated. It seems that there is an expectation that through reflecting on the process of learning, the student can, and should, exemplify the kind of 'creative criticality' discussed in relation to essays. Failure to do so implies a 'mistake' of some kind. This may be the result of moves within higher education towards research driving practice, or, in the context of the discussion so far, it may be because the argumentative 'musicological' essay underscores thinking about writing in music.

This example suggests something of a fuzzy boundary between conceptions of the essay and the research report within certain music sub-disciplines (perhaps better thought of as genre fluidity). Criticality is clearly central to notions of good writing in music, not least in the way that it acts as a marker of creativity, whether in the development of original ideas and interpretations or in the reflection upon the creative process. Yet the way in which criticality cuts across (and thus causes interpenetration of particular characteristics of) genre means that academic tutors and students alike need to be clear on what 'shared understanding' means in specific sub-disciplinary and writing contexts, and how this understanding is articulated. Failure to do so, as we observe in Jack's quotation above, runs the risk of generating 'mistakes' when the demands of a genre are interpreted incorrectly.

Developing a position, finding a voice

> On the broader level it means not leaving the reader in any doubt as to where the argument is heading ... [avoiding] leading your reader up the garden path or on a magical mystery tour.
>
> (Sam, aesthetics, staff)

The types of creative criticality discussed above are enabled by the fact that writing genres act as 'broad guides to action rather than as constraining templates' (Hyland 2015: 33). On the one hand, these guides to action reflect the norms of and expectations of communities of practice;[5] on the other, 'individuals are able to exploit genre options to create some personal wriggle-room and express a persona they feel comfortable with' (ibid.). The tension between adherence to rhetorical conventions and authorial presence in writing manifested itself in the data thematically in the way that participants identified the importance of clear written communication, and the nature of that communication. Whilst participants did refer to the need for careful and correct presentation (referring particularly to grammar, punctuation and referencing), discussion about structure was particularly prevalent (especially in relation to essays and research reports); students valued structural signposting as a means to justify their approach and for 'setting up your work in a way that the reader can understand' (Seren, music psychology, student). The student views were echoed by the majority of staff: 'it's the structural thing ... clear introduction and clear conclusion and "this is what I'm gonna do" ... the clarity of, of what you're doing so that nothing really is a surprise' (Lennie, musicology, staff). This is perhaps unsurprising, given Wingate's (2012) discussion about the role of 'formal schemata' (structure signposting, style/register, referencing) in serving the presentation of a position.

---

[5] While EAP literature in general tends to refer to 'discourse communities' as a functional grouping (Swales 1988), within music education literature it is more common to refer to 'communities of practice' (see Wenger 1998).

Moving beyond structure and surface features

Wingate suggests that structure and style are vital for successful argumentation, but highlights how focusing on surface features can hide the true purpose of essay writing – developing an argument. This is exemplified by Charlotte's comments:

> So [points to some student work], there are problems with the structure, it doesn't fit the structure you would expect to see in a psychology dissertation … so they introduce some hypotheses at the end of the introduction, which was a bit weird, results and discussion should have been standalone potentially … it's the sort of style. (Charlotte, music psychology, staff)

Good writing in music psychology (and in technology and management too) was expected to follow a standardized (highly structured) format that participants understood as enhancing, or disrupting, the quality of the work (which is to say the structural conventions of the genres in question, mediated by the specific sub-disciplinary communities of practice in which they occur). The example above relates to a piece of work which was not considered to represent good writing and the explanation points solely to the fact that it does not follow the structural expectations of the 'research genre' (Gardner and Nesi 2013) to which this kind of work belongs. In this example, a focus on the weak structural elements becomes a distraction from the argument.

The interaction between structure and good writing within music is clearly not a straightforward one, and, depending on the sub-discipline and genre, greater or lesser adherence to conventional structure can be perceived positively or negatively. Good writing in those sub-disciplines with a more applied focus (like music psychology, management, technology) seems to be defined by conformity to standardized conventions; sub-disciplines which involve the synthesis and evaluation of theories and content (Bloom 1956) may demand a more flexible and creative approach to structure.

For example, there was a suggestion from some colleagues that there is a relationship between structural sophistication and good writing: 'Those kind of very standard kind of signposting things which I would recommend to a weaker student to orientate themselves, but … at a certain stage we need to get beyond because otherwise … the essay is gonna sound clunky' (Sam, aesthetics, staff). He goes on to say: 'There's an extent to which you can break the rules and, and there's a kind of flair that the very best students have, erm, where the reader is almost lulled into ignore kind of things like a, sort of, absolute kind of structure' (Sam, aesthetics, staff).

There is an echo of Wingate's ideas here; these examples suggest that surface features, such as structure and signposting, are indicative of a lower level of writing competency than work which has an authorial presence (or 'flair'). If we consider criticality too, then a kind of hierarchy begins to emerge: surface features provide a framework through which knowledge and content can be explored critically in order to develop a position with an identifiable authorial voice. Reflecting on the data that has been presented so far, it is also interesting to note that the first two elements were discussed fully by participants; concrete conceptualizations of authorial voice (and how it could be recognized or achieved) were noticeably absent, though it was clear that this was perceived as essential to good writing across different genres and sub-disciplines.

Finding a voice

The reflections presented in the interviews around good writing in music noted approaches used to engage the reader, as well as creative criticality applied in relation to existing literature and practice. Students can find it difficult to develop their writing skills, and to find their own authorial voice, and this is further complicated if they are required to produce work in different genres and sub-disciplines in parallel. The institutional context (with its generalized study skills support) can also mean that surface features of writing are prioritized over a richer understanding of the discipline (cf. Lea and Street 1998).

Hints of what authorial voice might look like in good writing suggest that it should also reflect the expectations of the discipline:

> They [a student] really understood what was motivating that style of writing and they were even able to reproduce quite a lot of the features of it … being able to engage with the idiom but perhaps not having the structure yet … cultivating a deeper sense for this more ambiguous and sort of questioning and perhaps even aesthetic playful style of prose.
>
> (Sam, aesthetics, staff)

The expectation that students should engage with the 'deeper epistemological issues associated with knowledge in different disciplines' (Lea and Street 1998: 167) was discussed directly only by Sam (aesthetics, staff) and Lennie (musicology, staff), although it was implicit elsewhere (see the above discussion on 'creative criticality'). It is also worth noting that criticality is mentioned here too – again highlighting the complexity of unpicking and defining the essence of good writing in music.

Staff representing the more applied areas seemed to expect a more detached writing style, avoiding the use of metaphor (Arthur, Management, staff) and 'flowery' language (Charlotte, Performance, staff), but it was clear that writing style was important for stance and connecting with the reader: 'I wouldn't say it's particularly interesting writing ... but I was rereading it this morning and thinking, this is very functional, systematic, clear, logical, but it's not setting the world on fire in terms of style' (Charlotte, music psychology, staff).

Style of writing is clearly significant and this comment supports the suggestion that adhering to surface features alone are not enough to create good writing (Lea and Street 1998) and a deeper engagement with the conventions of the sub-discipline is required. It is perhaps worth noting that students did not necessarily think of their readers in the same way as the staff. The student respondents seemed acutely aware of their readers, making efforts to ensure that they are 'not just assuming previous knowledge of the topic and that you're introducing them to different terms in a way that people can then use that knowledge throughout your writing to understand what you're saying' (Ellie, musicology, student).

Some of this concern was perhaps borne of the students' experiences (and perhaps frustration) of reading for their studies and discussing ideas in class, but it is clear that they identified good writing as being meaningful for a potentially non-specialist audience, moving away from jargon to ensure that their position is correctly communicated. The need to position oneself in relation to previous work was also articulated by one of the composition students: 'it's more just pointing out how you've done this ... why you've done and also why it's original as well ... Which is the hardest part, I think, of it all ... to say why your work's different to like loads of other work when so many people have done so many things. It's hard I think' (Fran, composition, student).

Fran's comment above is reminiscent of the discussion above regarding criticality, and the need to justify the approach taken in relation to existing work (whether that is focused on practice or literature). Fran acknowledges the challenge of this aspect of her work, and this may in part be because this kind of writing may belong to a kind of 'occluded genre' (Swales 1996) of writing; the level of justification and reflection that often appears in such work is not always a visible part of professional practice and this can make it difficult for students when they are trying to develop their own position and voice within their writing. Ellie and Fran (and staff members too) seem to (subconsciously, at least) consider writing as more than just an assessment activity; it is a way to engage with, and contribute to, a community of practice that extends beyond the immediate pedagogical context, yet this is rarely expressed as a conscious intention.

One of the challenges in understanding good writing in music, and perhaps an explanation for why surface features may be mistakenly identified as the main indicators of good writing, is that many of the sub-disciplines connect with other discipline areas (e.g. psychology, business). Students and staff, particularly working in these particular sub-disciplines, will be acutely aware of the cross-disciplinary contexts of their work and finding a way to create and navigate a shared understanding of good writing may inevitably end up focusing on the more tangible surface features rather than on the more inscrutable process of using those features to develop a position.

Teaching and learning good writing

The emphasis on creative criticality and authorial presence in good writing begs the question of how students learn what is appropriate to the particular communities of practice in which they seek to integrate. There is certainly a gatekeeping element to teaching and learning – Lea and Street note the complex conceptual and ideological forces at play within such terms as 'structure' and 'argument' (1998: 168–9) that students are required to understand if they are to develop good writing (see also Murray and Sharpling 2019). But there is also a question of how explicitly students are instructed in such matters, or whether they are expected to learn the rules of the game through observation rather than direction.

The most prevalent strategy for improving writing to emerge related to learning from good practice. This may relate to seeing examples of similar work submitted by previous students, or examples of high-quality work. These may be helpful for understanding how to structure the writing for a particular assignment (Fran, composition, student), but also useful in terms of the style of writing required:

> Any point that you're making of good writing followed up by 'and this is what that looks like in practice' because … you can sort of nod and go 'hmmm, yes that makes sense' when someone explains something but then … you don't know how to apply it to your sentence. And examples of it in your area as well … bearing in mind that your example needs to be specific to the subject because good musicology writing is subtly different from good English Literature writing.
>
> (Ellie, musicology, student)

Applied examples that relate to general advice on writing are perceived positively by students, but it is important that these examples relate specifically to the area of work; there is an acknowledgement here that there are 'subtle' differences between different disciplines which can be difficult for students themselves to identify. Enhancing student writing therefore relies on subject tutors being able to identify and explain the specific characteristics of good writing within their areas of expertise, and emphasizes the need for volumes such as this! The other model of good practice relates to learning from published writing within the discipline/sub-disciplines. Ellie (musicology, student) points out that 'reading lots of examples' is the best way to develop writing skills. However, she also acknowledged that 'a lot of the times when you were reading the books … they wouldn't always stick to the rules that had been laid out by my lecturers!'. It is clear that the student is observing the tension between rhetorical conventions and 'personal wriggle-room' (Hyland 2015: 33), though it is less certain if they feel confident in using this tension productively in their own writing.

One piece of advice offered by Charlotte (music psychology, staff) to her students was to try 'to think more about the craft of writing within those published pieces of work' and she went on to describe her practice in supporting student writing, primarily around the areas of rhetorical convention (structuring, critical argumentation): 'I did mock up a few examples of a good bit of critique and put it up on Powerpoint, highlighted in different colours to show that here they are providing the context, here they're engaging with some wide sources, here they're kind of evaluating in a balanced way.'

This approach to scaffolding learning was also described by Lennie (musicology, staff), and the psychology student identified that this would have been a useful way for her to begin to build confidence in critiquing research ('I always thought in Case Studies [one of her modules] that it would have been really great if we'd gone through and done one together, like just talked it through' (Seren)). There is an implicit assumption that students should know about the mechanics of the language since this receives little detailed discussion within the data. At the same time, encouraging students to read and immerse themselves in the subject area, and examples such as Charlotte's, highlight the ways in which students are taught how to construct and develop an argument. However, there is little discussion of how the more nebulous art of communication and authorial voice are understood by staff and taught to students.

The student participants suggested that practice was important in the process of developing writing skills, but this was most effective if coupled with useful feedback. Useful feedback took a range of forms. It might point to frequent errors requiring attention where the student could use that feedback 'to address those areas that I'm weaker in and then try and build up more confidence in doing those aspects well' (Seren, music psychology, student). Other forms of feedback might offer opportunities to discuss pieces of writing in person and learning from those discussion (Fran, composition, student), or offer more specific indicators of how to improve the structure and argumentation of the writing:

The aesthetics essay that I got back [the annotated essay], that was really helpful for my writing style, would have things like 'expand on this', 'substantiate this point' but then it would also have things crossed out like 'you don't need to say this because you can put that in a footnote' ... so having feedback where it feels like the marker has thought about your restrictions was really helpful.

(Ellie, musicology, student)

These suggestions reflect established good practice surrounding feedback in higher education (Jackel, Pearce, Radloff and Edwards 2017), but there is one other suggestion from Seren (music psychology, student) following an experience researching in another country with different supervisors:

It was really interesting to see somebody else's point of view on my writing and I think that definitely has helped me as well to have that other perspective on how I can improve ... good writing is different for everybody, so I think getting different people's opinions on a piece of work is really valuable ... so whether that's like, discussing in class about, like, particular piece of work and going through it, like, methodologically, I think that could be quite good.

Perhaps a useful strategy is to find new ways of engaging students in the process of giving and received feedback; this may help to overcome the challenges associated with 'occluded genres' which in turn will serve to strengthen student writing.

It seemed from the interviews that students struggle with the kind of critical reflective writing expected within some of the sub-disciplines (management, technology and composition); part of the challenge may be that students do not understand what is required of them in this type of exercise (perhaps in the way it sits against the background of the traditional musicological essay), cannot understand the relevance of the assignment or perhaps feel uncomfortable with a more personal style of writing:

They asked us to kind of evaluate our own selves and our work and our feelings and everything and then put it into the context of the literature which is like, 'I'm sorry, but, how do you do that?' [laughs] ... I was struggling with that so much because ... like, how does it; maybe some theories do relate to me but it was, I remember it was really, really forced. I had to like really pull out, really irrelevant stuff from books and read different studies to make it all stick together. It didn't make much sense to me.

(Layla, management, student)

This points to a need for greater clarity in task requirements and purpose (this will be revisited below), but also suggests that good writing depends, at least in part, on student understanding and buy-in to the task in hand. This relates to aspects of confidence, as discussed above, but also suggests that such writing requires a more critical focus.

It is perhaps significant that these suggested strategies emerged mainly from the more discursive sub-disciplines. One final strategy relates to the value of contextualizing writing within the real world which emerged in relation to three of the more applied sub-disciplines (psychology, composition and technology). This may be as simple as recognizing that there are word limits on academic publications to help students to 'understand why there's a word limit in place … it's reflective of what happens in the real world' (Seren, music psychology, student). Highlighting the relevance of writing to the way in which a composition or technology student might experience the real world was also suggested by Jack (staff):

> As a composer, if someone just says, 'well I just want to write music', well that's lovely, you can do that, but what happens when you get into a rehearsal and the ensemble are asking you to communicate … how did you come up with this? Or what's the aesthetic significance of this element? And if you just sit there dumbfounded and say 'I just wanted to write some music' that's not going to be great.

This strategy perhaps reflects an increasing move within higher education to embed transferable/employability skills within curricula (Higher Education Academy 2015), or suggests that students are now more attuned to thinking about how their courses prepare them for life after graduation. However, good writing does not occur in a vacuum and it is perhaps useful to encourage students to think more carefully about how their work fits within a broader context of creative and professional practice, and how engagement with different writing genres can contribute to this.

Conclusions and implications

Throughout this chapter we have highlighted that perceptions of good writing in music are underpinned by the ways in which staff and students conceptualize the 'musicological (argumentative) essay'. Criticality is one of the key features of our data, and to some extent the participants' understanding of how this relates to good writing in music aligns with Nesi and Gardner's (2013) description of the essay genre. However, good writing in music is also characterized by *creative criticality* – an expectation for originality which involves creating new insights through critical engagement with the literature and/or with creative practice and which transcends genre and sub-disciplinary areas. It is difficult to be sure about the source of these expectations, but it is likely that the interdisciplinary nature of music, where students may work in several different sub-disciplines within a single programme, leads to blurring and borrowing between genres and sub-disciplines. This kind of genre fluidity, or fuzziness, points to a need for greater precision in how we define (as well as teach and assess) writing tasks in relation to the sub-disciplinary areas of music, and points to the need for those working in music to develop new meta-linguistic clarity in relation to its writing tasks.

Criticality is an important part of developing a position, which is also perceived as a marker of good writing in music. Surface features (such as writing structure) play an important role in facilitating argumentation and criticality, although the ways in which this is enacted within different sub-disciplines are delicately nuanced and seem to vary according to the broader disciplinary connections beyond music (e.g. with psychology, management), yet also appeared to reflect the extent to which the sub-disciplines may be seen as applied or more rhetorical. However, there is an implied hierarchy in the features of good writing, suggesting that its pinnacle relates to authorial voice, building on aspects of criticality and argumentation. Equally, conceptualizations of authorial voice and stance are nebulous; staff and students alike struggled to articulate clearly how this is exemplified in writing about music, and were unclear about how such a skill can be developed or taught. In some ways, these data reflect Wingate's (2012) discussion of argumentation, although here participants' conceptions of authorial voice transcended genre alignment, in a way that reflected the distinctions associated with criticality. Instead, the data seemed to speak to communities of practice as discussed by Hyland (2015: 34): 'To work in a discipline, then, we need to be able to engage in these practices and, in particular, in its discourses. We need to proximate to the rhetorical conventions it routinely employs to claim membership and learn how to use these conventions to take positions on matters the community values.' Hyland later says (p. 36): 'The community's collaborative practices do not just crush users into conformity but are also the options which allow writers to engage in a community and perform an identity. In other words, identity is what makes us similar to and different from each other and for academics it is how they both achieve credibility as insiders and reputations as individuals.'

Comments from Charlotte, Lennie and Sam point to the expectation that good writing in music should adhere to structural conventions, yet demonstrate a unique flair or voice; framed within Hyland's view above, this suggests that academic staff are hoping to see evidence of their postgraduate students engaging with their communities of practice and performing their position or identity as scholars. The students themselves seem to implicitly recognize that this is a necessity, as demonstrated by their recognition that reading widely is key to learning about good writing. Yet our participants do not describe what engaging with the literature achieves or transmits specifically: they do not recognize that this allows them to engage with their community and learn its discourses and practices. This reinforces the suggestion above that as a discipline, music needs to reflect further on the markers of good writing such that it has a clearer sense of its own meta-language and how this can be taught and revealed to its students. It may be that good writing in music is best framed in terms of Communities of Practice, but this requires more exploration and moves beyond the scope of the data presented here.

There is a clear need for a more detailed investigation of good writing in music that goes beyond a single institution and which utilizes a much larger sample. Our data have led us to focus on communities of practice, but there is perhaps work to be done on how assessment criteria contribute to, and shape, the expectations of these communities. It has been valuable to triangulate the perceptions of staff and students, not least because this more strongly highlights the fuzziness in perceptions relating to good writing, reinforcing the divergence between staff, who are likely to be more fully integrated within their own community of practices, and students who need to learn how to do the same, and why this is important. To add further triangulation through the analysis of specific writing examples would undoubtedly enrich the research further, and this might be an interesting approach in future studies. We have included some insights into how our participants have tried to teach and learn good writing in music, but it is clear that more work is also needed: a study to explore the impact of different interventions for teaching and improving good writing in music would be welcome, as would further research to verify and enrich the findings outlined here. In a rapidly changing educational climate (speaking here of pre-tertiary as well as tertiary settings), it is perhaps an important moment for us to scrutinize our practice and articulate the tools of our trade more transparently such that we can improve our skills as educators and researchers.

References

Australian Tertiary Education Quality and Standards Agency (2017). [Online: Search results for 'music'] Available at: https://www.teqsa.gov.au/search/music (Accessed 20 December 2018).

Bloom, B., Englehart, M. D., Furst, E. J., Hill, W. H., and Krathwohl, D. R. (eds.) (1956). *Taxonomy of Educational Objectives: Handbook 1. Cognitive Domain.* White Plains, NY: Longman.

Braun, V., and Clarke, V. (2006). 'Using Thematic Analysis in Psychology'. *Qualitative Research in Psychology* 3 (2): 77–101.

Burnard, P., and Haddon E. (eds.) (2015). *Activating Diverse Musical Creativities: Teaching and Learning in Higher Music Education.* London: Bloomsbury Academic.

Calella, M., and Urbanek N. (eds.) (2013). *Historische Musikwissenschaft: Grundlagen und Perspektiven.* Stuttgart: J.B. Metzler.

Cook, N. (2000). *Music: A Very Short Introduction.* Oxford: Oxford University Press.

Cooper, A., and Bikowski, D. (2007). 'Writing at the Graduate Level: What Tasks Do Professors Actually Require?' *Journal of English for Academic Purposes* 6: 206–21.

Cooper, T. (2018). 'Towards a Creative Criticality: Revisiting Critical Thinking'. *Integral Leadership Review* 5 (31) Available online: http://integralleadershipreview.com/16019-toward-a-creative-criticality-revisiting-critical-thinking/ (Accessed 3 July 2018).

Ding, A, and Bruce, I. (2017). *The English for Academic Purposes Practitioner: Operating on the Edge of Academia.* London: Palgrave Macmillan.

Gardner, M., and Springfeld, S. (2014). *Musikwissenschaftliches Arbeiten: Eine Einführung.* Kassel: Bärenreiter.

Gardner, S., and Nesi H. (2013). 'A Classification of Genre Families in University Student Writing'. *Applied Linguistics* 34 (1): 25–52.

Harper-Scott, J. P. E. (2009). 'Introduction'. In Harper-Scott, J. P. E. and Samson, J. (eds), *An Introduction to Music Studies*, 1–4. Cambridge: Cambridge University Press.

Harper-Scott, J. P. E., and Samson, J. (eds.) (2009). *An Introduction to Music Studies.* Cambridge: Cambridge University Press.

Heile, B., Moreda Rodríguez, E., and Stanley, J. (eds.) (2018). *Higher Education in Music in the Twenty-First Century.* Abingdon: Routledge.

Hentschel, F. (ed.) (2018). *Historische Musikwissenschaft: Gegenstände, Geschichten, Methoden, Probleme.* Laaber: Laaber-Verlag.

Herbert, T. (2001). *Music in Words: A Guide to Researching and Writing About Music.* Oxford: Oxford University Press.

Higher Education Academy (2015). *Framework for Embedding Employability in Higher Education.* York: Higher Education Academy Available online: www.employability.ed.ac.uk/documents/HEA-Embedding_employability_in_HE.pdf (Accessed 3 July 2019).

Hyland, K. (2015). 'Genre, Discipline and Identity'. *Journal of English for Academic Purposes* 19: 32–43.

Jackel, B., Pearce, J., Radloff, A., and Edwards, D. (2017). *Assessment and Feedback in Higher Education: A Review of Literature for the Higher Education Academy.* York: Higher Education Academy.

Johnston, B., Mitchell, R., Myles, F., and Ford, P. (2011). *Developing Student Criticality in Higher Education: Undergraduate Learning in the Arts and Social Sciences.* London: Continuum.

Lea, M. R., and Street, B. V. (1998). 'Student Writing in Higher Education: An Academic Literacies Approach'. *Studies in Higher Education* 23 (2): 157–72.

Mei, W. S. (2006). 'Creating a Contrastive Rhetorical Stance: Investigating the Strategy of Problematization in Students' Argumentation'. *RELC Journal* 37 (3): 329–53.

Moreda Rodríguez, E. (2018). 'Writing about Music in the 21st Century'. In Heile, B., Moreda Rodríguez, E., and Stanley J. (eds.), *Higher Education in Music in the Twenty-First Century*, 126–37. Abingdon: Routledge.

Murray, N., and Sharpling, G. (2019). 'What Traits Do Academics Value in Student Writing? Insights from a Psychometric Approach', *Assessment and Evaluation in Higher Education* 44 (3): 489–500.

National Association of Schools of Music (2018) 'Basic Competency Index'. Available online: https://nasm.arts-accredit.org/accreditation/standards-2guidelines/basic-competency-index/ (Accessed 20 December 2018).

Nesi, H., and Gardner, S. (2006). 'Variation in Disciplinary Culture: University Tutors' Views on Assessed Writing Tasks'. In Kiely, R., Clibbon, G., Rea-Dickins, P., and Woodfield, H. (eds.), *Language, Culture and Identity in Applied Linguistics (British Studies in Applied* Linguistics *21)*, 99–117. London: Equinox Publishing.

Quality Assurance Agency (2015). *Characteristics Statement: Master's Degree* Available online: https://www.qaa.ac.uk/docs/qaa/quality-code/master's-degree-characteristics-statement.pdf?sfvrsn=6ca2f981_10 (Accessed 2 July 2019).

Quality Assurance Agency (2016). *Subject Benchmarking Statement: Music* Available online: http://www.qaa.ac.uk/docs/qaa/subject-benchmark-statements/sbs-music-16.pdf?sfvrsn=1f9af781_10 (Accessed 20 December 2018).

Rink, J., Gaunt, H., and Williamon, A. (eds.) (2017). *Musicians in the Making: Pathways to Creative Performance*. Oxford: Oxford University Press.

Sarath, E. (2014). '*Transforming Music Study from Its Foundations: A Manifesto for Progressive Change in the Undergraduate Preparation of Music Majors*'. (Report on the Task Force on the Undergraduate Music Major, The College Music Society). Available online: http://www.mtosmt.org/issues/mto.16.22.1/manifesto.pdf (Accessed 20 December 2018).

Swales, J. (1996). 'Occluded Genres in the Academy: The Case of the Submission Letter' in Ventola, E., and Mauranen, A. (eds.), *Academic Writing: Intercultural and Textual Issues*, 45–58. Amsterdam: John Benjamins Publishing.

Swales, J. (1988). 'Discourse Communities, Genres and English as an International Language'. *World Englishes* 7: 211–20. doi:10.1111/j.1467-971X.1988.tb00232.x

Swales, J. (1990). *Genre Analysis: English in Academic and Research Settings*. Cambridge: Cambridge University Press.

Wenger, E. (1998). *Communities of Practice: Learning, Meaning, and Identity*. Cambridge: Cambridge University Press.

Wingate, U. (2012). '"Argument!" Helping Students Understand What Essay Writing Is About'. *Journal of English for Academic Purposes* 11 (2): 145–54. doi: https://doi.org/10.1016/j.jeap.2011.11.001

Woodward-Kron, R. (2002). 'Critical Analysis versus Description? Examining the Relationship in Successful Student Writing', *Journal of English for Academic Purposes* 1 (2): 121–43.

Appendix One: Interviewee Information

Pseudonym	Level	UG degree/place	Programme/Specialism
Seren	PGT Student	University of Leeds	MA Music Psychology
Fran	PGT Student	UK non-Leeds	MA Critical and Experimental Composition
Ellie	PGT Student	University of Leeds	MA Critical and Applied Musicology
Layla	PGT Student	US, then UK non-Leeds	MA Music and Management
Lennie	Staff		Musicology, performance
Jack	Staff		Composition, technology
Charlotte	Staff		Music Psychology, performance
Arthur	Staff		Music Management
Sam	Staff		Aesthetics, musicology

Appendix Two: Indicative Interview Questions

For academic staff

How many master's students have you supervised?

What kinds of written work do your students tend to produce (commentaries for composition/technology work, empirical reports, traditional dissertations)?

What makes a good piece of written work in your opinion (can you provide some specific examples (drawing on the samples provided, perhaps))?

What tends to characterize a poor piece of written work (Can you provide some specific examples (drawing on the samples provided, perhaps))?

What makes a good introduction? Is this different from other sub-disciplines within music?

What is the most effective structure for a piece of written work in your discipline? How is this different from other sub-disciplines within music?

What makes a good conclusion?

What have students told you that they find challenging in relation to their academic writing? Do you have a sense that there are aspects of academic writing that they find more straightforward? To what extent do you think these concerns/views are specific to your discipline? What advice do you tend to offer when they express those concerns?

What tools do you use to try to help students understand how to develop their writing skills to a high level?

For students/graduates

What is your experience of academic writing whilst at university?

What is your experience of academic writing during your master's?

What lessons have you learned about the characteristics of good writing during your higher education?

How have you developed good writing in music?

What do you think constitutes poor writing in music?

What different experiences of writing in music have you had? Does good writing look different for different areas of musical study?

Good Academic Reflective Writing in Dentistry

Marion Bowman

Introduction

[Academic Reflective Writing] is trying to encourage transformative learning ...
part of it is about them – what they have learned about themselves.
(Interview with ARW Marker 2 in this study, 2019)

Academic reflective writing (ARW) is a relatively new 'genre' of student writing which has arisen as a vehicle for assessing learning from work experience in vocationally oriented higher education courses (Ryan 2011; Vassilaki 2017). ARW is significantly different from the traditional academic essay, as it is a complex blend of personal thoughts (reflections) and academic analysis or reasoning. Doing ARW is a 'complex, rigorous intellectual and emotional exercise' (Rogers 2002); thus if students are not given explicit guidance and time to develop their ARW practice, the resulting reflections are often superficial or technical (Jonas-Dywer et al. 2013; Tsang 2012; Ryan 2013). Unfortunately, ARW is assessed more often than it is explicitly taught in higher education (Ryan 2011, 2013). In addition, the literature base contains very few studies that analyse the discourse features of student reflective writing (Luk 2008; Ryan 2011). The aim of this chapter is to analyse a sample of high-scoring ARW student texts from dentistry to bring to light the overall structure and linguistic features of these reflective texts and the purpose they serve in a healthcare discourse community. Whilst the example texts are taken from dentistry (which is a discipline that is not often discussed in the English for specific purposes (ESP) literature), the pedagogical recommendations based on this analysis should be applicable to ARW in other disciplines.

Academic reflective writing (ARW)

Due to its blended nature, ARW relies on the student being able to competently write through a range of levels of reflection (see Table 5.2) to discuss a chosen episode/s from their work experience (Ryan 2011). In this chapter, in alignment with Ryan and Ryan (2013), it is argued that the student writer must attend to all of levels of reflection, as these provide a framework for systematic reflective thought (Rogers 2002). Each level of reflection is dependent on the other levels in order to provide context, personal framing, intellectual rigour and considered judgement. Working through these levels of reflection can lead to the ultimate goal of arriving at a transformed perspective that could influence future work-based practice (Rogers 2002). As such, ARW is holistic and is about achieving balance in order to meet the end goal convincingly.

The importance of ARW in Healthcare

Reflective writing has been used in training nurses and medical students in higher education since the 1980s (Fragkos 2016). Initially personal reflective writing (journaling and diary writing) was encouraged, but more recently ARW (which is thought to bridge the gap between practical experience and theory, according to Schon (1995)) has been used to assess reflection on practical experience. The requirement for reflective practice is now embedded in the regulatory codes of medicine, nursing and dentistry. This requirement applies to both the training of undergraduate healthcare professionals, and as a vehicle for demonstrating continuing professional development (CPD) after registration (General Dental Council 2012). For example, in dentistry there is a requirement for registered professionals to reflect on whether each CPD activity they have undertaken has led to changes in their practice and individual learning needs or not (GDC 2013).

The requirement for health professionals to be able to reflect is framed as being important for practitioner self-awareness and meta-learning, which is thought to make a contribution to ensuring continuous improvement in clinical safety and ultimately patient care (Dube and Ducharme 2015). Indeed, a practitioner's level of self-awareness and their ability to reflect are something that are assessed in fitness to practice proceedings, which are held if there are complaints about dental or medical care (Brindley 2018). It could be argued that this way of framing reflection (and reflective writing) places a significant amount of responsibility for transformative change on the individual practitioner or student, rather than on the healthcare team, institution or system. Dirkx and Mezirow (2006) postulate that reflection should go further than this and should critically appraise the workplace setting that the student or practitioner is embedded in, in order to suggest wider transformative changes.

Constraints to ARW

Reflective writing, especially ARW, places a very high rhetorical demand on students, due to the differing types of language required at each level of reflection (see Table 5.2). At the level of a whole text, students may be confronted with a range of challenges, including how to structure the text and how to balance the different required elements (Bowman and Addyman 2014a). Often in the early years of a degree course, a structure, for example, the Gibbs cycle (Gibbs 1988), is given to help the students organize their ARW piece. This may not be the case in the later years of a degree course.

Whilst the complexity of ARW could be thought of as one constraint, it is argued, in line with the thinking of the academic literacies movement, that teaching student ARW in a healthcare context encompasses more than just ensuring skill acquisition. Instead, ARW could be thought of as a 'site for social positioning' (Hyland 2002) where the student is developing their professional identity through writing, whilst simultaneously attempting to satisfy the expectations of the power structures that influence the kind of discourse that is expected (Lea and Street 2006). Significant power exists in terms of the dental and medical regulatory bodies that expect students to demonstrate compliance with a set of standards and core values, in order for them to register as trained professionals. For example, a student writer might hesitate before explaining their actual negative feelings towards a particular patient for fear of questions being asked about their fitness to practice.

Students can also be concerned if they are writing about critical incidents which involve their dental tutors. I have been asked by students, 'Is it ok for me to write about something that the clinical tutor did wrong in clinic?' In this case, student writers may choose to write to satisfy the perceived reader, but not to include their genuine thoughts (Bowman and Addyman 2014b; Vassilaki 2017). This constraint is arguably even more pressing for practising registrants. A recent medico-legal case appeared to use the honest reflections of a practitioner in her e-portfolio as part of a body of evidence that resulted in her being de-registered as a medical professional after a patient in her care had died (Kaffash and Gregory 2018). This led to an outcry from medical professionals who called for the privacy of registrants' reflective writing to be protected, to allow for genuine transformative reflection.

Method

Methodology

This study is situated within ESP, which foregrounds practical concerns, notably meeting the communicative needs of specific groups of students studying or working in a particular discipline (Dudley-Evans and St John 1998). In ESP, ways of expressing knowledge in a discipline are explored through analysing the structure and language used in texts of particular genres within that discourse community as this acts as a powerful heuristic (Dudley-Evans and St John 1998; Flowerdew 2011; Swales 1990).

The two ARW tasks

Table 5.1 shows the two tasks that will be analysed in this chapter and shows how possible prompt questions would be quite different for each task. As shown in Table 5.1, the two tasks are written in Year 4 of a five-year course, a point at which students are expected to be fairly competent dental professionals already, able to perform a range of procedures. Task B is a shorter reflective section at the end of a longer clinical case study of the dental care given to a medically compromised patient. The first section of Task B contains detailed clinical information about the patient's medical, oral and social history, as well as the diagnosis, prognosis, treatment and the care pathway. These clinical case notes are written in short, dense bullet-pointed notes using medical terminology, whilst the reflective section at the end of the report is discursive in nature and has no prescribed structure. In contrast, Task A is a stand-alone reflective text of 1500 words which is comprised of three mini-essays reflecting on the ethical aspects of three incidents involving teamwork with colleagues. In both tasks, the student writer has to choose the aspects or incidents to reflect upon.

Recruitment of participants

Tasks A and B above were selected in order to illustrate how different ARW tasks at the same level in the same programme can have a contrasting character. The exemplar texts that were chosen for analysis in this study were those of high-scoring students. Ethical permission to conduct the study was obtained from the Arts, Humanities and Cultures Faculty Research Ethics Committee (LTSLCS-089). The top scoring five students for each task were initially approached, if there was no response from these students then other students (moving down

Table 5.1 Tasks A and B which were selected for analysis in this study (both tasks are at Year 4 level)

Reflective Level (See Table 5.2)	Task A: *Write a reflective assignment of not more than 1500 words regarding three significant incidents from your clinical practice that relate to teamworking.* (Marked by ethics tutors external to the Dental School)	Task B: *Write a reflective section based on the preceding clinical case report which details the dental treatment of a medically compromised patient (no set word limit). Select significant points from the case history to reflect upon in this section.* (Marked by dental tutors within the Dental School who specialize in Oral Medicine)
1	What were the main aspects of the incident that relate to teamworking between health professionals that went well or badly?	What were the main aspects of your management of the medical aspects of the case, and whether you met the patient's needs, that went well or badly?
2	How did this affect your feelings as a professional?	Did you have the skills/knowledge to deal with this? What was new to you? What did you feel about this case in relation to your expertise in handling medically compromised cases?
3	Using your own reasoning or ethical principles, your regulatory code or the literature, can you explain what went well or badly in this case in more detail?	Using your own thoughts or the practical medical literature or the broader literature on communication/professionalism/patient care, can you analyse why aspects of the case went well or badly?
4	Was this a good or poor example of teamworking?	Was your management of this patient's medical needs successful or not?
5	What have you learned about teamwork from this? What would you do if a similar situation arose? How could the system be changed to prevent this kind of incident happening again? If the influences/values base of practice changed, how could things be different? If the constraints were removed how could this kind of teamworking change?	What have you learned from this case (about yourself, about treatment in medically compromised patients, and about patients/patient care)? As a consequence of your experiences, how, if at all, would you change the management of a similar case in the future? Do you view patients/patient care in the same way as a result of being involved in this case?

the grades list sequentially) were contacted. In this way, three high-scoring texts from Task A were identified, and four texts from Task B.

Insider identity of the author

It is worth noting here that my position as an English for academic purposes (EAP) practitioner is a bit unusual, as I am based within a Dental School all year-round, instead of operating from a central University Language Centre. My job role includes supporting international and home students academically through one-to-one appointments. This insider student-facing view means that I am familiar with what is required of students in the Dental School's ARW tasks and with the student experience of doing ARW.

Analysis of the texts

After recruiting participants to this study, the analysis of the texts began. In line with Luk (2008), the analysis of the student texts proceeded in several steps. Firstly, analysis started with the identification of the major reflective issues discussed in the texts. For Task A, each mini-essay was an in-depth analysis of one reflective issue linked to one teamworking incident. In contrast, in Task B, a number of reflective issues were identified from the case, for example, reflecting on treatment, management or communication, and were explored more concisely. Once the reflective issues had been identified, these issues were analysed into the constituent levels of reflection shown in Table 5.2. Using these levels for analysis made it possible to identify patterns for each reflective issue. The final step in analysis was to identify any micro-level linguistic patterns per reflective level in order to work out which language structures would be useful to students for expressing different levels of reflection across the two tasks.

Interviews with markers of the texts

Whilst I do have some insider knowledge of these ARW tasks, it was important after the textual analysis to triangulate my ideas with those of markers of these texts. To this end, interviews were conducted with an experienced marker of each task in order to elicit insights into what they regarded as the successful features of ARW in the high-scoring examples. Ethical permission for the interview component of the project was granted (LTSLCS-102), and markers of both texts were approached. The two interviewees who were subsequently recruited to the study are referred to as Marker 1 (2019) and Marker 2 (2019) in this chapter.

Results

The levels of systematic reflective thought in ARW

Table 5.2 shows five levels of reflection with their associated key questions and example sentences. This table was developed after the textual analysis of the high-scoring ARW tasks in this study, in conjunction with the literature, particularly Ryan (2011), Ryan and Ryan (2013) and Gibbs (1988). It is worth noting that the Gibbs cycle contains six levels of reflection. In Table 5.2, Gibbs' (1988) 'Conclusion' and 'Action Planning' levels have been consolidated into one level for the purposes of this study, as it was found that statements in students' texts at these two levels often overlapped, with 'future action' often being implied in 'concluding' statements. In addition, student texts in this study also showed an overlap between Gibbs' (1988) 'Evaluation' and 'Conclusion' functions at times; thus, a five-level analytical structure was thought to be more appropriate for this data. In contrast, Ryan (2011, 2013) sets out four levels of reflection, with the equivalent of Gibbs' (1988) 'Evaluation' level being absent and the 'Conclusion' and 'Action Planning' levels being combined as a 'Reconstructing' level. For the purposes of this study, having an 'Evaluation' level was deemed important, as reaching a judgement on the critical incident being discussed is a requirement of both tasks. In this study, the levels of reflection in Table 5.2 will be referred to either by their level numbers, that is, 1–5, or by their Gibbs' cycle (1988) level descriptors, as healthcare students tend to be familiar with the Gibbs level names. The example sentences in Table 5.2 have been drawn from the student texts to illustrate the linguistic patterns at a micro-level.

Good ARW for Task A

In Task A, students must select three incidents from their clinical experience that relate to teamwork and then reflect on the ethical underpinnings of these cases in three mini-essays bounded by an overarching introduction and conclusion. According to Marker 1 (2019), there are three key aspects vital for being able to demonstrate transformative learning in this assignment: choosing appropriate case (choice), reflecting on the case (reflection) and analysing the ethical and/ or teamwork issues associated with each case (reasoning), before charting the way forward.

Table 5.2 Levels of reflection (adapted *from Ryan 2011 and Ryan & Ryan 2013; and ^from Gibbs 1988)

Level of Reflection	Nature of each level	Detail of each level with example prompt questions for Tasks A and B	Example sentences from high-scoring students essays (Tasks A or B)
1	Description^ Reporting and responding*	Write a brief and focussed description of the key aspects of the case (related to the required themes for each task)- - What happened?^	Relevant linguistic features here include: adverbial phrases for context, simple past tense for narrative, clinical dental terms, and noting who was involved, e.g. *As I was positioning to insert the needle, I pricked my finger, and immediately I declared what occurred to my assistant and tutor who were present' (Task A)*
2	Feelings^ Relating*	Relate the incident to yourself: Use 'I' (your feelings/level of experience) - What were you thinking and feeling?^	**Prior to treatment or incident:** *'My own lack of knowledge regarding [medical conditions] … '(B)* **During treatment or incident** ('I felt +adjective statements'): *'I felt ashamed to alert them to what had happened … ' (A)* Or *'it was/this was ± adjective … ' statements:* *'It was comforting that the tutor' … [was] understanding … ' (A)* **After treatment** *'I'm glad that I eventually took the initiative to research her condition' (B)*
3	Analysis^ Reasoning*	Analyse the case/incident: Consider different perspectives - What sense can you make from the situation?^	Cause and effect language is important here and citations may be present or absent: *'Several General Dental Council guidelines (2018b) were involved, including principle 6 … ' (A)* *'Cyclophosphamide causes myelosuppression'. (B)*
4	Evaluation^	Reach a judgement on this case - What was good and bad about the experience?^	*' … both the tutor and I should have worked together … ' (A)* *'The benefits of the drug outweighed the risks … ', (B)* *'Prior to this patient, I had not considered the psychosocial aspects[of chronic disease]' (B)*
5	Conclusion and action planning^ Reconstructing*	Think about possible future actions as a result of what you have learned - What else could you have done?^ - If it arose again, what would you do?^	*'If I am hesitant about a tutor's instruction I will ask for further guidance to understand the reasoning behind this.' (A)* *'I have learned that in these circumstances, it is important to.. (B)'* *'I will employ this scale in future … ' (B)*

Choosing an appropriate case

In Marker 1's (2019) view, it is advisable for a student to choose cases where something perhaps went a bit wrong, 'not necessarily clinically, but something where they could have handled the situation better – where they could have acted differently in terms of teamworking or ethics'. Having said that, not every case where something has gone wrong was seen as a suitable case to pick, as 'something could have gone wrong and [the student could have] responded like a hero' (Marker 1 2019). This would mean that it would be more difficult for the student to demonstrate that they would act differently in a similar situation in the future. Marker 1 (2019) acknowledges that sometimes 'people don't like to admit mistakes and they pick cases that show them in a good light, and try to think of words which admit to something, to some minor failing, just to meet the guidelines without really soul searching'. Having said that Marker 1 (2019) explained that it would be 'fine to choose a positive case (where things went well) occasionally, … although I would prefer to see just the one [positive case out of the three]'. This interviewee explained that positive cases 'tend to be quite similar in terms of the issues they raise' (Marker 1 2019). Another important consideration relating to the choice of cases for a portfolio type assignment like this would be for the student to choose cases that 'raise slightly different issues from each other' to avoid repetition (Marker 1 2019).

Demonstrating reflection

Once students have chosen an appropriate case, they need to show their reflections on: 'what went well, what went badly, what they've learned from it, what they are going to do differently in future, and any wider implications [the case] may have' (Marker 1 2019).

The following extract from Author 3 (see Table 5.3) is an example which shows 'a depth of self-awareness', where the reflection 'was done at the time of the incident' which is 'unusual' (Marker 1 2019). The case involved the student repeatedly asking for assistance from the dental tutor, but not receiving it. The following abbreviated extract shows the student's reflections and consequent actions: (*the numbers in brackets below refer to the levels of reflection in Table 5.2).

I shared these feelings [of frustration and disappointment] with my group and it became apparent that they felt the same (2*) … we decided that this was poor leadership (4) - most importantly we felt uneasy treating patients during these sessions (2). Recognising these flaws, resulted in us arranging a meeting with a senior member of staff (1) …. Within just a week of raising the concern, I personally noticed a drastic change on clinic (4) … this was echoed by my group too (4). … This scenario was particularly significant for me in that this was the first time I had stopped just thinking about the fact I should speak up … and actually spoke up … (4)

Whilst Marker 1 (2019) regarded the example above as highly reflective, it was interesting that this marker felt that they might not give the essay a first-class pass as it lacked 'ethical reasoning' which was seen as another essential ingredient for success in this task.

Reasoning

Marker 1 (2019) explained that 'we are always looking for awareness of where ethical principles come to bear' on a case. In particular, a feature of a high-scoring essay would be one in which the student writer has identified where 'principles point in different directions' or 'conflict with each other' (Marker 1 2019). In these sorts of situations a student would need to 'exercise ethical judgement, and in some circumstances there's no substitute for that … when you can't find a manual of exactly what to do in the General Dental Council (GDC) guidelines' (Marker 1 2019). The following extract from Author 1 (see Table 5.3) outlines an ethical dilemma in which the student dentist had treated the patient for a dental issue that had not been specified in the original referral.

> This incident also raises a conflict between the principles of beneficence (Beauchamp and Childress 1983) and integrity, as leaving a patient in pain out of loyalty to the referral could be viewed as not acting within their best interest, especially when one feels competent to provide treatment which could alleviate that pain (3).

The student writer then linked the exploration of this ethical dilemma to convincing future action:

> In hindsight, had I been aware of the referral protocol, I perhaps would have opted to place a temporary restoration on the second molar only and advised the patient to see their GDP [General Dental Practitioner], therefore striking a balance between the relief of pain and commitment to the bounds of the referral (5).
>
> (Author 1)

The extract above does have a citation that refers to the literature. However, according to Marker 1 (2019), 'compared to other essays, reference to sources is not as important' (see also Table 5.3, Author 3 who did not cite literature and yet produced a successful essay). Instead, what is valued is the student being explicit about their individual thinking process using ethical principles or values, whether referring to the literature or not. Interestingly, for this particular essay Marker 1 (2019) felt that the quality of the ethical reasoning was impressive enough for the essay to be awarded a first-class pass even though 'the reflection was OK, I felt there could have been more frankly'. This stands in contrast to the essay discussed above (Author 3) in which the student showed self-awareness and had led an exercise in group reflection, but there was a perceived lack of ethical reasoning in the essay. It is possible that for Marker 1 (2019), whilst both reasoning and reflection were important, quality ethical reasoning may have been regarded more highly in this kind of ARW task. Marker 1 (2019) did acknowledge that it was possible that there could be differences in opinion within the marking team on this.

Other features of a successful essay of this type (Task A)

Other than choosing an appropriate case and including genuine 'soul searching' reflection and relevant in-depth ethical reasoning related to teamworking, Marker 1 (2019) was looking for an essay that is concisely written without too much initial description of the clinical aspects of the case. Marker 1 (2019) explained that only 'the clinical detail that is actually relevant to the ethical teamwork issues that are being raised' should be included. This series of three mini-essays should also be bounded by an overarching introduction and conclusion which may or may not set out a theme for the three essays (Marker 1 2019). In the case of Author 3, there was a clear reflective theme of 'learning to speak out when something seems wrong on clinic' with each mini-essay showing progressive personal development linked to this theme. This is likely to have contributed to this essay's high score.

Observable patterns in the structure of the high-scoring texts for Task A

Marker 1 (2019) explained that in terms of the structure of each discrete essay, what was sought was an initial concise description of the incident, a reasoned discussion of the underlying ethical/teamwork issues and then a reflection on the issues and detail of the lessons learned. For Task A, each of the three mini-essays could be regarded as one discrete reflective issue. Within each issue, the

Table 5.3 An analysis of the sequence of levels of reflection (see Table 5.2) in the Task A high-scoring essays

Author and mini-essay	Levels of reflection in each mini-essay or semantic unit
Author 1 essay 1	Intro sentence: 1-1-2-3-1-3-3-4-1-1-3-4-4-3-5-3-5
Author 1 essay 2	Intro sentence: 1-1- 2-1- 4-1-3-4-4-3-3-5-3-5-3
Author 1 essay 3	Intro sentence: 1-1-2-1-3-4-5
Author 2 essay 1	Intro sentence: 1-1-1-2-3-2-3-3-3-3-4-5-5-5
Author 2 essay 2	Intro sentence: 1-1-2-1-2-1-2-2-2-4-3-3-3-3-2-4-4-5-5-5
Author 2 essay 3	Intro sentence: 1-1-1-1-1-1-3-1-2-4-3-3-3-2-3-4-5-5-4
Author 3 essay 1	Intro sentence: 2-4-1-1-3-1-1-1-2-4-1-1-1-4-5-4-5-4-5-5 (no literature)
Author 3 essay 2	Intro sentence: 1-2-1-2-2-2*-2*-4-3-2-1-4-5-4-5-5-4 (min literature, *consulted peer group for their perspective on issue)
Author 3 essay 3	Intro sentence: 1-4-4-1-2-1-5-3^ (^analysis without literature)-5-4

pattern of reflective levels discussed followed a roughly 1-2-3-4-5 pattern (see Table 5.3), perhaps with the exception of Author 3, who was highly reflective and very explicit about his/her feelings and judgements in discussing the case as they went along.

Although this is a limited sample, it suggests that good advice to give to students attempting this kind of ARW (mini-essays each on one incident) for the first time might be to try to proceed through the reflective levels (1–5 of Table 5.1) using prompt questions for guidance (see Table 5.1).

Good ARW for Task B

Showing a transformation in perspective

In common with Marker 1 (2019), Marker 2 (2019) sees the purpose of Task B as being to encourage transformative learning in students through ethical reasoning and reflection. Task B's aim is to encourage students to move from an inevitable focus on developing their technical dental skills, to a more well-rounded appreciation of the patient's perspective (Marker 2 2019). In this way Marker 2 (2019) sees a role for reflection and reflective writing in developing students' identity as patient-centred healthcare professionals. Good ARW here is seen as showing that a student has made, or is starting to make, the leap from their worldview, which is often that of a driven, healthy and highly literate young adult, to a greater understanding of the world of patients who often have a very different experience of life (Marker 2 2019). What follows below are extracts that were identified by Marker 2 (2019) as showing that a student is developing 'insight … that starts to relate to the individual, so that is starting to take that step away from the technical to the reality of people'.

> Although I feel I was well informed in terms of the medications and conditions which applied to my patient (4), I have considered that my patient may not be informed or remember all of the details (4), even with tactical prompting (3). In the future I may be drawn to contact the patient's GMP (General Medical Practitioner) sooner (5), in order to ensure I am aware of all the relevant details and can discuss any issues (3), especially if more stressful or longer appointments are scheduled, and if the patient's conditions appear to worsen (5).

Marker 2 (2019) viewed the extract above as 'good insight because that is the absolute reality', that is, that patients don't always know the details of their own medical conditions. Interestingly, the extract above does not proceed in a stepwise fashion through levels 1–5 from Table 5.2. Instead the description of the case (1) is not referred to, as it was contained in the earlier clinical sections of this assignment. The student does not refer to their personal feelings here (2) but instead there is more of an emphasis on evaluation (4) or making a judgement, but the judgement made is not just from the student clinician's perspective, but on what might be happening for the patient. There is detailed concluding/action planning (5) with some elements of analysis (3) being included to explain reasons or give conditions supporting what is being said. Similarly, the extract below hints at the beginnings of a transformed perspective for the student writer:

> Despite delivering smoking cessation advice, making the patient aware of the potential risks associated with smoking for both oral and general health, (1) it was clear that there was no intent to stop (4). This concerned me (2) however, it became apparent that smoking was an enjoyable comfort (4) and perhaps offered a stress relief (3).

According to Marker 2 (2019) the extract above represents a 'refreshing' realization in which a judgement (4) is made on what might be going on from the patient's point of view. Marker 2 (2019) then explained that in their entire career they had not met a patient who was not already informed of the negative health impact of smoking, that it is more of the health professional's role to support patients in relation to smoking cessation, rather than to provide information; therefore, this extract again showed how the student writer was moving closer to 'the reality of people' (Marker 2 2019). Whilst the extract above showed evaluation from the patient's perspective (4), it could be argued that there could be a more explicit reference to the student's intended future actions (5), in the light of this new patient-centred perspective on smoking cessation.

Another instance of showing signs of the start of a transformed perspective concerned a student who encountered a patient who was illiterate. Marker 2 (2019) explained that reflecting on this could be 'quite a leap to make that some people who you come across in your daily life don't have basic reading and writing skills'.

Whilst the sections detailed above could be thought of as 'critical reflection' (Jonas-Dwyer et al. 2013) as the student writers seem to be viewing an aspect of a case from the patient's perspective for the first time, according to Marker 2 (2019) quite a bit of what was written in the other paragraphs of the high-scoring example texts could be thought of as scientific reflection. It was explained that: 'what you often get from students is they are quite scientific about it … and they give some technical answer, and actually whether it truly has a pragmatic relevance or not, is a different matter' (Marker 2 2019). Arguably the following extract from one of the high-scoring texts represents useful reflection that does have a pragmatic relevance to the patient's dominant medical condition, which is Raynaud's phenomenon.

> After the adverse drug reaction in response to Lidocaine HCL 2% (1:80 000 adrenaline), any subsequent procedure requiring local anaesthetic was performed with Citanest 3% with Octapressin to avoid such symptoms (1). However, in hindsight, I should not have used Lidocaine with Epinephrine even though the patient confirmed having it previously (4). Adrenaline can cause adverse cardiovascular effects in susceptible patients and exacerbate the symptoms of Raynaud's (3). My own lack of knowledge (2) regarding the medical conditions for which Lidocaine HCL 2% with Epinephrine is contraindicated put the patient at increased risk (4). Stimulation of beta1 adrenergic receptors can cause palpitations, tachycardia and increase cardiac workload (3). Stimulation of alpha-1 adrenergic receptors causes vasoconstriction which can exacerbate symptoms of Raynaud's phenomenon, hypertension and pulmonary arterial hypertension (3).

Interestingly, the extract above spans most of the reflective levels 1–5 (Table 5.2), with the exception of explicit ideas on future action (5). Again, future action (5), in this case not using lidocaine in Raynaud's patients, is implied. The extract above is a bit different from the earlier extracts about patients' knowledge of their own medications, giving smoking cessation advice and working with illiterate patients, all of which were transformative, as the student was starting to think of care from the patient's point of view. It seems that the presence of examples showing transformative learning or 'critical reflection' (Jonas-Dwyer et al. 2013) in the full texts will have helped the students achieve high grades for this task. However, Marker 2 (2019) holds the view that if an ARW piece is usefully reflective (like the lidocaine extract above), and shows evidence of learning, even if the learning is not necessarily transformative (i.e. does not fully consider the patient's perspective), it is still possible to do well in an ARW assignment. According to Marker 2: 'I think reflection does have its value because it shows that they are thinking about – how does the Science link to my clinical decision making … it's ultimately about clinical decision making.' Successful reflective writing, in the view of Marker 2 (2019), will not just list clinical information but instead the pieces of information will be connected by the writer and interpreted in the light of the case.

Observable patterns in the macrostructure of the high-scoring texts for Task B

In terms of the overall structure of the four high-scoring texts for Task B, the student writers have each chosen different ways to structure their reflective sections. One of the students used subheadings to distinguish different reflective issues from the case, for example, Medical Knowledge, Communication, Patient Management and Implications for the Future. In the other students' texts there were no subheadings, but in a similar way, each paragraph corresponded to a discrete theme or reflective issue unit arising from the case.

In contrast to the fairly predictable pattern of reflective levels per issue seen in Task A (moving roughly 1-2-3-4-5 for each mini-essay overall), the pattern of reflective levels for each issue (which roughly corresponds to one paragraph per unit in Task B) was fairly random. In Task B, whilst there was no discernible pattern, once an initial point had been made about the issue, it was explored using a variety of reflective levels, for example, for Author 1 the patterns were as follows:

- 4-2-1-4-3,
- 2-1-4-3-4,
- 1-2-3-4
- 3-1-1-4
- 4-3-5
- 3-2-1-2-4-5

In Task B Authors 2, 3 and 4 also showed no discernible pattern in the distribution of reflective levels per reflective issue, similar to Author 1 above. In my experience as a student adviser I have found that students can find it difficult initially to identify relevant issues from the case (semantic units) to reflect upon. It is interesting that the four high-scoring student writers have used a variety of starting points for their semantic units, which is something that could help students who are not sure how to start their ARW assignments. For example, the introduction of an issue could begin with the student writer's judgement (4) or feelings (2) on an aspect of the case, before further analysis, as shown below:

> I do feel (2) I have built a good rapport with the patient (4) as she does feel comfortable informing me (3) of changes to her medication, her disease status and providing me the details of her consultant rheumatologist and cardiologist (3). [further analysis of referral and information exchange with other medical professionals followed, and then future actions and intentions].

Less commonly, the issue being explored could begin with medical information (3) linked to the case, e.g.:

> Xerostomia is very relevant for those with polypharmacy and comorbidities (3) and I was mindful of this during treatment (2).

Alternatively, a paragraph could begin with an evaluation (4) and implied lesson that the student has learned from the case (5), e.g.:

> This case has taught me that recording a detailed and accurate medical and drug history is irrelevant unless you understand the implications of such medication and medical conditions on the patient's general and oral health (4/5) [further analysis of aspects the medical history followed and what the student would do in future].

Another characteristic noticed in the high-scoring examples of Task B was that the technical medical information that was included to support what was being said was seldom accompanied by literature citations. Most of the medical information used by student writers may have come from the British National Formulary (a kind of dictionary of medications), anyway, perhaps negating the needed for repetitive citations.

In summary, though, for Task B, it is probably good advice to recommend to students to fully explore each reflective issue arising from the case by paying attention to all of the reflective levels (with perhaps the exception of level 1 as this is included in the earlier clinical sections of this kind of task). For a task like Task B, though, it would also be advisable to place emphasis on reaching a judgement on the case both from the writer's point of view and the patient's point of view, if possible, and to include detailed intended future actions which could show a transformed perspective in practice.

The linguistic features of Tasks A and B

The actual language used at each level for both Tasks (see Column 4 of Table 5.2) was broadly similar, but with some subtle differences. Due to the nature of Task B (a reflective section following medical case notes) there were fewer level 1 descriptive statements than in Task A, as most of these had already been made in earlier sections of Task B. As such, the level 1 statements tended to imply reference to earlier detailed description. Also, in contrast to Task A, the statements at level 2 for Task B tended to be less directly linked to feelings, with the word 'feel' being used less often. Instead, statements tended to focus more on the student's prior level of medical experience in relation to the case, and what the student was thinking during treatment. Evaluative overall feelings of professional satisfaction or otherwise instead emerged instead towards the end of the discussion of the case. Perhaps this may be due to the nature of Task B, with students wanting to appear clinical and objective. Arguably, difficulties with teamworking (Task A) could be less threatening to patient safety than clinical difficulties (Task B).

Using a formal academic tone, and cause and effect language for the analysis of detailed clinical information, is key to success at level 3 (analysis) for both Tasks A and B. No literature citations were noted in the Task B examples, and no dilemmas or contrasting explanations were explored in Task B texts either. In terms of level 4 (evaluations), in Task A, evaluations unfolded gradually, and were linked to the self (2), to aspects of the case (1) and are supported by analysis (3). The evaluative reflective statements tended to begin with initial evaluations employing varying degrees of certainty, and later in the text reached more conclusive judgements. In contrast in Task B, a higher level of certainty was evident possibly because of the nature of the task (patient care). Also, judgements were made from the practitioner's and the patient's point of view. Modal verbs (should have or would have) were used in Task A and B for looking back with the benefit of hindsight on what the writers think they should have done differently (level 4). Finally, future simple with 'will' or 'must', or statements showing learning, for example, 'I have learned that in these circumstances it is important to … ' were used at level 5 in both Tasks A and B to indicate intended future actions.

Discussion: Effective and less effective ARW generally

The first challenge facing the student undertaking ARW, before even beginning a description (level 1 of Table 5.2), is to choose a suitable case or example from their experience to reflect on. According to Marker 1 (2019), choosing a suitable case to discuss is key, as a student will be 'up against it' if they have chosen a case where either there is very little to reflect on, as very little could be done differently in hindsight, or where there are very few relevant academic issues emerging from the case that could be further discussed. Ryan and Ryan (2013) explain that if an appropriate focus is not chosen for reflection in the initial stages, then it is unlikely that the student will be able to reflect in sufficient depth later on. There may also be insufficient room for analysis that sheds new light on the experience if there is too much description (Jonas-Dwyer et al. 2013). Unfortunately, retelling the story of an incident in an unfocussed, descriptive way which includes details that are not relevant to the main learning point arising from the incident, is a common error in student ARW (Marker 1 2019; Ryan and Ryan 2013).

Overly descriptive ARW pieces can be regarded as non-reflective (Jonas Dwyer et al. 2013). In Jonas-Dwyer et al.'s (2013) study conducted with third-year dental students, lecturers estimated that between one third and one half of the written reflective assignments they had marked were non-reflective. This finding is echoed by the present study. According to Markers 1 and 2 (2019), a common error for the dental students writing to two particular ARW briefs was to get carried away with a detailed description of a clinical dental procedure at the expense of identifying relevant underlying principles, or putting across convincing learning points for future practice. Luk (2008) found that a descriptive focus on the practical application of routine pre-learned skills left little room for the questioning of current practice.

On the other hand, an ARW piece that is reflective would keep description to a minimum, relate the incident to one's own knowledge, experience or feelings (level 2 of Table 5.2) and would engage in a reasoned analysis of the links between practice and theory (level 3 of Table 5.2) (Jonas-Dwyer et al. 2013). In addition, a reflective piece would evaluate the incident (level 4 of Table 5.2) and identify some learning opportunities for the future at level 5 of Table 5.2, but these points would not show a significant change in perspective or involve the questioning of one's own initial assumptions (Jonas-Dywer et al. 2013).

Demonstrating transformation through reframing the incident could be thought of as critical reflection. In the study by Jonas-Dwyer et al. (2013), only a very small proportion of the student ARW pieces studied were found to be critically reflective; the majority were either non-reflective or simply reflective. Ryan (2011) and Ryan and Ryan (2013) make the point that systematic reflection, leading to critical reflection, is not intuitive, and that it is a thinking process that needs specific explicit teaching and scaffolding in order for students to develop as ARW writers. Troyan and Kaplan (2015) further argue that ARW is hard to do well without support, even if students are competent writers in other genres.

Conclusion

The close analysis of high-scoring student texts from two ARW tasks in Dentistry has shown that in order to earn high grades for this kind of task, students are required to show signs of transformation in their thinking and ways of acting in relation to particular cases or incidents from their professional experience. ARW places very different demands on the student writer to the traditional essay, and students who are new to this genre can find it 'peculiar' (Vassilaki 2017). In ARW the student writer is expected to show honesty, openness and self-awareness, situating themselves as the central reflective agent 'I' in the piece, moving from a brief and focused description of an incident, to personal feelings, to a judgement on the incident and then to specific ideas for future action. This may be difficult for students, as true transformative learning is easier to demonstrate in cases where something has gone wrong. Student writers, thus, need to be willing to discuss their own errors or misjudgements, or those of colleagues, against the potential constraints of the required values set out in the regulatory healthcare code, or in the knowledge that a tutor who is being discussed in the essay could be one of the markers of the task. A further significant constraint to this kind of ARW is the inherent complexity of this type of writing, which necessitates at least five different levels of reflection and their associated linguistic resources (see Table 5.2) to arrive at a sense of transformation in perspective. These levels of reflection could either be followed roughly in a 1–5 order for each mini-essay on a discrete incident (Task A) or could proceed in any order in different paragraphs for each aspect of a general clinical case (Task B).

In order to be fully able to demonstrate transformative personal reflection, these reflective thoughts have to be supported by reasoning, using some kind of external source material (in this case, ethical principles for Task A or medical facts for Task B) or by internal thought processes. Interestingly, unlike the traditional essay, for the two ARW tasks discussed in this chapter, citations referring to external literature were not seen as essential for success in these tasks. However, this is not necessarily the case for all types of ARW tasks. It is also interesting that whilst attention was needed at all five levels of reflection success in both tasks, the markers highlighted different levels of reflection as being most important in each task. According to White et al. (n.d.), different healthcare tutors can have different interpretations of the nature of reflection and reflective practice, even from within the same discipline. In this case, Marker 1 (the ethics tutor) seemed to value ethical analysis for resolving ethical dilemmas (level 3) slightly above reflection (levels 2, 4 and 5 of Table 5.2). However, for Marker 2 (a clinical tutor), being able to make reflective judgements (level 4) on what was important for not only the student practitioner, but also for the patient, was very important. In both tasks choosing appropriate aspects for discussion was seen as important, as was keeping clinical description of the event to a minimum, and linking all levels of reflection to pragmatic future action.

In conclusion, this chapter has endeavoured to contribute to the literature on what actually characterizes good student ARW from an empirical student text-based perspective and as informed by tutors within the discipline. It is argued here that while ARW tasks may have elements in common; for example, the levels of reflection (see Table 5.2), different tasks and different markers (even in the same discipline and at the same level) place different demands on the student writer. There are also subtle differences in emphasis noted at the linguistic level of analysis for these two Tasks. These differences negate the idea that ARW is a coherent genre of academic writing, which is in line with the academic literacies model of academic writing.

Recommendations

In supporting student writers doing ARW, it is recommended that EAP professionals or subject tutors:

- Make sure students have had a sufficient quality and quantity of work-based experience to generate reflection (Jonas-Dywer et al. 2013).
- Make explicit the safe ways of negotiating the power imbalances associated with this personal kind of writing. Be clear about what is safe to write about, what is not, and what bounds of confidentiality exist surrounding the writing. Also explain when/if/how confidentiality will need to be broken, for example, if potentially dangerous incidents are discussed in the reflections that need action in order to prevent future harms.
- Set aside times when students can safely discuss their reflections with each other prior to writing (Jonas-Dywer et al. 2013).
- Consider using visual and creative approaches to stimulate reflection if needed (McIntosh 2010).
- When setting the assignment, use real example texts for each task (with permission from students in previous years). Give students the opportunity to analyse and compare example texts that were awarded different grades in an interactive workshop setting.
- Introduce the students to a framework containing levels of reflection (e.g. Table 5.2) which students can use to assist their analysis of example texts and to frame their own writing (Ryan 2011).
- Make available examples of the kinds of language associated with each reflective level, for example, use a bank of example sentences, especially if there are English Second Language students in the cohort (see Table 5.2).
- Give students the opportunity to analyse their own written drafts of ARW, which Ryan and Ryan (2011) regard as a particularly powerful way of enhancing learning. This could be in the form of a second short interactive workshop a few weeks before the deadline.
- During drafting, also make sure students have the opportunity for one-to-one discussions with support tutors about their writing that stimulate reflection (if they need it). During the discussions, give students formative feedback on the levels of reflection attained as well as using prompt questions (see Table 5.1) to deepen reflection on the issues discussed (Bain et al. 2002).
- Allow for the development of criticality in ARW over time through repeated practice with feedback (Tsang 2012).

References

Bain, J. D., Mills, C., Ballantyne, R., and Pakcer, J. (2002). 'Developing Reflection on Practice Through Journal Writing: Impacts of Variations in the Focus and Level of Feedback'. *Teachers and Teaching* 8 (2).

Beauchamp, T. L., and Childress, J. F. (1983). *Principles of Biomedical Ethics*. Oxford: Oxford University Press.

Bowman, M., and Addyman, B. (2014a). 'Academic Reflective Writing: A Study to Examine Its Usefulness'. *British Journal of Nursing* 23 (6).

Bowman, M., and Addyman, B. (2014b). 'Improving the Quality of Academic Reflective Writing in Nursing: A Comparison of Three Different Interventions'. *Journal of Learning Development in Higher Education* 7.

Brindley, J. (2017). 'The Mirror Crack'd … : An Illuminative Evaluation of the Use and Relevance of Reflection in Undergraduate Dental Care Professionals' Education'. PhD Thesis, 10 October 2019. Available online: https://ethos.bl.uk/OrderDetails. do?uin=uk.bl.ethos.740081

Brindley, J. (2018). 'The Role of Reflection in ECPD'. *BDJ Team Feature: British Dental Association*, 1 August 2018. Available online: https://www.nature.com/articles/ bdjteam201827.pdf

Dirkx, J. M., and Mezirow, J. (2006). 'Musings and Reflections on the Meaning, Context, and Process of Transformative Learning: A Dialogue Between John M. Dirkx and Jack Mezirow'. *Journal of Transformative Education* 4 (2): 123–39.

Dube, V., and Ducharme, F. (2015). 'Nursing Reflective Practice: An Empirical Literature Review'. *Journal of Nursing Education and Practice* 5 (7): 91–9.

Dudley-Evans, T., and St John, M. J. (1998). *Developments in English for Specific Purposes: A Multi-Disciplinary Approach*. Cambridge: Cambridge University Press.

Flowerdew, J. (2011). 'Action, Content and Identity in Applied Genre Analysis for ESP'. *Language Teaching* 44 (4): 516–28.

Fragkos, K. (2016). 'Reflective Practice in Healthcare Education: An Umbrella Review'. *Education Sciences* 6: 27.

General Dental Council (GDC). (2012). Preparing for Practice [Online]. Available from: https://www.gdc-uk.org/ (Accessed 22 May 2019).

General Dental Council (GDC). (2013). Standards for the Dental Team [Online]. Available from: https://www.gdc-uk.org/ (Accessed 22 May 2019).

Gibbs, G. (1988). *Learning by Doing: A Guide to Teaching and Learning Methods*, Further Education Unit. Oxford: Oxford Polytechnic.

Hyland, K. (2002). 'Authority and Invisibility: Authorial Identity in Academic Writing'. *Journal of Pragmatics* 34: 1091–112.

Jonas-Dwyer, D. R. D., Abbott, P. V., and Boyd, N. (2013). 'First Reflections: Third-Year Dentistry Students' Introduction to Reflective Practice'. *European Journal of Dental Education* 17: e64–e69.

Kaffash, J., and Gregory, J. (2018). 'Revealed: How Reflections Were Used in the Bawa Garba Case', 20 May 2019. Available online: http://www.pulsetoday.co.uk/news/gp-topics/legal/revealed-how-reflections-were-used-in-the-bawa-garba-case/20036090. article

Lea, M. R., and Street, B. V. (2006). 'The Academic Literacies Model: Theory and Applications'. *Theory into Practice* 45 (4): 368–77.

Luk, J. (2008). 'Assessing Teaching Practicum Reflections: Distinguishing Discourse Features of the 'high' and 'low' Grade Reports'. *System* 36: 624–41.

Marker 1. (2019) Interview with M. Bowman, 13 March, Leeds.

Marker 2. (2019). Interview with M. Bowman, 14 March, Leeds.

McIntosh, P. (2010). *Action Research and Reflective Practice*. Abingdon: Routledge.

Mezirow, J. (1998). 'On Critical Reflection'. *Adult Education Quarterly* 48 (3).

Neville, P. (2018). 'Introducing Dental Students to Reflective Practice: A Dental Educator's Reflections'. *Reflective Practice* 19 (2): 278–90.

Rogers, C. (2002). 'Defining Reflection: Another Look at John Dewey and Reflective Thinking'. *Teachers College Record* 104 (4): 842–66.

Ryan, M. (2011). 'Improving Reflective Writing in Higher Education: A Social Semiotic Perspective'. *Teaching in Higher Education* 16 (1): 99–111.

Ryan, M. (2013). 'The Pedagogical Balancing Act: Teaching Reflection in Higher Education'. *Teaching in Higher Education* 18 (2): 144–55.

Ryan, M., and Ryan, M. (2013). 'Theorising a Model for Teaching and Assessing Reflective Learning in Higher Education'. *Higher Education Research and Development* 32 (2): 244–57.

Schon, D. (1995). *The Reflective Practitioner: How Professionals Think in Action*. Aldershot: Arena.

Swales, J. M. (1990). *Genre Analysis: English in Academic and Research Settings*. Cambridge: Cambridge University Press.

Troyan, F. J., and Kaplan, C. S. (2015). 'The Functions of Reflection in High-Stakes Assessment of World Language Teacher Candidates'. *Foreign Language Annals* 48 (3): 372–93.

Tsang, K. L. (2012). 'Oral Health Students as Reflective Practitioners: Changing Patterns of Student Clinical Reflections over a Period of 12 Months'. *American Dental Hygienists' Association* 86 (2): 120–9.

Vassilaki, E. (2017). 'Reflective Writing, Reflecting on Identities: The Construction of Writer Identity in Student Teachers' Reflections'. *Linguistics and Education* 42: 43–52.

White, P., Laxton, J., and Brooke, R. (n.d.). 'Reflection: Importance, Theory and Practice. Article for the Assessment and Learning in Practice Settings Centre for Excellence'. Available online: http://www.alps-cetl.ac.uk/documents/Reflection_BAA_article_submission.pdf (Accessed 4 January 2020).

6

Dissertations in Fine Art

Sara Montgomery

Introduction

Writing in fine art can take many forms and includes reference to visual images, sound, video and other media. Artists regularly need to write grant proposals in order to apply to exhibit their artwork; this may involve writing descriptions of their work or concepts to inform others of where their inspiration comes from. However, artists are unlikely to write an analysis of their own studio practice, which is more likely to be done by a critic or other 'outside' person. On the other hand, throughout university study, the requirement for students of fine art to write critiques (crits) is commonplace. These are varied in structure but generally require students to explain their work to peers and tutors (Orr and Shreeve 2018: 40).

Compared with the writing that artists undertake in their grant proposals, students studying fine art at master's (MA) level are asked to write texts that are more extensive, analytical and researched. In this type of work, students are required to adhere to an appropriate academic style, use appropriate language and structure, follow conventions for referencing and construct appropriate research questions. Their research methods are expected to be well considered, building to a coherent argument with a critical approach.

Fine art as a discipline is predominantly about creative and visual elements. Although writing is also required, the ways in which it is linked to studio practice are varied. This study takes an investigative approach into a practice-based MA fine art course, looking into the form the writing takes and how it is linked to studio practice. Specifically, I will consider the purpose of the writing, asking what it does and why, but also considering how this identified purpose is achieved. It should be noted that the samples of student writing examined in this study achieved high grades, and I take this to indicate that the scripts are examples of good student writing in fine art. In this chapter, 'studio practice' will refer to the visual artistic work created by students. The 'practice-based' nature of the MA programme under scrutiny means that the dissertation holds less weighting in assessment compared to the studio practice and that, therefore, the visual element is the central feature on the course.

This small-scale study involves (a) textual analysis of three MA-level dissertations, (b) analysis of the task instructions and assessment rubric directing the student writers and (c) semi-structured interviews with three subject specialists. Firstly, I will provide some brief discussion of issues relating to writing in fine art. Secondly, I will outline the methodology for data collection (interviews) and then give some context to the dissertation task. The results of both my textual analysis and the interview data are considered in the Discussion and Conclusion. This study generates many questions and ideas for future research around the issue of what is perceived to be good writing in fine art.

The purpose of writing in fine art: what, why and how?

Several existing studies have addressed the question of what types of writing are employed in academic fine art, or art and design contexts, and why they are undertaken. Such studies have questioned the purpose of writing on practice-based art and design courses. An issue raised is that the linear thought processes needed with some genres of academic writing are in opposition to the non-linear and creative thought processes called for on a practice-based course in a creative discipline. This can expose a disjunct for the student writer, between writing skills and practice-based skills (Lockheart et al. 2004). Traditional academic writing genres often provide the structure for the writing tasks, and they may not be the best fit for creative disciplines (Melles and Lockheart 2012). However, institutions may feel obliged to include academic writing, in these traditional genres, on their practice-based courses in these creative disciplines, in order for the courses to be considered academic (Lockheart et al. 2004). Considering these potential barriers to good academic student writing in fine art, more information is needed about its current characteristics and requirements, and further evidence is needed on how, and to what extent, fine art students struggle with traditional academic writing genres, such as the dissertation.

MacDonald (2009) provides a clear vision of the purpose of writing in an artistic context, arguing that writing can help an artist to comprehend their work and consider their artistic identity and the 'construction of an autography' (2009: 97). Artists can consider, through the writing process, how their studio practice is positioned. Although, she does not specify the genre of the writing which may be produced, MacDonald (2009) focuses on how artists, as doctorate-level students, engage with the writing process to enrich and comprehend their studio practice.

Also examining what and how writing is produced in fine art contexts, Paltridge et al. (2012) conducted a small-scale study that considered the variety of genre, content, style and use of author voice in high-level dissertations. The study highlighted the range of approaches by focussing on and comparing two dissertations, out of their selection of examined writing, which they perceived to be at 'opposite ends of a continuum' (Paltridge et al. 2012: 989). In one dissertation, 'parallel "codes" or "voices" are presented; that is, the artist and the academic' and in the other, 'these two may be more closely combined, where one code or voice recontextualizes the other' (2012: 998). Paltridge et al. (2012) draw upon Elkins' categorization of three types of doctor of philosophy (PhD) dissertation:

1. The dissertation is research that informs the art practice.
2. The dissertation is equal to the artwork.
3. The dissertation is the artwork and vice versa.

(Elkins 2009b cited in Paltridge et al. 2012: 998)

Borg (2004) proposes that the aim of the MA dissertation is to do your own research around themes that inspire your studio practice through critical engagement with artists and sources. MacDonald (2009) situates the aim of the writing with equality or even symbiosis with the studio practice, linking to the second and third of Elkins' categorizations (Elkins 2009b cited in Paltridge et al. 2012: 998).

Lockheart et al. (2004) find that the genre of good writing in art and design may be varied or manipulated, and that creativity can be explored, via such means as having text represented in more visual ways (Edwards 2004). Lockheart et al.'s 'Writing-PAD'-Writing purposefully in Art and Design (2004: 89) was created to support many genres of writing in this field. Allison (2004) investigates creativity in students' academic writing in terms of how the writing task may be adapted by the student, unique argumentation or viewpoint presented, and content. EAP tutors commenting in his study describe creativity as a 'fresh approach' (Allison 2004: 198), and Allison concludes that 'creativity is positively valued though not elaborated or defined' (2004: 200). Creativity (in student academic writing) seems to be an area which is difficult to determine.

Also, of importance in the fine art context seems to be students' demonstration of critical engagement with sources and/or other artists; interacting, creating questions and new lines of inquiry and achieving an 'internally persuasive' voice (Borg 2004: 193). Haas (2018) argues, in her paper proposing her Reader Engagement Framework, that effort should be made by the student writer to view things from the perspective of the reader. She identifies a component of writing which is subjective, but which could provide advanced engagement for the reader, labelled as 'something extra done for visual or tactile appeal' (2018: 143). This component can manifest in the criticality of the argument or perhaps via more creative, visual methods.

What constitutes good student writing within disciplines usually means writing that adheres to the particular expectations of the discipline in which it occurs. Across most disciplines, aspects of writing, such as critical thinking, structure, language use and argument are valued, but discipline-specific requirements must also be acknowledged (Nesi and Gardner 2006). Engagement with the literature and demonstrating depth of understanding and argumentation are considered to be favourable features (Murray and Sharpling 2018). Tardy (2015) finds that student writers can be rewarded for risk-taking if this is done in ways that the tutor considers to be legitimate. She suggests that the tutors accept when student writing tests the limits but only if the tutors feel the student knows what they are doing. In arts-based writing, the issue of knowledge representation is significant. What is valued is 'the greater use by "arts" students of orienting themes that represent knowledge as perspectival rather than factual' (North 2005: 530). This seems to indicate that knowledge representation, alongside an understanding of the culture of the discipline in the particular institution, is important for good writing in fine art.

Individual academics' impressions of a piece of student writing can be different; features of the writing which receive more scrutiny in the marking process may vary for each individual, and what one tutor identifies as being the best aspect(s) of a piece of writing may not be the same as another. Assessment rubrics help align differing views, but tutors are not always able to explain why certain features are considered to be good (Lea and Street 2000 cited in Nesi and Gardner 2006; Murray and Sharpling 2018). A useful observation to make at this point is that the Reader Engagement Framework (Haas 2018) could be used to ascertain opinions of good features of writing, the features which Haas (2018: 143) categorizes under 'Advanced Engagement', those features which gain high engagement or engrossment from the reader.

In addition to Lockheart et al.'s (2004) Writing-PAD, created to provide support for all writing in art and design, and Edward's (2004) MADD – Matters around Art and Design Dissertation website, giving more specific dissertation guidance; it is hoped that this study could further add to knowledge for students navigating the textual element of their practice-based fine art courses. The following research questions guided this investigative study which takes a close look at dissertation writing by MA fine art students using a small sample:

1. What purpose does the dissertation serve on this practice-based fine art course?
2. Is the dissertation genre a challenge for the student writers and what writing support is provided?
3. What can be identified as good features of student writing in this context?

Methodology

This study focussed on dissertations from an MA-level programme. There were three stages to the methodology. The first two stages involved textual analysis of student writing (dissertations) and analysis of the task instructions and assessment rubric, and the third stage consisted of interviews with subject specialists. I initially chose face-to-face interviews as the method to collect data at the third stage; however, because it was not possible to meet the three subject specialists face-to-face, two out of three interviews were conducted over the telephone, and only one was face-to-face. I sent the questions in advance of the interviews (see Appendix) so that the interviewees could consider their responses. Before organizing the interviews, I contacted the department with details of the scholarship project in order to provide context for the data collection.

The three interviewees were the same subject specialists who had supervised or graded the dissertations. I conducted three individual interviews, each of 30–35 minutes; these were recorded for my purposes with consent from the interviewees. The interview questions provided the structure, and I chose structured interviews for two main reasons: in order to make the different interviews more objectively comparable and to allow the subject specialists, rather than myself, to speak as much as possible. I read out the questions and then gave the subject specialists time to answer. The interviewees provided lengthy responses to the general task questions, but fewer details relating to the second part looking at specific dissertations. The questions are given in full in the Appendix.

In the next section, for context, I have provided a description of the dissertation task brief which shows what instruction and guidance the student writers were given. Following that is a textual analysis of introductions, then an analysis of the assessment rubric and finally the results from the interview data followed by the discussion.

The dissertation task brief

The dissertation task explored in this study has a word count range of 7,500–9,000 and requires student writers to include the following steps:

1. Diagnose their artistic concerns.
2. Investigate contemporary culture finding key individuals, or groups, undertaking work that shares relevant concerns and/or themes to their own.
3. Critically contextualize their artistic practice.

The task appears to be dynamic and creative, involving current ideas and links to concepts influencing the students' studio practice. Much as Borg (2004: 193) describes, this dissertation task explores issues around which the students' own studio practice is based. Step 3 (critically contextualize their artistic practice) chimes with MacDonald's (2009) description of the positioning of the studio practice through the writing. This dissertation task exists alongside the studio practice and students are asked, in the dissertation task brief, to allow the dissertation and studio practice to 'positively enable one another'.

Student writers create their own research questions to investigate their chosen area. Structured support is built into the task brief in the form of stages of work; guidance and written feedback are given on initial plans. Students also deliver presentations of their more developed plans in order to receive feedback from tutors and peers. This aims to help shape their research questions and highlight any issues. Each student has a supervisor with whom they meet regularly for structured support. Although this would mostly be about the content, written samples are submitted to supervisors early in the process to gain feedback on language.

The cohort on this practice-based fine art course often has a variety of writing experience on entry to the course. However, all students undertake writing assessments of around 3,000 words for other credit-bearing modules; the teaching and assessment on these modules should give students further experience of academic writing, which could improve the quality of their dissertations. These assessments are usually academic essays, but some modules involve a reflective portfolio based on a group project. On these modules students must engage critically with sources; written assessments are graded using the same rubric as the dissertations, which specifically calls for critical analysis. By the time student writers are preparing research questions for their dissertations, they would be familiar with the requirements of the assessment rubric.

Student writers are required to adhere closely to task instruction, transferring written instruction into practice. Their writing needs to have appropriate tone, style and self-direction; below are excerpts from the instructions directing students to incorporate these three factors.

Appropriate tone

A writing sample* [part of your plan], in terms of style and formatting, should be written as you plan to write the final submission, with references and an appropriate tone.

*This writing sample, as part of the dissertation plan, is submitted to supervisors for feedback in the planning stages which allows for support with tone and style of the writing.

Style:

The questions, methods and writing style you choose are all open to appropriate forms of experimentation.

Self-direction:

You need to write from and with the concerns that motivate you as a practitioner. You are always the centre and driving force of your project. Remember that your project is self-directed and so establishing its field, questions, method and findings must all be driven by you.

Textual analysis of dissertation introductions

The following are brief textual analyses of the introductions of three MA-level dissertations written by fine art students to illustrate the range of approaches (to dissertation writing) that exist. My analysis shows the variety of approaches to the task in terms of structure of content, style and use of language.

Introduction 1

The paper opens with several direct questions, which challenge the writer's choice of research area and provide immediate context. Their use could be compared to how rhetorical questions function in an oral presentation to engage the audience.

The passive tense is used to introduce the selected works for analysis and describe their structure and materials, but it is rarely used throughout the rest of the text. Personal pronouns do not feature in the introduction and the most common verb forms are past and present simple, which seem to contribute to the 'direct' style.

The writing is precise, 'lean' and 'content-heavy'. Points are not reformed, and the pace is rapid, moving from one description or statement, to the student writer's voice making an evaluation.

Overall, the writing conveys a certain confidence through aims which are stated clearly and purposefully, for example – *the aim of the following … is to uncover …* The student writer seems to be generating new inspiration (for their studio practice) as they claim the theory used in the paper's analysis will '*invigorate*'. There is a bias towards positive connections or outcomes in the application of this theory, but if this absence of objectivity creates ideas, then it seems to be meeting the requirement of the task.

Introduction 2

The first four paragraphs introduce several interesting ideas, but they are not expanded on, and there is some ambiguity over whether these areas will be covered in the main body. In the overview, from Paragraph 5 on, there are many instances of clear, systematic writing with sophisticated use of cohesive devices. Topic sentences are given, followed by sequencing cohesion introducing descriptions of content. Linking is sometimes also present between paragraphs. There is a general to specific structure going from historical chronology to modern case studies.

Introduction 3

The writing starts with a direct question, in a similar way to Introduction 1, gaining the attention of the reader. What follows is a combination of personal narrative, description of events/process and passively written statements, which add theory to the practical artistic process. There are questions directly relating to the student writer's art practice referred to with frequent use of personal pronouns.

Statements of the student writer's position on certain art practices are given. Many questions which explore the topics are introduced, and perhaps aim to be answered during the dissertation; but it seems more open than that, like a stream of consciousness with ideas being shown to the reader for consideration. The author's voice is at the forefront of the work, guiding the reader through the practice and influences.

Table 6.1 describes the content in each paragraph across the three introductions, which allows for comparison between them. The analysis here shows that there is significant variety between the structure and content choices of the dissertation introductions. The first two have more similarities in that they provide some background information followed by a more focused explanation of their studies, then the aim and overview of the contents are given. These are typical features of introductions in academic essay writing and probably in line with typical dissertations. The third introduction is much longer than the other two and does not seem to contain the genre-specific features of a dissertation such as an aim, definitions or an overview. It does provide some background though, and a new approach, and questions are raised towards the end.

Table 6.1 Table of Description of Introduction Paragraph Contents.

Paragraphs: P1, P2…		
Introduction 1	Introduction 2	Introduction 3
P1: 3 direct questions introducing the research area/ Thesis question given. P2: Introduction of 1 artwork, brief background and description of piece/ brief analysis and evaluation of artwork. P3: Clarification given of term/ and link made between artwork and chosen theory. Aim given/ methodology.	P1: General background of main topic. P2: More focused background and introduction of concept to be investigated, which is explained plainly using present passive and simple tenses. P3: Student writer's link to their area of interest. P4: Aim of writing given. P5–7: Detailed overview of contents of each section. Clear writing with signposting and cohesive devices.	P1: Direct question and description introducing the student's artwork. P2: Detail of personal creative methods. P3: Historical background information and explanation of terms relating to the creation of the artwork. P4–7: Description of artwork in situ in a gallery. P8: Introduction of influential artists or related artwork. P9–13: Explanation of new approach and questioning of scope and impact.
250 words	**420 words**	**1,600 words**

Considering that the three dissertations received good grades, the three introductions could demonstrate how genres can be successfully manipulated by student writers, as considered in Tardy's (2015) study, and provide evidence towards there being a range of practices demonstrated for one task in student academic writing (Paltridge et al. 2012).

Features of language use, choice and style

I selected excerpts, displayed in Table 6.2, to demonstrate how the student writers' language choices achieved certain functions in the dissertations. These are what I consider, as an EAP specialist, to be examples of good writing. My labels are given in the Function column and my explanation is provided in the third column.

Table 6.2 Table of Selected Excerpts of Good Writing.

Function	Excerpt from dissertation	Explanation
'Direct style'	*In what follows, the guiding question is this…* *This enables the piece to adapt and change almost constantly…* *Made in the early 1980s, this…* *is created from…*	The phrases serve to allow the writing to proceed at a pace which is engaging to the reader through the clarity and tightness.
'Direct style' as topic sentences	*The investment of time, dedication and… to my practice is evident and made more palpable to an audience when they interact with the work. The themes also challenge current art practices of over-preservation and over-commodification of artwork.*	These topic sentences give an impression of confidence in the student writer and a purposeful impression of their content, these factors are favourable to the reader.
Cohesive devices	*Furthermore…* *To summarize, the aim of the following chapters…*	Adding to the flow of the writing and helping the reader anticipate what is next.
Stylistic vocabulary choices which serve to illustrate (visually evocative)	*Transmute with every successive appearance… in a process of constant reconfiguration…* *Encapsulated…* *… shimmering vision…* *… tales spawned…* *Under the spotlight of… this disparate tableau is not a mortician's slab.*	Helping the reader to visualize the content and follow the writing, like with a story.

Function	Excerpt from dissertation	Explanation
Highly descriptive vocabulary choices including 'playful' choices (also visually evocative)	*… terrifying demons…* *… engulfed a village…* *… gaping jaws of hell.* *… rhythmical and repetitious twists and turns.*	As above, perhaps with more poetic or surprising vocabulary choices.

Analysis of the assessment rubric

On this practice-based course, subject specialists mark the student writing using assessment Rubrics which have been designed for use with writing tasks across all taught MA programmes in the faculty. Student writers are introduced to the rubric from the beginning of their course through the Virtual Learning Environment. This section looks at what instruction the student writers receive and when they receive it.

The assessment rubric for marking written tasks has four main criteria:

1. Selection of sources – focusing on the student's ability to select and manipulate sources.
2. Analysis, understanding and argument – considering how students demonstrate understanding of those sources by the extent to which they engage in arguments which are clearly communicated, original and compelling.
3. Design – looking at students' approach to their chosen research question and their research methods.
4. Presentation and impact – highlighting student adherence to academic conventions and the effectiveness of the overall impact of the work.

The four criteria contain questions and descriptors which guide the subject specialists when grading the student writing and the students when producing it. For example, in the criteria under 'Analysis, understanding and argument' the following questions are provided: *How clear is the intellectual engagement with issues and ideas informing the work? What is the level of critical analysis?*

The student writers' language is addressed in the final criteria, 'Presentation and impact', where the subject specialist assesses the level to which academic language has been applied. For student writers to achieve a grade of high merit or above in this section they must satisfy the following descriptors:

Excellent use of language; highly accurate proofreading; excellent application of academic conventions ... The overall impact of the work is compelling.

or

Effective use of language; accurate proofreading; accurate application of academic conventions ... The overall impact of the work is very strong.

'Impact' does not feature in the instructions in the dissertation task brief; however, student writers will have had written work assessed using this rubric already, and had access to it from the start of their MA course, so theoretically they will have a good understanding of the descriptors and what they are asking.

Table 6.3 displays the features seemingly required in 'good' writing (e.g. impact) and where and when the information/instruction to consider them is provided. Some features are stated as required before the task – in the task brief and/or assessment rubric – but some became apparent after the task, emerging from the interview data and my observations as an EAP specialist. This analysis gives an idea of what information/instruction the student writers receive and when they receive it, but it is likely the requirement of these features may be communicated to students through meetings with their supervisors.

Table 6.3 Table of Analysis of Instructions Including Required Features.

Features (required in 'good' writing as stated in the task brief, assessment rubric or post-task)	Where information/instruction provided
Appropriate tone Style – open to appropriate experimentation Precision – in reference to academic language Self-direction	Task brief (pre-task)
Impact Compelling	Assessment rubric (pre-task)
Openness/ flexibility/ flux Newness – creativity in research Risk taking	Subject specialists' comments obtained from interviews and discussed in more detail in the Results section (post-task)
Direct style (differing from self-direction)	EAP specialist's observations (post-task)

Results

Summary and analysis of the interview data

This section provides a summary of the data from the interviews with the subject specialists.

In response to my first research question I found that the purpose of the dissertation is to provide a platform from which students can explore their studio practice, and contextualize it within the wider world of art. Two of the subject specialists commented that student writers should 'Situate [their] artistic concerns in the broad field of fine art' and '[Find] areas of interest in similar fields.'

One subject specialist explained that the aim of the dissertation task was not for student writers to be critiquing or explaining their own studio practice, but rather to be exploring the topic and related theories. Another subject specialist made the following comment in reference to the task aim: '[The] dissertation adequately articulates what the studio work is about- [a] good reflection of what they actually do, appropriately evaluating what [the] work is about.' It was felt by one subject specialist that because the same topic is chosen for the dissertation as for the studio practice, there could be a danger of student writers producing descriptive monologues of their work and not embracing the theoretical inspirations or displaying enough criticality.

It was felt by one of the subject specialists that, in the dissertation task, less emphasis is placed on rigorous research, but rather on the selection of sources by the student writer that help to explore the context of their studio practice. This subject specialist explained that student writers were not expected to have significant knowledge at this stage, and could be 'borrowing rather than knowing.' Student writers could show a surface-level understanding of their research findings but should still be able to position themselves in that area. Another subject specialist felt that this superficial approach could mean the students opted for less challenging sources, selecting artists whose work was like theirs, resulting in more description than the sparking of inspiration. They also raised the concern that sometimes the student writers might not be giving sufficient time to understand, in full, the artists' intentions and so were possibly misrepresenting them.

The selection of a traditional dissertation genre was considered by most of the subject specialists to be giving student writers an advantage in the sense that they were not required to consider another genre type, but could be quite methodical in their approach to the writing, as described in the following subject specialist comments:

'Formatting straightforward – should not use creative formatting- [student should conserve the majority of their creative] energies for [the] studio practice.'

'Creative formatting- opens [too] many possibilities- [an MA programme of] 12 months needs some focus [as it goes by very quickly].'

'Straightforward [formatting]- useful for moving forwards. Feed on to PhD-helps to focus. Feeding into future career.'

The final comment above touches on how the dissertation, as a piece of academic writing, can evidence the student writers' abilities when applying for PhDs or other further areas of academic study. It was felt by two of the subject specialists that the dissertation genre, including the linear thought processes required which were identified as an issue by Lockheart et al. (2004), would not pose a challenge. However, for some student writers, becoming accustomed to academic writing was more difficult because it was new to them, or because they had had long breaks in their university study.

There were a few comments made considering the engagement of student writers with the task. One subject specialist stated that writing has a significant role in artistic practice, and is a fundamental skill, but perhaps not in an academic form. They felt that it acted as more of a communicative or functional tool needed for applications or proposals. Levels of familiarity with the dissertation genre could affect engagement with the task. The genre required in this task would be familiar to those student writers with experience of academic writing; however, there is (typically) a range of knowledge and experience in the cohort. Those student writers less familiar with the dissertation genre may experience difficulties engaging with the task. Additionally, for some students, artistic practice was not their principal career, which could also impact on their engagement with the writing. An additional factor that could affect engagement is that the dissertation task on the course is worth less of the overall grade than the studio practice, therefore, perhaps having less time and/or effort spent on it. This is referred to with the following comment from a subject specialist: 'Writing is subservient to the course aim.' The lesser status of writing on this MA programme may mean the student does not feel inspired to do more than the basics.

In considering my second research question about what writing support is provided for student writers, I was told by subject specialists that guidance on the dissertation task is given in ten structured stages, with tasks broken down weekly to help with time management. In one weekly task students prepare and deliver presentations to explain their content ideas at the developmental stage, and their initial research questions, in order to receive feedback from peers and tutors. Student writers also attend meetings with their supervisors as well as skills workshops to support them with academic skills such as referencing.

There seems to be flexibility in the way student writers can express themselves in terms of, for example, use of image, what sections to include and language style. One subject specialist explained that student writers could express themselves in slightly unconventional ways and push boundaries, but that they would need to follow the conventions of the dissertation genre; this was described as 'experimentation within realms'.

It is considered good by the subject specialists if the student writers are able to draw on inspiration from carefully selected areas and perhaps from unexpected subject disciplines. For example, if they are able to combine theories in music with their artistic influences, this could create fruitful and exiting new combinations. One challenge is to put theory into practice and apply the knowledge they have gained, making judgements about what to include which one subject specialist described as 'selection of what is pertinent'. There are a lot of theories and concepts presented to student writers through their optional modules, as well as gleaned from their own research, and it was felt by subject specialists that it was sometimes a challenge for student writers to make effective choices and apply the content/theories. The amount of choice and range of interpretation could mean disengagement and vagueness in writing content if students are unable to make effective selections. According to one subject specialist, successful student writers choose one case study only and utilize, up-to-date lines of theoretical thought; often ones not commonly used in the discipline. They should demonstrate an intensity of research, taking ideas to their limits and viewing the case study from differing perspectives – reinterpreting old work through a new lens.

A subject specialist reflects on a dissertation which received a high grade: '[The] student is dealing with live issues in art, contemporary issues which are in constant flux, [and] they have laudably taken a risk.' This good dissertation made clear links between the student's studio practice and the case study which was chosen. The student raised questions to challenge the case study which also reflected on their studio practice and provided some theoretical grounding to the dissertation. As the dissertation took shape and developed, the subject specialist explained that it seemed as though the student's writing and their studio practice were continuously informing each other. It was as though each existed to inform the other because they were so closely intertwined, one sometimes leading, and then following. In the dissertation, cross-disciplinary primary research provided unique perspectives and brought these together in the artistic context. The subject specialist commented that the student structured their arguments clearly and was convincing.

Critical engagement with sources and linking the content closely to studio practice is a key element of success in this dissertation task. One subject specialist explained that a successful student writer should be visualizing and expressing ideas from the first stages of their planning of the dissertation. Generally, the subject specialists felt it was a challenge for student writers to make the final edit as relevant as it could be, and students needed to keep adapting and re-drafting the writing to accommodate the most up-to-date content. One subject specialist explained that in general a student who produces good writing has the capacity to understand what the dissertation task is and is not. It is not necessarily carefully constructed writing, research and arguments you might have in humanities essays – it is demonstration of 'ideas in progress' that is important. In the writing process there is an element of risk-taking and self-belief, and a need to keep the content flexible and in a state of flux even up to the later stages of writing, allowing changes to be made constantly. One subject specialist advised that students 'hammer it out in the last few weeks!' They also described how '[the dissertation is] a late edit of the research process'.

Subject specialists considered expressive language appropriate to the dissertation genre. An excerpt of student writing: '*Under the spotlight of ... this disparate tableau is not a mortician's slab*' was considered to be 'quite descriptive, made it enjoyable to read'. The subject tutor said, 'The writing can be expressive; an overuse of adjectives would be bad but if it helps to describe environment and is effective then it is fine.'

Discussion

This dissertation task requires exploration of the students' studio practice, specifically, extended consideration of the main themes and influences. These themes should be communicated and contextualized within contemporary art practice through extensive and well-selected research, which should involve critical engagement with sources and artworks (Borg 2004; Nesi and Gardner 2006). Students are permitted to show a surface understanding of content, but an understanding of how the chosen elements can interact to create something new is a requirement. The student writer should use the space of the task in order to consider their position of self as an artist within the wider community of contemporary art, perhaps constructing what MacDonald refers to as an 'autography' (2009: 97). Through the task, ideas can be researched which generate potential routes for artistic exploration, allowing the dissertation task to act as a springboard of inspiration. The purpose of the fine art dissertation echoes the findings in Borg's (2004) study. Student writers are expected to explore an area of studio practice through critical engagement with artists and sources which resonate with them, thereby contributing to their developing artistic identity. Examples of subject specialists reflecting this purpose in their student feedback are:

'Provides new possibilities for a continuing and developing practice.'

'To solicit from the artist a wider view of the place of their own practice in contemporary art and in debates that art incite and issues that are confronted by artistic practice.'

'Produce insights for the artist in the terms of her own practice.'

The theme of newness emerges as valuable within this practice-based course. Features of the student work are described as 'refreshing' or 'interesting'; communication of an original idea is seen as good. This matches with creativity being described as a 'fresh approach' (Allison 2004: 198), new ideas are tied in with creativity and creativity stems from originality. One subject specialist reflects on this idea: 'New lines of theoretical thought - up to date - refreshing. Intensity of research to take to limits. [Offering up] differing perspectives.'

Successful student writing focuses on well-chosen case studies, but then brings in alternative, sometimes cross-disciplinary, perspectives. The subject specialists asserted that it is expected that student writers will incorporate ideas from other disciplines, perhaps using theories from art history, music or philosophy; adopting a new lens with which to view their contemporary artistic influences, as one subject specialist commented: 'It is encouraging to see a student engaging with comparatively new strands of theoretical and philosophical thought.'

One aim of the student dissertations is to produce a piece of extended writing which can be added to a portfolio of work for application to further higher education, such as a PhD. For this reason, the dissertation conforms to traditional dissertation genre expectations which allow it to be interpreted in several contexts. This accords with Hyland's view that 'genres thus provide an orientation to action for both producers and receivers, suggesting ways to do things using language which are recognizable to those we interact with' (2009: 26). Similarly, Nesi and Gardner state, 'Writing of this type may simply serve as evidence of educational achievement, or it may reflect the output of the professional academic' (2006: 10).

The dissertations are part of a process, not an ending; they are a cog in the structure, the structure being the course as well as the students' future artistic career. The writing must interact with and underpin the studio practice, but also stand-alone and convey its aim to the reader. The writing task is submitted in the same month as the studio practice output; therefore, the two tasks will naturally influence and inform each other, whether leading or following.

Directional changes in the studio practice could mean a shift in focus of the writing topic, or the two could diverge. They move backwards and forwards, feeding off one another. 'Writing and art making are both processes, … they are porous and dynamic. They can flare up, or act off one another' (MacDonald 2009: 101). 'The text "positions" the practice – suggesting a spatial metaphor. It also looks back from a position – having travelled –or looks towards the movement of the work away from a position that has acted as a point of departure' (MacDonald 2009: 95). The student's research does not support or inform the studio practice, but instead complements it. However, this finding does not quite fit in with Elkins' (2009b cited in Paltridge et al. 2012: 998) PhD dissertation categorizations as this type of dissertation is not equal to the studio practice and neither is it truly informing it. It is important to note here that the categorizations are based on PhD-level writing rather than MA.

It has been identified in previous studies that writing for art and design courses is required in order for the course to be considered academic (Lockheart et al. 2004: 94; Melles and Lockheart 2012). Edwards (2004) provides ideas on how academic writing can be approached more creatively for visual subjects. However, the main motivation for the selection of dissertation genre for this writing task, by the subject specialists who developed the course, appears to be so that the writing genre does not detract from the content. The dissertation genre is one which is familiar in academic contexts and therefore the genre of the writing will not overshadow the content, and the task could be an example of the student's academic writing ability in a genre which is widely recognized. However, there may be difficulties with students understanding the purpose of the task. Although its requirements are outlined fairly clearly by the subject specialists, perhaps producing a piece of writing for the sake of having academic writing to progress in academia does not resonate with those concerned solely with studio practice.

Nevertheless, subject specialists in fine art in this study felt that the style of the writing could be expressive and descriptive if done effectively, which demonstrates the existence of genre testing (Tardy 2015) or even Haas' observation of 'something extra done for visual or tactile appeal' (2018: 143), where students confident in their linguistic abilities can give the reader something extra. Conforming to the typical dissertation genre allows the written work to remain clear, uncomplicated and easily identified in its purpose, structure and content.

However, the data presented in my textual analysis of dissertation introductions (Table 6.1), and the summary of interview data, show that creativity can exist within this traditional dissertation genre and is indeed expected by the subject specialists. Tutors want innovation and impact, and this probably entails individual tutor preference (Murray and Sharpling 2018; Tardy 2015).

There can be a difficult-to-navigate relationship between artistic practice and written theory. The written element seems to be an integral part of artistic practice, although it is debatable what genre it should be in and in this academic context it is a dissertation. On this practice-based course, the variety of the cohort leads to a range of academic writing experience. There tend to be around 20 per cent L2 speakers of English, mature students, as well as UK students, all of whom could be part-time or full-time students. It is quite common for part-time students to have alternative careers alongside their MA study, which means they have other significant responsibilities. Considering this variety of student profile and motivations for taking the course in terms of their future artistic identities and careers, perhaps the writing task would make more sense as a reflective piece if the student was not continuing their academic study. However, the requirement of in-depth engagement with theory and case studies hopefully has the positive outcome of inspiring the students' practice.

Because of most credits on this practice-based MA programme being gained through studio practice it seems important to focus on how visual images are used in the student writing; they were present in the three MA dissertations that I read for this study. There are challenges when deciding what choices have been made with respect to the modes (visual, textual) because it is not possible to know why certain choices have been made without talking to the student writer. For example, the decision to divide the text into distinct sections and insert a full-page visual image could have been done because the text and image are perceived to have equal weight of meaning. Kress and van Leeuwen (2006: 19) state that there are limitations of these modes of communication but go on to explain how they can be used to communicate the same ideas in varying ways. Additionally, either mode, visual or textual, could be the main communicator of meaning (Bateman 2014), so for potentially useful future research, investigation into what informs the image choices made by the student writers would be beneficial.

Reference to use of image was made in the interview (Question 4e, Appendix), but no specific comments were provided by subject specialists. However, to provide some context, I have analysed one dissertation and made the following observations on the student's use of image. Two photographs in the dissertation function as bookends to the body of the text, providing a visual beginning and end to the writing which is achieved in two ways. The first is through the positioning of the images – one is on the title page and the other after the conclusion, but prior to the references. Positioned in this way, the photographs gain meaning by working as a pair. Secondly, the images are photographs of the same object taken first from the front and then from the back. There is a sense of playfulness in using them in this manner, visually signifying the beginning and end of the text. They are not referred to in the main body of the text, so their purpose seems to be ornamental. To reiterate an important final comment, I observed that all the dissertations I analysed for this study incorporated visual images, so future research focusing on this seems to be pertinent.

Conclusion

The fine art dissertation task analysed in this study aims to give the student space to research their artistic interests (some of which are very wide-ranging and reach into other disciplines) without needing to produce the practical artwork. The student writers have a framework (structured steps) as well as a supervisor to guide them through the dissertation process. Good writing means keeping the content adaptable and up to date. Student writers are gathering ideas and theories and through this process are sparking new ideas, but not necessarily needing to follow up on all of them in their dissertation task or their studio practice. However, this surface-level of contact with sources could result in some misunderstanding of other artists' work or theories.

All of this takes place within a dissertation genre, which means that the student writers have to produce a piece of writing in which these ideas are presented and explored but adhere to this traditional academic writing genre. The variety of academic experience and motivations of the cohort could mean that the dissertation genre is not always the most inspiring or best fit. In addition, the topic being the same as the students' studio practice caused some student writing to become quite descriptive (of their studio practice) rather than critical.

The interview data showed that demonstration of an overall understanding of well-selected sources presented through well-constructed arguments seems to be of more value to subject specialists than specific language use. In the early stages of information gathering I spoke to an international student studying on this practice-based fine art course. The student had received feedback on their writing and expressed some trepidation about what shape the future (dissertation) writing was to take but they understood, from feedback comments on their work, that direct style was perceived to be good by their tutor. I have observed direct style in the dissertations analysed in this study through the student writers' use of direct questions. These are elaborated on in the section 'Textual analysis of dissertation introductions', in Introductions 1 and 3. Although not articulated in my interview data, it seems that direct style is seen as a feature of good writing, this is hinted at in the quote from one subject specialist reflecting on writing that was given a high grade: 'Clearly made own views and was convincing'.

In further studies I could involve more perceptions of what is considered to be good writing in fine art by showing subject specialists the excerpts I selected as representations of good writing (Table 6.2) and seeing if they agree. Haas' (2018) framework could be implemented to analyse student writing, addressing the question of what makes writing engaging. Aspects of writing identified by Edwards (2004) as visual/verbal terms, particularly metaphor and use of image, would also be interesting to analyze in student writing in fine art.

Another further study could be a focus on the range of student writing which is presented in response to a task. Variety in student response is demonstrated in Paltridge et al.'s (2012) research where, from the sample of student writing collected for the study, two pieces of writing considered to be 'at opposite ends of a continuum' (989) were selected, analysed and compared. As Paltridge et al. (2012) suggested, having a collection of high-level dissertations available for students as models to view may help them to understand the task in more detail and the parameters within which they can experiment. The experimentation could happen in any area within a single writing task, for example, in the overall structure of the writing, how images are used or the interplay between the writing and the studio practice.

It has been proposed that subject specialists are not always able to articulate adequately and unambiguously the 'discursive requirements of their disciplines' (Ding and Bruce 2017: 9), and that EAP specialists must try to devise methods to help students to meet those requirements. Providing EAP specialists with a clearer idea of the writing required for assessment in fine art departments, through closer links between the department and EAP specialists, can develop into an environment where course content, student attainment and student challenges are more commonly spoken about across both the EAP and fine art disciplines (Edwards 2004). This type of ongoing activity can, hopefully, result in developing cohesive support networks that enable the development of a better and more clearly articulated understanding of disciplinary writing requirements to the benefit of students and tutors alike.

Appendix. List of questions from the interviews with subject specialists

General task questions:

1. What is the purpose of the fine art dissertation?
2. Are there requirements/restrictions on the content or style of the dissertation task? Would you be flexible, as the one grading the work, if these factors were atypical, but you felt that the student had 'got it'?
3. In which areas might you use a more holistic 'instinct' or 'implicit rubric' involved with good writing?

Looking at specific dissertations:

4. What makes this dissertation earn the grade of merit/distinction?

for example,

a) Originality 'newness'/creativity?
b) Criticality/argumentation?
c) Content?
d) Use of theory or explanation of methodology?
e) Use of image?
f) Language?
g) Structure?
h) Something else?

5. Can you identify an aspect of the work which exemplifies this?
6. Can you identify a specific paragraph or sentence that exemplifies 'good' writing? What's special about it?
7. Referring to the feedback given on this dissertation, can you comment on what you said here? (*interviewer selects comment*).

References

Allison, D. (2004). 'Creativity, Students' Academic Writing, and EAP: Exploring Comments on Writing in and English Language Degree Programme'. *Journal of English for Academic Purposes* 3: 191–209.

Bateman, J. (2014). *Text and Image: A Critical Introduction to the Visual/Verbal Divide*. London: Routledge.

Borg, E. W. (2004). Internally Persuasive Writing in Fine Arts Practice'. *Art, Design & Communication in Higher Education* 3 (3): 193–210.

Borg, E. W. (2009). *The Experience of Writing a Practice-Based Thesis Is Fine Art and Design*, PhD Thesis University of Leeds.

Ding, A, and Bruce, I. (2017). *The English for Academic Purposes Practitioner: Operating on the Edge of Academia*. Cham, Switzerland: Palgrave Macmillan.

Edwards, H. (2004). 'Art and Design Students Employing Aspects of the Visual and Metamorphic to Structure and Create Meaning in Writing. An Insight from the MA dissertation-writing Intranet Site at the Royal College of Art'. *Art Design & Communication in Higher Education* 3 (2): 119–35.

Elkins, J. (2009b). 'The Three Configurations of Studio-art PhDs'. In Elkins, J. (ed), *Artists with PhDs: On the New Doctoral Degree in Studio Art*, 145–65. Washington, DC: New Academia Publishing.

Haas, S. S. (2018). 'Aargh! This Essay Makes Me Want to Poke Sticks in My Eyes!' Developing a Reader Engagement Framework to Help Emerging Writers Understand Why Readers Might (Not) Want to Read Texts. *Journal of Academic Writing* 8 (2): 137–49.

Hyland, K. (2009). *Academic Discourse: English in a Global Context*. London, New York: Continuum.

Kress, G., and Van Leeuwen, T. (2006). *Reading Images: The Grammar of Visual Design* (2nd ed). Oxon: Routledge.

Lea, M. and Street, B. (2000). 'Student Writing and Staff Feedback in Higher Education: An Academic Literacies Approach'. In Lea, M., and Stierer, B. (eds), *Student Writing in Higher Education: New Contexts*, 1–14. Buckingham: The Society for Research into Higher Education and Open University Press.

Lockheart, J., Edwards, H., Raein, M., and Raatz, C. (2004). 'Writing Purposefully in Art and Design (Writing PAD). *Art, Design & Communication in Higher Education* 3 (2): 89–102.

MacDonald, C. (2009). 'How to Do Things with Words: Textual Typologies and Doctoral Writing'. *Journal of Writing in Creative Practice* 2 (1): 91–103.

Melles, G., and Lockheart, J. (2012). 'Writing Purposefully in Art and Design: Responding to Converging and Diverging New Academic Literacies'. *Arts and Humanities in Higher Education* 11 (4): 346–62.

Murray, N., and Sharpling, G. (2018). 'What Traits Do Academics Value in Student Writing? Insights from a Psychometric approach, Assessment & Evaluation in Higher Education'. Routledge. Available online: https://www.tandfonline.com/doi/full/10.1080/02602938.2018.1521372.

Nesi, H., and Gardner, S. (2006). 'Variation in Disciplinary Culture: University Tutors' Views on Assessed Writing Tasks'. In Kiely, R., Clibbon, G., Rea-Dickins, P., and Woodfield, H. (eds.), *Language, Culture and Identity in Applied Linguistics*, 99–118. London: Equinox Publishing.

North, S. (2005). 'Different Values, Different Skills?' *A Comparison of Essay Writing by Students from Arts and Science Backgrounds, Studies in Higher Education* 30 (5): 517–33.

Orr, S., and Shreeve, A. (2018). *Art and Design Pedagogy in Higher Education.* Oxfordshire, New York: Routledge.

Paltridge, B., Starfield, S., Ravelli, L., and Nicholson, S. (2012). 'Doctoral Writing in the Visual and Performing Arts: Two Ends of a Continuum'. *Studies in Higher Education* 37 (8): 989–1003.

Tardy, C. (2015). 'Bending Genres, or When Is a Deviation an Innovation?' In Artemeva N., and Freedman, A. (eds.), *Genre Studies around the Globe: Beyond the Three Traditions*. Canada: Inkshed Trafford publishing.

7

Good Writing in Linguistics

Diane Nelson and Valentina Brunetto

This chapter aims to describe good academic writing practice in the discipline of linguistics. Linguistics – unlike the well-studied related field of applied linguistics – has received very little attention in the EAP literature. It is often characterized as a field that spans several broad approaches to research, including social science, physical science and arts/humanities. Across this diverse discipline, the presentation and analysis of linguistic or language-related experimental data are of central importance. This may take the form of quantitative data analysed using statistical methods, or language-based examples (representations of individual sounds or syllables, words, sentences, transcribed sections of discourse) or other forms of data. Linguists also adopt a great deal of technical terminology and make use of abstract representational schema (e.g. sentence trees, phonological schema or tableaux). This chapter starts with a historical overview of the field, which integrates methods and approaches from both natural and social sciences. We will then identify two varieties of linguistics writing, theoretical-descriptive and experimental, which are conditioned by the type of data being analysed. We will analyse selected student texts from master's and outstanding final-year undergraduate dissertations, investigating their strengths with a focus on the use of authorial voice and presentation of different types of linguistic data to support evidence-based critical argumentation. Finally, we present interview data and related teaching materials from an experienced UK linguistics lecturer that aligns with our characterization of discipline-specific writing practice.

Introduction

Since Becher's (1987) classification of academic disciplines along the *hard-soft* and *pure-applied* dimensions, empirical research in the field of textual and genre analysis has shown that there is extensive variation between writers in different fields, which reflects, at a deep level, different epistemologies and academic identities. *Hard* disciplines, such as physics and biology, have long histories and established paradigms; their object of enquiry is factual and the methods of study tend to be well established. In contrast, *soft* disciplines, such as the social sciences and humanities, focus on phenomena that are less universally recognized and can be approached with different, competing frameworks. Surface features of texts, such as vocabulary or academic style, often bear an important connection to the values and culture of the academic community within which research is conducted.

These disciplinary differences have been widely documented in both professional published academic articles and in different genres of student assignments (Yeo and Boman 2019). Some of these differences emerge early in student writing. In a series of interviews with students from arts and science backgrounds enrolled on a history of science course, North (2005) found that students from 'hard' disciplines tend to view the phenomena studied as given and uncontested, whereas students from 'soft' disciplines are more prone to see knowledge creation as a complex, relativistic process; these attitudes reflect differing academic cultures and approaches to the nature of knowledge. Arts students were seen to be at an advantage because they were more sensitive to the tutors' expectations of criticality and logical argumentation in their essays.

Taken together, these ideas have important pedagogical implications. Academic discourses are permeated by implicit expectations about the nature of knowledge, the role of the researcher and their communicative purpose in disseminating new knowledge. The challenge for students entering a discipline is not only to become accustomed to those values and expectations, but also to master the stylistic means to successfully convey those in their writing.

In this chapter we focus on good writing in linguistics. Linguistics may be seen as a relatively new discipline, and linguists approach the study of human language(s) from a very broad range of perspectives that interface with many other disciplines. Linguists may study the physical science of speech sounds (instrumental phonetics), the abstract representations underlying language structure and meaning (phonology, morphology, syntax and semantics), the ways in which children and adults learn language (language acquisition/ language learning), the ways in which language interacts with social identity (sociolinguistics), the properties of language in wider communicative and discourse contexts (pragmatics/discourse analysis), and the way the brain stores and processes language (psycholinguistics). Across all of these core subfields of linguistics, evidence to support different theories and approaches comes from language data, ranging from sound recordings of individual words to million-word corpora. Increasingly, research in linguistics draws on experimental methodologies to support more abstract models. This means that as a discipline, linguistics lies at the intersection of the 'hard' and 'soft' sciences.

For this chapter we focus on writing in 'pure' and theoretical linguistics, which has received virtually no attention in the EAP or genre analysis literature. We distinguish theoretical linguistics from the related field of applied linguistics, which has been extensively studied in the EAP literature, to the point that Swales (2019) describes ESL/applied linguistics as 'over explored' and questions the value of numerous circumscribed studies (Swales 2019: 76). In the first part of this chapter, we situate linguistics in the landscape of academic disciplines, and discuss its emergence as a uniquely interdisciplinary field. In the second part of the chapter we identify good writing in linguistics master's-level dissertations (theses), and, where relevant, advanced undergraduate-level dissertations. Dissertations represent an important object of study for EAP practitioners for several reasons. First, a dissertation represents the culmination of an entire degree in the discipline, a piece of work designed to showcase both the research skills and discipline-specific writing skills of the student. One primary aim of a master's degree in linguistics is to prepare the student for doctoral study and/or a career as a researcher in the field, so students learn to emulate the writing that gets published in journal articles and monographs. Second, the global market for postgraduate degrees in linguistics is buoyant in many English-speaking countries, particularly in the United States and the United Kingdom (at the time of writing, at least thirteen UK universities offered taught MAs in 'pure' linguistics alongside of or instead of applied linguistics programmes); EAP practitioners are increasingly in demand to prepare international students for these programmes.

Moreover, linguistics affords a unique opportunity to explore what makes good writing in a highly interdisciplinary subject where the boundary between hard and soft is not clear-cut. This relatively young field claims connections to philosophy, philology, cognitive science, brain science, even mathematics – all disciplines that constitute strong backgrounds for postgraduate students in linguistics. In the section that follows we aim to show how distinctive 'good' features of linguistics dissertations count as 'statements of knowledge' (Bazerman 1981: 362) in a field that situates itself at an interesting intersection between the social and natural sciences.

Linguistics as a science

In order to understand what stylistic and literacy practices are valued in linguistics research – and therefore in students' writing – we start by situating these practices along the following four dimensions, following Bazerman (1981):

a.   What is the object of inquiry?
b.   How is the author's claim linked to the literature in the field?
c.   What is the level of persuasion invested in the claim?
d.   How is authorship and authorial identity represented in the text?

Focusing on three academic articles from different disciplines (molecular biology, sociology of science, literature), Bazerman noted that each text represented a different way of integrating these four questions in a meaningful discourse. While the phenomenon presented in a molecular biology paper is 'real' and the language to describe it is universally accepted in the scientific community, in the case of a sociology paper the phenomenon may not even exist prior to the paper itself. In the 'soft' discipline of sociology, choice of terminology is not neutral, nor is there a single theoretical framework that the author can refer to. This means that the writer carries the more onerous task of having to build a framework in which to place their claim, to justify its validity while drawing on an effective synthesis of the literature, and to persuade the reader not only of the claim itself but of the entire framework adopted. Importantly, this is a complex process which cannot be reduced to a simple opposition between hard and soft disciplines; rather, it is a fluid process, possibly different for different texts even within the same discipline. So where does linguistics stand in this picture? Does good writing in linguistics more closely resemble writing in molecular biology, or writing in sociology?

The object of study in linguistics is, strictly speaking, language data. A key paradigm change in the study of language, however, happened in the mid-twentieth century with the pioneering work of Chomsky and Lenneberg, which broke with the American structuralist tradition in pursuing a scientific investigation of the capacity for language as a property of the human mind. According to Chomsky and many other generative linguists, language can be studied as an *internal* object, which is not directly observable, but can nevertheless be investigated like other natural phenomena. Linguistics under this perspective is a branch of cognitive science, and the method of study is the scientific method of generalization by induction, hypothesis testing and theory building, similar to a 'hard' science like molecular biology. On the other hand, many linguists did not adopt Chomsky's generative approach, and continue to see language as an *external* property of human behaviour and societies. According to this view (variously known as usage-based or cognitive-functional linguistics,) linguistic behaviours can be measured empirically by collecting and analysing spoken and written language, but the mental representations that underlie the use of language cannot be studied directly. Within both generative and non-generative theories, proposals are refined, new paradigms are formulated and alternative theoretical approaches compete to characterize abstract models of language. At the same time, methodologies to study language are in constant development; the explosion of neuroscience techniques for the study of language processing, for example, has propelled our understanding of the brain processes implicated in the production and comprehension of language. (It is possible that these abstract models of the mental capacity for language will one day be fully integrated in the (hard) brain sciences, but that future is still relatively distant.)

Linguists therefore ascribe great importance to their theories, and it is curious that this young field has already seen academic disputes which were so heated they were dubbed 'linguistics wars' (documented in the homonymous book by Harris 1993). This strong theoretical orientation is reflected in the distinctive rhetorical devices linguists employ to navigate their academic discourse. Technical terms must be defined carefully. Linguists strive to demonstrate that the phenomena they investigate are no less real than the reality studied by biologists and physicists, that they have 'psychological reality'. Linguists working in various theoretical approaches have introduced technical, original, vocabulary to describe grammatical phenomena; generative linguists focus on constraints, formal parameters and grammatical structures such as *islands, parasitic gaps, pied-piping, sluicing, scrambling* and so on – many of which we owe to the imagination of one single linguist called John Ross – while those working in usage-based (or cognitive-functionalist) approaches are more interested in patterns and constructions involving *schemas, hierarchies,* 'fuzzy' categories and *prototypes*. Some terms can be assumed to be understood and shared by the intended audience; others need to be motivated through argumentation. This, as we see in the next section, is also something the student has to master.

Compared with a neighbouring discipline such as psychology, linguistics, characterized by its competitive theoretical approaches, targets more niche audiences, as witnessed by the highly specialized nature of many academic conferences around the world, and this is typically reflected in academic texts in the communicative pact between author and audience. As noted above, the type of persuasion attempted in a paper in linguistics depends on several factors, such as how much of the framework is shared and what the aim of the article is. In theoretical linguistics, argumentation has a fundamental role due to not only the abstract nature of the topics under consideration but also to the ongoing development of the theory, in which the author intends to play a part. There tends to be a strong, quite individualistic, sense of authorship in linguistics precisely because it is a field where there is an accentuated sense of history. As Huybregts and van Riemsdijk write (in Chomsky 2004: 65):

> Precisely because the field is so young, the assessment of the structure, the health, the progress of the field is among the favourite discussion topics among generative linguists. In some sense we have all turned into amateur historians or philosophers of science.

This continuous engagement with theoretical developments in the discipline – both within and across broader theoretical approaches – sets linguists apart from 'hard' scientists. North (2005: 528) noted that the tendency among science students to see scientific knowledge as fixed and unproblematic should not be attributed to a lack of criticality but to the fact that 'science education tends to elide the process though which knowledge has been constructed, whereas students of other subjects are exposed to varying interpretations over time' – an observation that goes back to Kuhn (1970). The history of ideas is rich in the field of linguistics, in particular as it is taught at the postgraduate level, and this is reflected in the sense of authorial identity that emerges in linguistics writing. Although the author is often 'hidden' behind the language data, the writer's 'voice' is all in the strength of the argument (what Hyland (2001: 208) calls 'the persuasive authority of impersonality'). The writer has the task of assembling the evidence in the form of linguistic data, skilfully guiding the reader through the logical steps of the argument, and emphasizing how the data and the originality of the analysis will make a theoretical and/or empirical contribution to the field. Interestingly, in a case study reported by Lenze (1995) which focused on teaching approaches in linguistics and Spanish, 'argumentation' emerged as the core concept for linguistics academics, with students' development of analytical and theoretical understanding as key teaching aims, whereas for Spanish academics 'production' was the most important aspect of teaching. However, Lenze (1995) also noted that although these core concepts were reflected in the academics' teaching approaches, they were mainly assumed implicitly. A recent study by Lau and Gardner (2019) shows that this 'person-oriented' approach to knowledge may also be reflected in students' learning styles, with students from *soft-pure* disciplines (including linguistics, in their sample) preferring individualistic, as opposed to collaborative, modes of learning.

In sum, much work in twenty-first-century linguistics has a distinctive epistemological orientation which sets it apart from other social sciences and places it closer to the natural sciences. One of the goals of contemporary linguistics research is the scientific study of language as a cognitive capacity. However, unlike mature scientific paradigms, which tend to be conservative, linguistics lacks a unified framework, and this tension between different linguistic theories and models of language is reflected in a strong sense of authorial identity and theory-building in linguistics writing. Authority is accomplished with strong argumentation and the ability to move from description to generalization, with the ultimate goal to achieve a principled explanation of the aspect of language under investigation.

The study

Student writing in linguistics

Although there is an expectation that postgraduate dissertations should approximate the structure and style of a research paper, it is useful to ask to what extent students actually succeed in emulating professional writing. To begin with, the main goal of a student research project is education, not publication (Nesi and Gardner 2006), and it is not typically expected from student work to reach publication standard. Another complex question is to what extent tutors make explicit to students their expectations and assumptions about what counts as good academic practices in the discipline. A large body of research (e.g. Lea and Street 1998; Neumann 2001; Nesi and Gardner 2006) has shown that tutors' perceptions of good writing is indeed shaped by subject-specific epistemological orientations as members of an academic community, but these beliefs often remain implicit, even in the feedback that students receive. For example, the tutors who participated in Lea and Street's (1998) study often made reference to features of form (language, clarity, structure, argument) but struggled to fully explicate their meaning in the context of their discipline. It is possible, as Godfrey and Whong (this volume) point out, that an analysis looking only at surface textual features perhaps cannot give us the 'meta-language' to explain what makes certain features more effective than others. A good starting point, then, is to examine good student writing not as sets of atomistic, transferable, skills, but as effective literacy practices in a specific academic discourse which has been successfully internalized. In particular, we will focus on how this is achieved by the use of two features of academic writing in linguistics: authorial voice and the presentation of data in constructing an argument.

Focusing on student dissertations and research projects at postgraduate level, we identify successful features in two varieties of linguistics research project: theoretical-descriptive and experimental. Our goal is to explore not only the distinctive characteristics of each variety but also their commonalities, based on the assumption that surface traits in student writing often reflect deeper cultural orientations of a discipline, which students at this level of study are more likely to have internalized.

Our method is not quantitative, since our goal is not to find out which traits are 'typical' but, rather, which practices work and how their effectiveness can be linked to a specific academic discourse – in our case, that of a discipline which is young, interdisciplinary, oriented towards abstract theoretical argumentation and in which both the methods and the theories are in a fluid state of development. The excerpts of student writing which we discuss in the next two sections, therefore, are intended to be analysed not so much as features which fit particular academic conventions but, rather, as evidence of the writer's sensitivity to the broad academic discourse within which their research project is situated. For this chapter we will mainly focus on textual style of student writing in dissertations, rather than on the macro-structure of dissertations themselves (except where relevant for identifying differences between varieties of linguistics writing); for more on this topic the reader is directed to the relevant literature (e.g. Dudley-Evans 1999; Paltridge 2002). For recent work on other specific aspects of dissertation structure, see Hsiao and Yu (2012) on literature reviews and Basturkmen (2009) on discussion sections, and Abdullah (2018) on both of these section types; all of these works look at applied linguistics or ELT rather than theoretical linguistics.

Authorial voice

Most style guides emphasize the importance of 'impersonal' forms in academic writing in order to achieve a tone of scientific objectivity or neutrality, and a substantial body of work has been done on the expression of the author in academic writing and its role in EAP pedagogy (see Canagarajah 2015; Hyland 2001, 2002, 2008; Tardy 2012). As mentioned above, the assertion of authorial identity (and, by extension, theoretical alignment) is a key feature of published work in linguistics which postgraduate students may be expected to master. In an early study, Hyland (2001) explored the use of first-person pronouns to express authorial voice in academic texts. The data was collected from a corpus of 248 academic articles from eight disciplines, including the related field of applied linguistics, as well as final-year undergraduate projects in Hong Kong. The main finding was a general underuse of authorial reference in undergraduate student writing compared to published articles. Regardless of discipline, students were more hesitant to take authorship for their claims and to stress the originality and/or significance of their methods and findings.

This gap in authorial presence between professional and student writing, however, appears to narrow down in postgraduate writing. Samraj (2008) conducted a cross-disciplinary discourse analysis of introductions to MA theses in biology, philosophy and applied linguistics, focusing particularly on intertextual connections (including density of citations and prominence of other researchers) and author presence. She found that in terms of the rate of use of the first person and the density of citations, applied linguistics writing occupies an intermediate position, situated between writing in biology and philosophy. Interestingly, work in applied linguistics resembled the scientific writing of biology dissertations in the way that the justification for the study was grounded in the existing literature and, partly, in the potential implications of the findings. This supports our discussion above that linguistics aligns itself in some ways with the natural sciences. Samraj (2008) concludes that clear stylistic variation in the three disciplines shows that master's students have internalized the genre conventions of their respective disciplines.

The majority of work on authorial voice focuses on student writing in applied linguistics. For the current study, we will look at authorial voice in 'pure' and theoretical linguistics as strategies that (a) facilitate alignment with underlying theoretical approaches and meta-theoretical discourses and (b) promote authorial stance through the data itself, moving towards the 'impartial' style of writing in the natural sciences.

In most linguistics writing, authorship and agency are typically backgrounded. This is achieved through several stylistic devices, including (a) use of the passive voice; (b) limited use of the first person, usually plural, to suggest agency by a non-specific research team; and (c) using the data, evidence or results as the subject of the sentence with non-agentive verbs such as *show, suggest, demonstrate* or *reveal*, as in the following example written by a postgraduate native speaker of British English:

> In this analysis, the mean PDF of female speakers from the East Wirral is considered against the female informants studied by Sangster in her first experiment (2001, 2002). The results of these independent samples t-tests are

summarised in tables 7 and 8. **The tests reveal** that PDF is lower in female speakers from East Wirral than it is for both working and middle class speakers from Liverpool.

Students in linguistics need to situate their own studies within a theoretical and methodological context, as this is essential for hypothesis formulation and experimental design. The introduction and/or literature review section of a project report or dissertation are therefore crucially important, as they set out a context and lead to a rationale for the study. In the example below from an MA dissertation written by an international student who is a non-native speaker of English, the student skilfully extracts a research question out of a previous author's study, by shifting the domain of enquiry from language production to comprehension. The authorial voice, which implicitly identifies a gap in previous work, is embedded in the expression *This raises the question*:

> Similarly, an eye-tracking study by Libben and Titone (2009) demonstrated that the cognate facilitation effect for French–English bilinguals depends on the speakers' L2 proficiency: The cognate facilitation effect was smaller for bilinguals with a higher level of L2 proficiency. **This raises the question** of whether effects related to language proficiency observed in language production can also be observed in the comprehension of language switches, and to what extent the cognate facilitation effect decreases or increases based on language proficiency.

Work on genre in published research in applied linguistics (e.g. Samraj 2008) shows that integral citations showing the author as the subject of the sentence are more frequent than in the 'hard' sciences. We find similar tendencies in theoretical linguistics writing, consistent with the observation that linguistics is a field with strong author presence. This student, a native-English speaking final-year undergraduate student from the UK, has successfully internalized this convention, citing authors of an earlier study using an integral citation to Szostak and Pitt (2013) twice in order to point out a difference between the two sets of findings. The student's authorial voice and ownership are expressed in two ways, first by using the findings as the grammatical subject in *whereas the current data shows*, and then by the use of a plural possessive pronoun in *our far condition*:

> Whilst rates do not vary much across conditions, the pattern of marginal change is different to that found for false alarm rates, and also different to the findings of Szostak and Pitt (2013). **Szostak and Pitt (2013) found** a decrease in accurate identification of added stimuli from 89% in the near to 85% in the medial condition, **whereas the current data shows** as increase from 79.37% in the near

to 83.86% in the medial condition. The hit rates then decreased again **in our far condition** to 77.53%, lower than in the near condition.

In the excerpt below, the student (an international MA student who is a second-language speaker of English) shows an awareness of the relevant literature in Relevance Theory, and uses appropriate adverbial expressions (*however, although, therefore*) to critically connect earlier studies to each other and to the current study. By identifying methodological problems in earlier work, the student develops a research question. In this case the authorial voice emerges implicitly until the overt reference to *the present study*:

> This was also supported by Antoniou and Katsos's study (2016). However, the higher pragmatic ability of multilingual and bilectal children cannot demonstrate that Relevance theory is true. Although higher EF helped multilingual and bilectal children to derive pragmatic implicatures, it didn't mean pragmatic implicatures were more effort-demanding. [While] Antoniou and Katsos's study (2016) did provide some insights of the limitation of Slabakova's study (2010), it was possible that the advanced learners have higher EF than the monolingual natives, and therefore the comparison of these two groups may be influenced. **The present study** will state how to eliminate this bilingualism effect in the next section.

These excerpts show how students in linguistics use a variety of authorial voices to situate their own work within the larger theoretical landscape, including the use of integral citations.[1] The ability to internalize conventions around authorial voice is an important part of academic acculturation (Canagarajah 2015).

Presentation of data: Two varieties of linguistics writing

Data-driven argumentation plays a crucial role in linguistics writing. Linguists use language data to support a theoretical proposal or to fill a gap in the empirical literature, but often these two aims are concurrent. Importantly, however, the nature and source of the data shape the way it is presented and also shape the stylistic features of the written analysis. While acknowledging the difficulties around the notion of 'genre' discussed by Godfrey and Whong

---

[1] On a related point, it is interesting to note that while linguistics situates itself across both the social and natural sciences, discipline-specific conventions for referencing and citations are almost universally aligned with Harvard/APA styles, with in-text citation and references presented in a list at the end of the work rather than in footnotes. This is true for both linguistics journal styles and student work in linguistics.

in the introductory chapter to this volume, we feel motivated to identify two distinct influences on linguistics writing that emerge out of different empirical approaches within the field, especially when it comes to the presentation and analysis of linguistic data to support argumentation.

On one hand, some sub-disciplines in linguistics, particularly instrumental phonetics and psycholinguistics, derive their methodologies from the 'hard' sciences, and rely almost exclusively on quantifiable, experimentally controlled data. Quantitative approaches to data collection and analysis are also used by researchers in corpus linguistics, historical linguistics, typology, sociolinguistics, first and second-language acquisition and grammatical theory and description (syntax, semantics and morphology). Writing associated with these methods we will refer to as the 'experimental' variety.

On the other hand, much work in linguistics does not use experimental methodologies, and presents linguistic data in a way that is designed to allow inductive reasoning. Associated with this type of research, we identify a second variety in linguistics writing that we will call 'theoretical-descriptive'.

Experimental writing

Data collected in experimental linguistics is normally quantitative, so students develop skills in presenting data in the form of graphs, tables and charts, and then reporting the results in the narrative. Experimental MA dissertations and theses generally follow the 'traditional' IMRD (Introduction-Methods-Results-Discussion) macro structure typical of research in the sciences and social sciences (Swales 1990; Dudley-Evans 1999; Paltridge 2002). It is therefore important for students adopting experimental linguistics methodologies to master academic writing styles which set out research methods, experimental results and quantitative data analysis in a clear and concise way. In this sense, good writing in experimental linguistics shares important similarities with writing in psychology and related sciences.

As in 'hard' science writing, the description of statistical results is often presented in a condensed prose style that incorporates conventions from the natural sciences. This international student who is a second-language speaker of English has successfully adopted standard 'hard' science conventions:

> In model C, there was a significant main effect of cognate ($p < 0.001$), direction A.to.E ($p < 0.001$), direction E.to.A ($p < 0.001$), direction E.to.E ($p < 0.001$), and region MC1 ($p < 0.001$) on the RT. The intercept was significant ($p < 0.05$). Based on the estimates given above, directions A.to.E and E.to.A had longer RTs compared to direction A.to.A, and RTs after cognates were quicker than

those after non-cognates. The model appears to be significant, at $p < 0.001$. The adjusted R-square of 0.01681 for model C showed that model was able to explain 1.681% of the total variation in RT.

Hypothesis testing is a crucial skill for MA students using experimental approaches to research in linguistics, and is typically covered in classes for research methods. This native English-speaking UK postgraduate student's presentation of results has been framed in this way, adding a critical dimension to the reporting of data:

> However, the second Mann-Whitney U test revealed that the situation is more complex. When the results are separated by gender, the null hypothesis is rejected for female speakers, since p=.008, yet the null hypothesis cannot be rejected for male speakers given that p=.267, below the significance level.05. These results imply that there may be gender differences for East Wirral speakers in their use of Liverpool variants.

Theoretical-descriptive writing

The variety of writing associated with the analysis of non-experimental linguistic data is arguably unique to the field of linguistics, being used for writing in core theoretical sub-disciplines including phonology, syntax, semantics, and morphology, as well as much work in language acquisition, historical linguistics, sociolinguistics, pragmatics and others. While experimental writing in linguistics is clearly conditioned by stylistic conventions in the natural sciences, theoretical-descriptive writing owes more to the inductive argumentation found in pure mathematics writing (this can probably be traced back to Noam Chomsky's early collaboration with mathematicians at MIT). Student writing in dissertations and theses tends to deviate from the IMRD macro structure, particularly towards the 'topic based' structure (Paltridge 2002). While writing in the 'hard' subfield of experimental linguistics tends to be dense and concise, writing in theoretical-descriptive linguistics contains more discursive discussion accompanying the presentation of language data.

Another important feature of writing in this branch of linguistics is that it uses empirical linguistic data, often alongside formalisms (e.g. schema, rule sets, tables, tableaux, formal logic notation, tree diagrams) to support theoretical discussion or linguistic description. One of the main aims of a linguistics degree at any level, then, is to demonstrate mastery of theory-specific technical vocabulary, conventions around presenting linguistic data and the appropriate use of formalisms needed to produce good writing.

Theoretical-descriptive writing in syntax, semantics, phonology and morphology is typically presented in a series of relatively short descriptive paragraphs, interspersed with frequent linguistic examples and tree diagrams or other schema. Each set of examples or diagram is usually introduced by a descriptive statement followed by a colon or period.

The excerpt below from a non-native English-speaking international MA student shows a good grasp of the terminology and conventions for argumentation in syntax:

> The question now arises whether the scope of the present model is wide enough to also include the second type of to-infinitivals discussed by Ojea (2005: 62). These are clauses introduced by verbs such as 'believe', where the temporal deficiency of the embedded Inflection would give rise to a simultaneous rather than futurate meaning:
>
> (32) Mary is believed to be in Paris now/*next month.
>
> If we consider the lack of 'for' under the embedded C, one possibility that arises is that in this case we have two one-step dependencies, with the functions -Mood and -Tense travelling directly to the matrix V and I, as exemplified by the following tree:

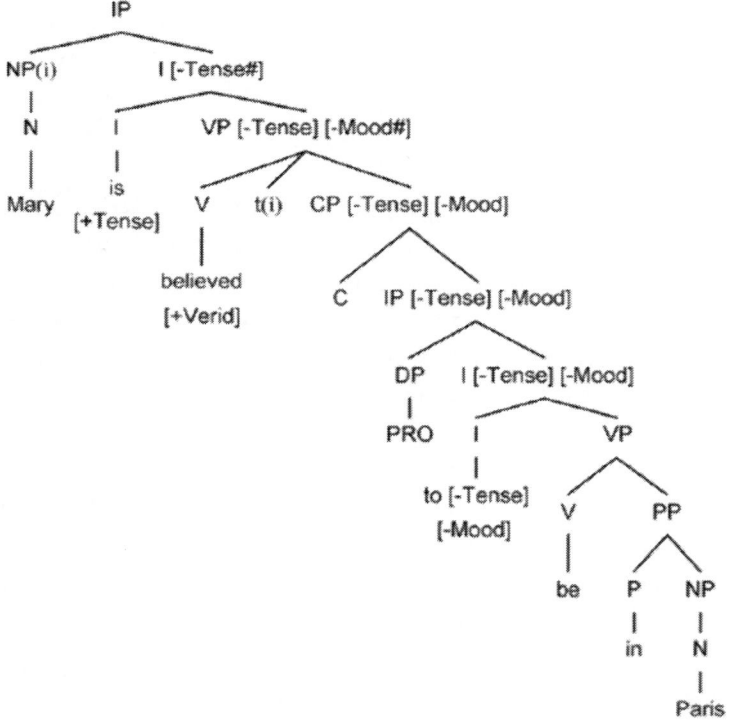

Figure 7.1

One way in which modern linguistics departs from other fields is that example sentences are generally not embedded within the discussion, but set out on a separate line for maximum clarity.[2] There are strict conventions around presenting linguistic examples, especially for work in syntax, morphology and phonology, where the reader needs a detailed breakdown of the structure of the linguistic example in order to follow the discussion. Good linguistics writers present information systematically, and describe and discuss examples in short chunks of text rather than in long expository passages. This international MA student, for example, constructs a minimal pair consisting of a grammatical sentence and an unacceptable or ill-formed sentence, a typical feature of theoretical-descriptive writing in syntax and morphology.

> Kurmanji has one neutral reflexive pronoun (*xwe*), which does not inflect. The A in an ergative construction still has control over this reflexive pronoun. This indicates the syntactic subjecthood of the A even though the verb does not agree with it. The reflexive pronoun *xwe* is used instead of a pronoun when it refers to the same syntactic subject.

> (24) Min sol-ê **xwe** guhêrî-n
>   1SG.OBL shoe-EZ.PL REF change-3PL
>   'I changed my shoes.' (SP02)
> (25) *1 Mini sol-ê **mini** guhêrî-n

> In example 24, *xwe* refers to *min* '1SG.OBL', which denotes that *xwe* is controlled by it. It would be ungrammatical if it is kept in a pronoun form as in example 25.

In theoretical linguistics writing, arguments unfold in a logical fashion, supported incrementally with each example presented. The linguistic data itself, often referred to by example number, may be the explicit subject of the sentence, or the sentence may be passivized to reduce the attention on the speaker and highlight the prominence of the example, as this international MA student's writing exemplifies:

> Another difference is that progressive and perfect are clearly distinguished and expressed by different grammatical forms in English, while they can be expressed with the same morpheme *teiru* in Japanese.

> (29) Kare-wa   choshoku-o   tabe-teiru.
>   He-TOP   breakfast-ACC   eat-TEIRU
>   He is eating / has eaten breakfast.

---

[2] However, the writing tradition in European philology still retains a preference for in-text examples.

Has eaten in sentence (29) can be also expressed by using *ta*.

(30) Kare-wa   choshoku-o   tabe-ta.
       He-TOP   breakfast-ACC   eat-TA
       He has eaten.

Sentence (30) reveals that perfective past marker *ta* is interchangeable with the imperfective present marker *teiru*, and can describe the same situation.

We asked a UK-based textbook author and linguistics lecturer of many years' experience to comment on what type of writing they were likely to award a high mark to. The same lecturer also shared their student guide to writing.

> In terms of a good mark, I'm looking for clear structure to the assignment; good argumentation, presented with evidence and not opinion; appropriate use of examples; good use of terminology, with definitions where relevant; prose style that is appropriate to an academic discipline and good command of English collocation etc.

From the writing guide:
A good dissertation has these features:

- *Is coherent*: Synthesizes the relevant literature; presents clear *arguments*, along with *evidence* for these positions, and contains appropriate *examples*.
- Demonstrates *understanding* of all issues mentioned by providing a full discussion. No point in mentioning that author X says this and author Y says that without explaining these concepts and arguments for the examiner.
- Makes it clear where ideas, definitions and hypotheses have come from – attributes all work to its author or authors appropriately.
- Does not rely on *opinions*, but instead is entirely based on firm evidence and argumentation. We are absolutely uninterested in your personal opinions; you are writing in a scientific discipline, and you are required to provide evidence, not ideas.

The set of criteria for good writing in linguistics given by this lecturer contains some generic features of academic writing (and, interestingly, mentions English collocations), but several key points support our characterization of discipline-specific features of good writing in linguistics. These include a focus on strong argumentation and presentation of evidence; the need to define technical terminology and demonstrate appropriate use of it; and the importance of citing individual authors as sources of ideas (which may prompt students to use integral citations). Finally, the lecturer explicitly characterizes linguistics as a scientific discipline where evidence is more important than 'opinion'.

Conclusion

In this chapter we have focused on 'pure' and theoretical linguistics, and shown how the unique nature and history of the discipline shapes good writing in this field. We have argued that as a new and interdisciplinary field with theories and methodologies still in a state of flux, linguistics writing combines stylistic features found in the social and natural sciences, and, to a lesser extent, in pure mathematics. Linguists use various stylistic devices used to situate the author's work within the theoretical landscape while maintaining Hyland's 'persuasive authority of impersonality' (2001). Most importantly, good linguistics writing is about the skilled presentation of language data and use of related technical terminology to make a coherent argument: we have shown how two broad methodological approaches to linguistics research are reflected in two distinct varieties of writing that students need to master when studying at postgraduate level.

References

Abdullah, F. (2018). 'Moves within the Literature Reviews and Discussion Sections of International Postgraduate Theses and Dissertations on ELT and Applied Linguistics'. *English Education and Applied Linguistics* 1 (2): 174–83.

Basturkmen, H. (2009). 'Commenting on Results in Published Research Articles and Masters' Dissertations in Language Teaching'. *Journal of English for Academic Purposes* 8: 241–51.

Bazerman, C. (1981). 'What Written Knowledge Does: Three Examples of Academic Discourse'. *Philosophy of the Social Sciences* 11 (3): 361–87.

Becher, T. (1987). 'Disciplinary Discourse'. *Studies in Higher Education* 12 (3): 261–74.

Canagarajah, S. (2015). '"Blessed in My Own Way": Pedagogical Affordances for Dialogical Voice Construction in Multilingual Student Writing'. *Journal of Second Language Writing* 27: 122–39.

Chomsky, N. (2004). *The Generative Enterprise Revisited, Discussions with Riny Huybregts, Henk van Riemsdijk, Naoki Fukui and Mihoko Zushi*. Berlin: De Gruyter Mouton.

Dudley-Evans, T. (1999). 'The Dissertation: A Case of Neglect?' In P. Thompson (ed.), *Issues in EAP Writing Research and Instruction*, 28–36. University of Reading: CALS.

Harris, R. A. (1993). *The Linguistics Wars*. New York: Oxford University Press.

Hsiao, C., and Yu, H. (2012). 'Knowledge Presentation in Thesis Writing–Examining Move Use in Reviewing Literature'. *English Teaching and Learning* 36 (3): 1–47.

Hyland, K. (2001). 'Humble Servants of the Discipline? Self-Mention in Research Articles'. *English for Specific Purposes* 20: 207–26.

Hyland, K. (2002). 'Authority and Invisibility: Authorial Identity in Academic Writing'. *Journal of Pragmatics* 34: 1091–112.

Hyland, K. (2008). 'Disciplinary Voices: Interactions in Research Writing'. *English Text Construction* 1 (1): 5–22.

Kuhn, T. S. (1970). *The Structure of Scientific Revolutions* (2nd ed). Chicago: University of Chicago Press.

Lau, K., and Gardner, D. (2019). 'Disciplinary Variations in Learning Styles and Preferences: Implications for the Provision of Academic English'. *System* 80: 257–68.

Lea, M., and Street, B. (1998). 'Student Writing in Higher Education: An Academic Literacies Approach'. *Studies in Higher Education* 23 (2): 157–72.

Lea, M. R., and Street, B. V. (2006). 'The "Academic Literacies" Model: Theory and Applications'. *Theory into Practice* 45 (4): 368–77.

Lenze, L. F. (1995). 'Discipline-Specific Pedagogical Knowledge in Linguistics and Spanish'. *New Directions for Teaching and Learning* (64): 65–70.

Nesi, H., and Gardner, S. (2006). 'Variation in Disciplinary Culture: University Tutors' views on Assessed Writing Tasks'. In R. Kiely, Rea-Dickins, P., Woodfield, H., and Clibbon, G. (eds.), *Language, Culture and Identity in Applied Linguistics*, 99–118. Sheffield, UK: Equinox Publishing.

Neumann, R. (2001). 'Disciplinary Differences and University Teaching'. *Studies in Higher Education* 26 (2): 135–46.

Neumann, R., Parry, S., and Becher, T. (2002). 'Teaching and Learning in Their Disciplinary Contexts: A Conceptual Analysis'. *Studies in Higher Education* 27 (4): 405–17.

North, S. (2005). 'Different Values, Different Skills? A Comparison of Essay Writing by Students from Arts and Science Backgrounds'. *Studies in Higher Education* 30 (5): 517–33.

Paltridge, B. (2002). 'Thesis and Dissertation Writing: An Examination of Published Advice and Actual Practice'. *English for Specific Purposes* 21: 125–43.

Samraj, B. (2008). 'A Discourse Analysis of Master's Theses across Disciplines with a Focus on Introductions'. *Journal of English for Academic Purposes* 7: 55–67.

Swales, J. M. (1990). *Genre Analysis: English in Academic and Research Settings*. Cambridge: Cambridge University Press.

Swales, J. (2019). The Futures of EAP Genre Studies: A Personal Viewpoint'. *Journal of English for Academic Purposes* 38: 75–82.

Tardy, C.M. (2012). 'Current Conceptions of Voice'. In Hyland, K., and Sancho Guinda, C. (eds.), *Stance and Voice in Written Academic Genres*, 34–49. Palgrave, Basingstoke.

Yeo, M., and Boman, J. (2019). 'Disciplinary Approaches to Assessment. *Journal of Further and Higher Education* 43 (4): 482–93.

Afterword

Ian Bruce

The different studies of disciplinary writing reported in the chapters of the 'Good Writing Project' collectively make a valuable contribution to the field of EAP in that the researchers have achieved what theorists of academic writing frequently urge us to do, but few actually carry out. That is, each has gone into a particular subject discipline and undertaken a close-up examination of its actual writing practices, texts and writers. It must be acknowledged that the planning, execution and reporting of these studies represent a considerable personal time investment by each contributor. Also to be acknowledged is the contribution of the researchers' participants, who gave their time, texts and ideas that enabled these investigations to be undertaken.

In this chapter, I will organize my reflections and ideas on the Good Writing Project in two parts. Firstly, I will revisit and reflect on the contributions of each of the projects reported in the chapters of this volume. In the second part, I will attempt to draw together some common themes and insights that emerge from the different chapters and relate them back to the field of EAP and specifically to the needs of the EAP writer and the knowledge base of the EAP teacher of academic writing.

Review of the chapter contributions

As a ground-clearing operation, Godfrey and Whong begin the volume with a chapter in which they seek to broaden approaches to EAP writing research and practice in two ways: widening the scope of the areas examined by EAP researchers and proposing a framework for new methodological approaches to pedagogical practice. After reviewing some of the recent issues raised around research of academic writing, they argue for further development in four areas:

- closer analysis and understandings of existing findings,
- larger and more varied data sets in academic writing research,
- a greater focus on the subject discipline tutor (who assesses student writing) and
- a more developed evaluative meta-language to discuss the why and how of good student writing in the disciplines.

As a framework for implementing some of these ideas for both teaching and researching EAP writing, they propose more close cooperation between EAP and subject discipline tutors as a basis for better investigations of student writing, for joint research of student writing and for developing a meta-language to articulate better the requirements of disciplinary writing.

This chapter raises the very relevant issue of the need to reflect on, and further extend approaches to researching academic writing in ways that are more pedagogically useful and involve closer collaborations with key stakeholders, such as faculty in subject disciplines and the student writers themselves. The broad approach proposed in this chapter accords with the comments by Cheng (2019) that 'very few genre analysis studies discuss the pedagogical implications in a pedagogically concrete manner'. Cheng proposes that 'students and faculty can become research partners who can contribute directly or indirectly to many genre analysis projects' (p. 44). Thus, rather than the researcher functioning as an 'outside expert', providing pedagogic information to practitioners (justified by quite general arguments about student needs), the collaborative scholarship model sees researchers as insiders, working with the other insider stakeholders to make transparent the writing practices, needs and textual resources of particular disciplines. Speaking from his own pedagogical experience and apparently supporting this view, Swales (2019), in an essay about the future of genre studies in EAP proposes, '[w]e can and should aim for an insider "emic" approach ... because the effort involved in trying to become something of an insider will often produce pedagogical and educational benefits' (p. 81). Essentially, what has been undertaken in the studies of this volume, in exploratory ways, are investigations of disciplinary writing from the inside with the type of emic focus that Cheng and Swales appear to advocate. These investigations begin to realize the broader approach to disciplinary knowledge about writing that Godfrey and Whong are calling for.

As an example of this more situated, emic approach to writing research, Webster (Chapter 2, this volume) reports a study that involved interviewing five university staff who taught digital media studies, focusing on the writing requirements and evaluative reasoning that related to their assessment of one competent example of student writing from their field. Although specific to one university context, this study provides an exploration that identifies both the genres of this relatively new branch of media studies and, importantly, the values and thinking of individual subject discipline lecturers around the assessment of these new genres. The genres of the discipline appear on a continuum, from more industry-related texts, such as different types of report and reflection, through to more conventionalized academic genres, such as the essay and research-reporting dissertation. By interviewing subject lecturers (about competently written examples of the genres), the study reveals the explicit expectations and preferences of teaching staff when assessing written student responses to these different types of assignment task. Drawing together insights from these interviews, Webster provides a summary of the expectations of the writing of the different assignment genres of this field, varying from the more industry-standard expectations of reports and reflections through to the structuring and valued elements of the more academic genres. In relation to the former category, it also reveals the extent to which examples of industry-related genres, guidelines, templates and criteria, specific to the digital media field, are provided to students as a way of initiating them into the structures, values and processes of writing in this field.

In continuing the proposal to undertake more emic, insider explorations of academic writing, Maxwell (Chapter 3, this volume) carries out a contextualized study in the area of postgraduate design courses, to discover what constitutes 'clarity' of writing in the perceptions of faculty in a particular design school – clarity being a fairly universal value among those evaluating academic writing in all disciplines. Maxwell uses two semi-structured interviews with three staff who teach design, and promotes discussion of examples of proficient student work in the subject during the second interview. Maxwell organizes her qualitative findings around a number of themes, including: the importance of clarity, ease of reading and language accuracy, language complexity, clarity of understanding, explicitness of links and clarity of purpose. Although the participant faculty claim that language accuracy is not the central factor in achieving clarity, it does appear that language is central to some of the key problems with clarity that emerge in the writing of EAL design students. Based on the findings of this study, Maxwell proposes a model for achieving clarity in writing in this field, a model that places language at its centre, surrounded by the four key variables of clarity of understanding, clarity of expression, clarity of purpose and explicitness of links. In relation to language, which is a key element of the model, the features of meta-discourse, cohesive devices, use of terminology, language complexity and accuracy emerge as key elements. In her conclusion, Maxwell provides a balanced, insightful view of issues relating to clarity. Importantly, she does not underplay the importance of the issue of the writer actually having *an appropriate understanding* of subject content knowledge and subject epistemology, and that these understandings provide the basis for achieving clarity of expression when writing in this subject area.

Burland, Venn and McLaughlin (Chapter 4, this volume) explore the concept of 'good writing' within music, collecting data through semi-structured interviews with five staff and four postgraduate (PG) music students. The interviews are concerned with examining the writing requirements of the compulsory assignments of taught postgraduate courses in: musicology, electronic and computer music, music management, composition and performance, the assignments being identified in terms of the academic genre families proposed by Gardner and Nesi (2012). Three overarching themes emerged as salient to music writing across the taught PG courses: criticality, developing a position (finding a voice) and teaching and learning argumentation. The interviews, however, identified differently nuanced views of what constituted criticality in the different branches of the field of music studies. For example, the role of critical engagement with literature in the extended case-building of essays establishes a basis for developing original interpretations. On the other hand, in research reports relating to technology and composition, it is expected that students will write reflectively and analytically about their own practice, including the successes and failures in their experience of the creative process. In terms of developing the skills and values of writing in music, staff reported providing textual examples as a form of scaffolding student postgraduate writing. Also the student participants in the sample emphasized the role of detailed feedback on their writing efforts. Overall, good writing in this field seems to require adherence to structural conventions as well as creativity and an individual voice in articulating student work.

Bowman (Chapter 5, this volume) reports an interesting study on the genre of reflective writing tasks (termed *Academic Reflective Writing – ARW*) that are a required part of the assignment load of dentistry students. The ARW is a professional task that reports and provides analytical reflection on practice events, integrating different aspects of the knowledge base of dentistry. Through this type of writing, novice practitioners demonstrate their developing professional competence in the field. The study involves analysis of five competent responses to two ARW tasks in terms of the levels of reflection undertaken and interviews with two markers of those tasks. The study reveals the challenging nature of the task, which combines science, professional practice, ethical standards and patient awareness. The use of a model for the five levels of reflection to analyse the tasks, combined with the insights of staff who grade these assignments together, provides understanding of the nature of the requirements and possible rhetorical structuring of this type of writing.

Montgomery (Chapter 6, this volume) presents a small-scale, practitioner study of dissertation writing in fine art. Specifically, she analyses three dissertations from the field, the guidelines and rubrics that relate to the dissertations and she carries out a semi-structured interview with a supervisor of each dissertation. In contextualizing her study, Montgomery refers more broadly to EAP and disciplinary writing research as well as previous studies of creative practice writing, identifying some of the key issues already raised about academic writing in this disciplinary area. In particular, she considers the issue of the suitability of fit between a linear, conventional dissertation structure and the requirements for fine art writing as well as the types of language and argumentation expected. Through a brief textual analysis of the introduction sections, she illustrates the variety of approaches that different students take towards this genre. Her analysis of the assessment rubric reveals that staff expectations of the genre are somewhat different from those of a dissertation in the social or physical sciences. Rather from the interviews with fine art dissertation supervisors, what emerges is the emphasis on the use of dissertation genre for the creative exploration and development of ideas, but the findings also emphasize that this development must be based on well-articulated understandings of the writers' sources.

Finally, Nelson and Brunetto (Chapter 7, this volume) explore writing in linguistics, and in particular, focus on the issue of authorial voice in two strands of the discipline: theoretical linguistics and applied linguistics. Between these two sub-branches of the discipline, differences in writer voice arise from epistemology and the types of investigation carried out. In more empirically driven, applied studies in linguistics, the study found author voice was constructed in ways that resemble other types of social science writing. On the other hand, writing in theoretical linguistics emerges as more descriptive and somewhat didactic, often interspersed with small, single-instance examples of a linguistic feature under discussion. As emerged in several of the chapters by previous contributors, Nelson and Brunetto emphasize the need for a grounded understanding of writing in the sub-branches of disciplines, which involves examining the influences of the epistemologies, research methods and genres. In common with other contributors, they argue against too many generalizations about the writing of a particular, over-arching discipline.

Themes and insights from the studies

In this section, I unpack and discuss key themes that emerge from the preceding chapters, highlighting the insights offered and consider their implications, including how they can be further investigated in the future. I will explore themes and insights that relate to firstly the student as a writer and secondly to the EAP practitioner and writing pedagogy.

The student writer

I have previously argued that the overall goal of EAP is the development of discourse competence, given the fundamental student need to process and create extended texts in academic contexts (Bruce 2008, 2011; Ding and Bruce 2017). For a comprehensive definition of discourse competence, I use Bhatia's (2004) concept of *discursive competence*, which is defined in terms of three subsuming competence areas: social, generic and textual (p. 144). In supporting the development of discourse (discursive) competence, much previous EAP research has focused on the characteristics of genres as categories of academic text to provide an important source of knowledge to inform pedagogy. Despite there being no single approach to genre theory, its various realizations have been widely used in EAP to provide insights, tools and meta-language to EAP practitioners to support pedagogy that relates to processing and creating larger academic texts. Although the earlier approaches to genre drawn upon in EAP were primarily textual, key ESP/EAP genre theorists (e.g. Bhatia 2004; Swales 1998) have long argued for combining textual and ethnographic investigations in order to have a more grounded, contextualized understanding of genres. This need for a more grounded, contextual approach to disciplinary writing (as part of the development of discourse competence) emerged in the interviews with the subject content lecturers in the studies reported in the preceding chapters. These insights were related to key assignment genres in each discipline, these written assignment outputs and the knowledge and dispositions relating to them often being the main focus of attention. From these studies, three, closely interrelated areas of student writer knowledge emerge as important for the development of discourse competence:

- understanding of subject content knowledge and epistemology (social competence);
- knowledge of assignment genres and their associated disciplinary expectations (generic competence); and,
- linguistic and textual knowledge (textual competence).

For student writers, the importance of knowledge of the content and epistemology of their subjects as key elements that shape disciplinary communication emerges in several of the chapters. For example, in the study of Burland et al. (Chapter 4), which examined writing in the subject of design, Maxwell reports that the 'tacit disciplinary conventions of meaning-making and knowledge-creation' are important to achieve effective writing in this discipline. Specifically, Maxwell emphasizes 'clarity of understanding' of subject content as a necessary prerequisite for successful academic writing. She summarizes the views of her informants (lecturers teaching design), who claim 'if students have not understood what they have read, they will struggle to express the rationale of their project or argument clearly' (p. 24). Similarly, in the chapter by Bowman (Chapter 5), relating to reflective practice writing in dentistry, what emerges as essential to that particular genre is understanding of its disciplinary practice role, in particular its importance 'for practitioner self-awareness and meta-learning' (p. 1) and 'developing their professional identity through writing' (p. 2).

Therefore, what emerges from these (and other) contributors' chapters is the importance of the aspect of discourse competence that Bhatia (2004) terms *social competence*, 'an ability to use language more widely to participate effectively in a variety of social and institutional contexts to give expression to one's social identity, in the context of constraining social structures and social processes' (p. 144). Consideration of the social dimensions of communication were particularly important elements of assignments that relate more closely to professional practice, such as the industry-related genres of reports and reflections in digital media studies and in the academic reflective writing, requiring self-analysis and self-critique of professional practice in the study of dentistry writing. The corollary of student need for this contextual, situated knowledge (and the discipline-specific processes involved in knowledge-transforming through writing) is the need for EAP practitioners to investigate and uncover this type of subject-related, meta-knowledge. In the different studies reported in the chapter contributions, this was achieved by practitioner engagement with the subject specialists, and particularly through targeted interviews relating to their expectations of subject practices and texts.

The second area of student writer knowledge that emerges from the contributors' chapters is the knowledge of the assignment genres that they are required to write in the different disciplines. In terms of Bhatia's discursive competence model, this type of knowledge is referred to as generic competence, which he defines as 'the ability to construct, interpret and successfully exploit a specific repertoire of professional, disciplinary or workplace genres to participate in the daily activities and achieve the goals of a specific professional community' (p. 145). Importantly, the focus in these studies tends to be on faculty expectations and requirements of student writing of different assignment genres. This is exemplified in Webster's (Chapter 2) summary of the expectations related to the different assignment genres of digital media studies. Differences in levels of formality, the relative importance of textual structuring and the use of meta-discourse and other elements are highlighted in relation to five assignment genres from the field. Similarly, examples of proficient student responses to different assignment genres in musicology are the focus of Burland et al. (Chapter 4). From their interviews with music staff and postgraduate students, the key themes of criticality, voice and argumentation are discussed, including how expectations relating to these elements vary between essays and research reports in this particular discipline. These findings relating to genre knowledge and generic competence suggest that the next step (following the types of ethnographic interview reported in the contributor chapters of this volume) would be targeted textual analyses of disciplinary samples of texts of these assignment genres to uncover in more detail how these valued elements of written communication are actually realized through written texts. However, to achieve this type of genre analysis requires a genre model that is able to account for the different elements that the contributor studies identify.

The third area of student writer knowledge that emerges as important from the series of studies in this volume is that of textual and linguistic knowledge. Bhatia (2004) describes this area as 'textual competence', which he defines as 'not only an ability to master the linguistic code, but also an ability to use textual, contextual and pragmatic knowledge to construct and interpret contextually appropriate texts' (p. 144). He notes that textual competence is wider than linguistic competence, relating to the ability to encode discursive meanings and implement academic stylistic elements and conventions appropriately in written texts. In the contributor studies in this volume, textual competence appears to emerge as important in realizing the more conventionalized academic genres. For example, one of Webster's (Chapter 2) informants in digital media studies talks about the need to make allowances and provide guidance for undergraduate students writing formal academic essays, but expects that by the time that they have to write masters dissertations, they will have a better understanding of formal academic style. Similarly, Maxwell's (Chapter 3) 'framework of clarity' places language in the central position linked to the elements of use of: terminology, language complexity, meta-discourse and cohesive devices. In the musicology study, Burland et al. (Chapter 4) find that key values of criticality and authorial voice are valued by the subject tutors that are interviewed; however, Burland et al. note that the same tutors find difficulty in articulating how these elements are actually realized in 'good writing'. The crucial point that emerges is that these are not discrete features to be studied and learned as part of an autonomous linguistic system, but rather textual elements that are crucial to encoding important discursive meanings that, in turn, relate closely to the generic form being used and the content and conventions of the discipline. Again, these insights appear to be evidence for situated analyses of competent writing in these disciplines to uncover those particular textual elements that need to be taught.

While Bhatia (2004) finds it convenient to articulate discursive competence in terms of the three different competences, it is still important to see them also as part of an integrated, functioning whole. Pedagogy that attempts to address them in this way requires a top-down analytic syllabus that includes activities related to both analysis and synthesis (Widdowson 1990).

The EAP practitioner

Building on the final point from the previous section, a key implication that emerges from these studies for EAP practitioners is the need for *holism* in relation to understanding and teaching the types of knowledge required by student writers. Achieving this type of holistic approach to addressing the writing needs of students, as has been implied in the previous section, requires pedagogically applicable knowledge that relates to context, genre and text.

Understanding of contextual elements, such as the epistemological basis for writing in a particular discipline, audience (faculty) expectations of student texts and the types of expected, knowledge-transforming processes to be communicated through the texts of different subject disciplines, taken together, constitute important areas for practitioner explorations and knowledge development. For some of these areas of knowledge, there are no ready-made, off-the-shelf descriptions. In understanding subject epistemologies as a major influence on disciplinary writing requirements, the EAP practitioner needs to begin with a clear understanding of the different 'approaches' to research in different disciplines (Cohen, Manion and Morrison 2017), such as the positivist, interpretive and critical theory approaches, their related theoretical tenets, methodologies and data collection methods. This knowledge provides a starting point for then examining the assumptions behind the knowledge-creating that shapes the writing within a particular discipline. In addition, the emic, insider investigative role for the practitioner that Swales (2019) advocates is also important for actually understanding the type of knowledge-transforming required of particular assignments within a discipline. In the contributor studies, these types of understanding were achieved by the contributors interviewing subject tutors about their expectations of certain types of assignment task. The value of this activity is well illustrated by Montgomery's (Chapter 6) finding about the role of the dissertation genre in fine art for the creative exploration and development of ideas.

In relation to genre knowledge, EAP practitioners often have access to quite developed understandings of the generic and textual dimensions of writing, exemplified in the use by Burland et al. (Chapter 4) of Gardner and Nesi's (2012) classifications of *genre families* in the musicology chapter. However, two points need to be made about the use of genre theory in EAP. The first is its lack of construct validity. That is, there is currently no agreement among theorists from the different approaches to genre theory about the nature of the constructs that relate to the concept of genre. Secondly, it must be emphasized that any theory of genre used to unravel and support the teaching of disciplinary writing must be sufficiently powerful to account for the social, cognitive and linguistic dimensions of knowledge that are integrated when constructing and processing extended disciplinary texts. The implication of these two points is that thought needs to be given to the particular theory of genre that is used in an EAP investigation and, in particular, *how well* that theory operationalizes all of the areas of knowledge that are integrated within the type of disciplinary writing that is under investigation. While the main focus of the contributor studies in this volume have been on the emic dimension of disciplinary writing, I feel that there is still also a case for a fine-grained genre analysis of larger samples of the assignment genre texts that the contributors were examining. However, that type of project would require a separate series of studies that would be reported in another volume.

The third thematic area that relates to the EAP writing practitioner is that of textual meta-knowledge. Although for convenience I write about this as a separate area of knowledge here, it is inextricably bound up with the two other areas already discussed (contextual and generic). In relation to the writing tasks discussed by the subject lecturers in the contributors' interviews, this area received the least mention. Understandably, the focus of these interviews was more on the 'what' that is communicated through disciplinary writing rather than the 'how', which is reasonable given that none interviewed was a text linguist. However, important points are still raised about textual competence in the preceding chapters, such as by Maxwell (Chapter 3), who examined the requirements of writing in design where the subject lecturers identified 'ease of reading' of student texts as important. Similarly, in the study of the musicology texts, Burland et al. (Chapter 4) identified the expression of criticality as important. However, what the interviews cannot reveal is how these attributes are actually realized through texts. Swales (2019) in his essay suggests that 'more attention could be given to (a) syntactic and phraseological patterns and uses, and (b) to local cohesive elements that will increase the "flow" of student texts' (p. 81). Generally, Swales claims this textual dimension is a somewhat neglected area in the EAP research literature, although there has always been some work on Halliday's (1985) concept of theme and rheme and his approach to different types of cohesive device. However, when considering the design lecturer's comment that 'ease of reading' is an important attribute of academic assignments, it is important to understand that *coherence* as a property of texts goes beyond the mere use of cohesive devices. A cohesive device may be used to signal a coherence relation, such as in: *Because it was threatening rain, he took an umbrella.* However, readers can still retrieve the same causative relation if there is no cohesive device, merely through the juxtaposition of the two propositions. *It was threatening to rain. He took an umbrella.* I suggest that an element often missing in the teaching of academic writing is a lack of focus on *coherence relations* (Knott and Sanders 1998). Possible taxonomies of coherence relations that could be considered here are those of Crombie's (1985) *interpropositional relations*, Mann and Thompson's (1987) *rhetorical structure theory* and Kehler's (2001) work on discourse coherence. My particular view has always been that the devices that promote 'ease of reading' of texts will differ according to general rhetorical purpose and that groups of coherence relations (and the ways in which they are signalled linguistically) will tend to be related to a larger textual whole. For examples of the linking of clusters of coherence relations (and how they are linguistically encoded) to certain text types and genres, see the section *EAP and Textual Grammar* in my book (Bruce 2011: 84–100).

Conclusion

The purpose of the investigations reported in the contributor chapters in this volume has been to explore the requirements of 'good writing' as it occurs in the academic assignment genres of the different disciplinary areas investigated. The studies have involved eliciting the views, expectations and requirements of the academic staff teaching courses and assessing written assignments in each of these disciplinary areas. Overall, these studies have served to emphasize the complexity and multifaceted nature of disciplinary writing in terms of the different areas of knowledge that it draws upon – epistemological, generic and textual. The implications of these (and other) studies are the breadth of the knowledge base required for academic writing pedagogy and student writer knowledge, and the important role of the writing tutor as a researcher and investigator of disciplinary writing requirements, especially in relation to developing awareness of the epistemological elements and social and generic conventions of writing within particular disciplines. The studies reinforce the importance of this researcher/investigator role of the writing tutor and the need for this type of research that uncovers the key features of disciplinary discourse creation. These studies are small-scale and local but they raise important issues that could be further investigated through larger-scale, linked ethnographic and textual research studies.

References

Bhatia, V. K. (2004). *Worlds of Written Discourse: A Genre-Based View.* London: Bloomsbury Publishing.

Bowman, M. (2020). 'Good Academic Reflective Writing in Dentistry: An Analysis of Exemplary Student Texts'. *The Good Writing Project.*

Bruce, I. (2008). *Academic Writing and Genre: A Systematic Analysis.* Bloomsbury Publishing.

Bruce, I. (2011). *Theory and Concepts of English for Academic Purposes.* Basingstoke, England: Palgrave Macmillan.

Burland, K, Venn, E., and McLaughlin, S. (2020). Musicology and Its Others. *The Good Writing Project.*

Cohen, L., Manion, L., and Morrison, K. (2017). *Research Methods in Education* (8th ed). Routledge.

Ding, A., and Bruce, I. (2017). *The English for Academic Purposes Practitioner.* Palgrave Macmillan.

Cheng, A. (2019). 'Examining the "Applied Aspirations" in the ESP Genre Analysis of Published Journal Articles'. *Journal of English for Academic Purposes* 38: 36–47.

Crombie, W. (1985). *Process and Relation in Discourse and Language Learning.* Oxford University Press.

Gardner, S., and Nesi, H. (2012). 'A Classification of Genre Families in University Student Writing'. *Applied Linguistics* 34 (1): 25–52.

Godfrey, J., and Whong, M. (2020). 'EAP Research and Practice. A Collaborative Scholarship Model'. *The Good Writing Project.*

Halliday, M. A. K. (1985). *An Introduction to Functional Grammar*. Edward Arnold.

Kehler, A. (2002). *Coherence, Reference and the Theory of Grammar*. Stanford, CA: CSLI publications.

Knott, A., and Sanders, T. (1998). 'The Classification of Coherence Relations and Their Linguistic Markers: An Exploration of Two Languages'. *Journal of Pragmatics* 30 (2): 135–75.

Mann, W. C., and Thompson, S. A. (1987). 'Rhetorical Structure Theory: Description and Construction of Text Structures'. In *Natural Language Generation*, 85–95. Dordrecht: Springer.

Maxwell, C. (2020). 'Exploring Clarity in the Discipline of Design'. *The Good Writing Project*.

Montgomery, S. (2020). 'What's Good Writing in Fine Art? A Focus on Dissertations;. *The Good Writing Project*.

Nelson, D., and Brunetto, V. (2020). What Is Good Writing in Linguistics? *The Good Writing Project*.

Swales, J. M. (1998). *Other Floors, Other Voices: A Textography of a Small University Building*. Routledge.

Swales, J. M. (2019). The Futures of EAP Genre Studies: A Personal Viewpoint. *Journal of English for Academic Purposes* 38: 75–82.

Webster, S. (2020). 'The Written Discourse Genres of Digital Media Studies'. *The Good Writing Project*.

Widdowson, H. G. (1990). *Aspects of Language Teaching*. Oxford University Press.

Index

academic discourse 12, 31–2, 160, 163,
    165–6
academic literacy 11–12, 24, 35, 74, 83 n.1,
    113, 162, 165
    Academic Literacies Model 13, 21, 130
academic reflective writing (ARW) 7,
    111, 181–2, 184. *See also* reflective
    writing
    constraints to 113
    in dentistry/healthcare (study and
        results) 112–13, 184
    good ARW 117, 119–27
    insider identity 116
    interviews with markers 116
    levels of reflection 117–19, 122,
        125–7, 130
    linguistic features of tasks 127–8
    methodology 114
    participants recruitment 114, 116
    tasks 114–15
    textual analysis 116–17
    effective/less effective 128–9
academic writing, student 2–5, 9–10,
    43–4, 140, 144, 148
    characteristics 48, 51
    clarity (*see* clarity in writing)
    creativity (fresh approach) 137, 152
    for digital media studies (*see* digital
        media studies)
    EAP research on 14–19
    in English 68
    feedback 93, 101
    generic features of 174
    genres 32, 51, 136, 154
    journal articles 68, 79, 161
    practitioner's analysis of 19–23
    problems 14
    quality of 49–50
    research 23–4, 36–7
        developments 178
        implementations 179
    simplicity in writing 67–9

Allison, D. 137
applied linguistics 8, 159, 161, 166–8, 182
argument/argumentation 42, 46, 51, 78,
    80, 92, 97, 100–1, 104, 138, 154,
    163, 172, 185
    argumentative essay 42–3, 50, 83, 85–6,
        88, 90, 160
    coherent 91, 135, 175
    data-driven 166, 169–75
    evidence-based critical 159
    quality of 45
    in theoretical linguistics 164
    Wingate on 104
art and design courses 136–8, 152
    arts students 138, 160
arts-based writing 138
Arts, Humanities and Cultures Faculty
    Research Ethics Committee 87, 114
assignments 15–17, 35–7, 63, 69, 78, 180,
    189
    ARW 125–6, 128
    compulsory written 88–9, 181
    digital media studies 49, 185
    genre 180, 183–5, 187–8
    'instructors' writing 33
    PG 44–5
    successful 33
    transformative learning in 117
    UG 38–42
authorial voice in writing 8, 98, 101, 104,
    159, 166–9, 186
autonomous linguistic system 186

BALEAP (British Association of Lecturers
    in English for Academic Purposes)
    framework 57–8
Barnard, I. 57, 59
    on clarity 63, 69
    view on 'jargon' 60
Basturkmen, H. 14, 166
Bazerman, C. 12, 162
Belcher, D. 13, 15, 34

Bhatia, V. K. 17
    discursive competence 183–4, 186
    social competence 184
    textual competence 185, 187
Borg, E. W. 137, 140, 151
British Academic Written English
        (BAWE) corpus 15, 59

Cheng, A. 24, 179
Chomsky, N. 162–3, 171
clarity in writing 5–6, 22, 40, 51, 57–8, 180
    categories of 75–6
    clarity of expression 22, 59–60, 65, 73,
        75–6, 180–1
    design 58–9, 71, 75, 77
    explicitness 60, 71–3, 75, 180
    findings 63–74
        clarity of purpose 73–5, 180
        clarity of understanding (skills and
            knowledge) 69–72, 75–7, 79,
            180, 184
        ease of reading and language
            accuracy 60, 64–7, 72, 74, 180,
            188
        importance of clarity 63–4
        language complexity 67–9, 77, 180,
            185
        terminology 71–2, 77
    implications 78–80
    in language 59–60, 76, 185
    linguistic features 77, 111
    study of 61–3
        analysis of programme documents
            63
        context 61
        sample data set 61–2
        semi-structured interviews 62, 180
classroom practice, EAP 16, 24
cognitive-functional linguistics 163
cognitive genre 12
coherence 3–4
    coherence relations 188
collaborative scholarship model 4–5, 9,
        23–5, 179. *See also* scholarship
community 13, 44, 52
    academic 10, 21, 32, 35–6, 49, 85, 160,
        165
    community of practice 6, 96–7, 96 n.5,
        99–100, 104–5

discourse 12, 60, 96 n.5, 111, 114
    professional 49, 185
    scientific 162
conservative genre 17, 49
content specialists/tutors 4, 9–11,
        17–18, 21–4, 60. *See also* subject
        specialists/lecturers
    on clarity 57, 64
    interview-based research with 12
continuing professional development
        (CPD) 112
corpora/corpus 15, 59, 161, 167, 170
creativity (fresh approach) 24, 93, 94 n.3,
        137, 151, 153, 181
    creative genre 58, 91
    formatting 148
critical discourse analysis 13, 17
criticality 6, 24, 79, 99, 104, 138, 147, 160,
        164, 185, 188
    creative 93, 95–6, 98, 100, 103
    in music 87, 90–6, 181
        and musicological essay 92–4, 103
        within research report 94–6
critical reflection 91, 102, 124–5, 129
critical theory 13, 186
critical thinking 44, 51, 88, 91, 94, 138
cross-disciplinary discourse analysis 167
cross-disciplinary primary research 149,
        151

digital media studies 5, 31, 33–4, 179,
        184–5
    academic writing in 34–5
    research 35–6
        argumentative essay 42–5
        findings 37–8, 50–1
        limitations 52
        methods 36–7
        project 47
        reflective task 45–7
        reports 38–41
        research proposal assignment 42
    written discourse genres of 48–9
disciplinary genre 31–2, 52, 59, 138
discipline-specific orientation 1–2, 11, 13,
        20, 24, 31, 34, 159, 161, 169 n.1, 184
discourse coherence 188
discourse (discursive) competence 183–4,
        186

discourse genres 5, 31–2, 38, 50–2
  of digital media studies 48–9
discourse markers 74, 77
dissertation 6–7, 180
  dissertation–level student writing 61–2
  fine art (*see* fine art, dissertations in)
  genre 148–9, 152, 154
  linguistics (*see* linguistics, good writing in)
  qualitative 13, 15
  task 47, 63
distinction-level work 15–17, 16 n.1, 36–7
doctor of philosophy (PhD) dissertation 137, 151–2

Edwards, H. 138, 152, 155
Elkins, J. 137, 152
embedded approach 10–12, 23
emic approach 35, 179–80, 186–7
English for academic purposes (EAP) 1, 83 n.1, 178
  complexity of clarity 78
  courses 1, 78
  objective of 10
  pedagogy 9–12, 14, 16, 19, 23, 33, 50–2, 59, 84, 160, 166, 178–9, 183, 186, 189
  practitioners (*see* practitioner)
  research frameworks 12–14
    on academic writing 14–19
  specialists 2, 23–4, 144, 146, 155 (*see also* content specialists/tutors; subject specialists/lecturers)
  tutors 11, 23, 137
English for General Academic Purposes 1
English for Specific Academic Purposes 1
English for specific purposes (ESP) 9–10, 111, 114
  genre model 4, 12–13
  second-language writing in 32
error(s) 72, 92, 101, 128–9
  genre 18
  language 65–6, 68, 70, 76, 79
essay 15–16, 32, 49, 51, 103, 121, 181, 185
  academic 140
  argumentative 6, 35, 42–5, 48, 50, 83, 85–6, 88, 90
  discursive 17, 47, 88
  extended undergraduate 85

humanities 150
  musicological 91–5, 103
  traditional 85, 111, 130
ethical reasoning 120–2
evidence-based critical argumentation 159
evidence-based teaching pedagogy 33
excerpts from good writing 141, 144–5, 150, 166
  Relevance Theory 169
experimental linguistic writing 159, 166, 170–1, 182
experimental research method 20

feedback 14, 21, 78, 93, 101, 131, 140–1, 148, 151, 154, 165, 181
  formal assignment 36, 44, 63
  in higher education 102
fine art, dissertations in 7–8, 135, 182, 187
  artistic practice 7, 140, 148, 153
  methodology/study 139–40
    analysis of assessment rubric 145–6, 182
    face-to-face interviews 139
    features of language (excerpts) 144–5, 150
    results 147–50
    task (student writers) 140–1, 146, 150, 152, 154
    textual analysis of dissertation introductions 141–4, 153, 155
  practice-based fine art course 135–6, 139–40, 145, 151, 153–4
  purpose of writing 136–9, 151
  research questions 139, 147–8, 156
  studio practice 135–6, 147, 149–52, 154
  subject specialists in 139, 147–53, 155
  visual images 135, 153–4
Freadman, A. 18

Gardner, S. 12, 15–18, 21–2, 33, 93–4, 94 n.3, 103, 151, 181, 187
General Dental Council (GDC) 112, 120
genre model 93–4, 104, 183
  academic 10, 12, 33, 83 n.1, 180–1, 185
  assignment 180, 183–5, 187–8
  awareness of 50–1
  cognitive 12
  conservative 17, 49

creative 58, 91
disciplinary 31–2, 52, 59, 138
discourse (*see* discourse genres)
dissertation 148–9, 152, 154
EAP research on academic writing
    14–19, 32
ESP 4, 12–13
genre traps 18
industry-related 180, 184
liberal 17, 50
occluded 99, 102
professional 58, 91
research 97
social 12
traditional assessment 58, 136
traditional dissertation 61, 147, 151,
    153
writing 6, 32, 83, 85–6, 88, 90, 92, 96,
    103, 137, 152, 154
Gibbs, G. 117
Gibbs cycle 113, 117
good student writing 2–3, 5, 8, 18–19, 21,
    23, 43, 45. *See also* poor student
    writing
    clarity in (*see* clarity in writing)
    excerpts from 141, 144–5, 150
    in fine art (*see* fine art, dissertations in)
    in linguistics (*see* linguistics, good
        writing in)
    in music (*see* music, good writing in)

Haas, S. S. 152, 155
    'Advanced Engagement' 138
    Reader Engagement Framework 138
Halliday, M. A. K. 12, 188
hard discipline 159–61, 168, 170. *See also*
    soft discipline
Harper-Scott, J. P. E. 84–5, 88
higher education (HE) 7, 83, 91, 95,
    102–3, 151
    ARW in 111–12
    UK 6, 9, 11, 31, 35, 88 n.2
Hirvela, A. 13, 15
historical linguistics 170–1
humanities 6, 16, 34, 83–4, 87, 150,
    159–60
Huttner, J. 15, 21
Hyland, K. 13, 15, 21, 83, 104, 151, 166
    persuasive authority of impersonality
        164, 175

IMRD (Introduction-Methods-Results-
    Discussion) 170–1
industry-related genre 180, 184
institution-wide approach 2, 50
interdisciplinary nature of music 6, 93,
    104
International English Language Testing
    System (IELTS) writing 15
international students 1, 10–11, 154, 161,
    168, 170
Internet policy report 38, 49
interpropositional relations 188

knowledge-transforming process 184,
    186–7

language 39, 42, 49–50, 59, 62, 80, 113,
    138, 180
    accuracy 64–7, 76–7, 79
    clarity in 59–60, 76, 185
    complexity (over-complex) 67–9
    and content 79
    dissertations in fine art 144
    error 65–6, 68, 70, 76, 79
    linguistics (*see* linguistics, good writing
        in)
    meta-language 22–4, 77, 105, 165,
        178–9
    of student writers 145–6
    transparency of 59–60
    understanding (skills and knowledge)
        69–71
Lea, M. R. 13–14, 57, 78, 88, 100, 165
Lenze, L. F. 164
lexico-grammar 9, 13, 16, 22
liberal genre 17, 50
Lillis, T. 13–14, 59–60, 71
linguistics, good writing in 8, 10, 16, 22–3,
    52, 68, 159–60, 169 n.1, 182
    applied 8, 159, 161, 166–8, 182
    authorship/authorial identity 162, 164
    cognitive-functional 163
    dissertations 104, 161, 166, 168, 170–1,
        174
    excerpts from student 169
    experimental 159, 166, 170–1
    features 10, 23, 52, 68, 74, 76–80, 111,
        127–8, 161, 166
    historical 170–1
    language 162–3

'linguistics wars' 163
linguists 159–60, 162–4, 169, 175, 187
meta-linguistic clarity 104
obstacles 59–60, 64, 67
research 162, 165
as science 162–5
study 165–75
  authorial voice 8, 166–9, 186
  data-driven argumentation 166,
    169–75
  student writing 165–6
  sub-disciplines in 160, 170–2
  theoretical-descriptive 159, 161, 164,
    166–8, 170–5
literature review 32–5, 47, 58, 65, 71–2,
  166, 168
Luk, J. 116, 128

MacDonald, C. 12, 136–7, 140
  autography 136, 150
markers 4, 21, 58, 70, 76, 94, 117, 119–25,
  129–30, 181
  ability of 65–7
  criticality 104
  discourse 74, 77
  interviews with 116
  lexico-grammatical 22
marking policy 65
Matters around Art and Design
    Dissertation (MADD) website 138
Melzer, D. 15, 33
merit-level work 16, 16 n.1
meta-disciplinary groupings of music 84
meta-language 22–4, 77, 105, 165, 178–9
molecular biology 162
Moreda Rodríguez, Eva 85
Murray, N. 11, 21, 76, 78
music, good writing in 6, 149, 181, 187
  challenges for students 84, 87
  interdisciplinary nature of music 6,
    93, 104
  programmes for students 88–9, 91, 94
  rhetorical practices of 83, 85
  semi-structured interview 86–7, 181
    data on interview 108
    questions 108–9
  study and results 87–8, 90–103
  sub-disciplines 84–6, 88, 91–2, 94, 97,
    100–1, 103–4
    composition 84, 88, 90, 95

music management 88, 90
musicology 84–6, 88–90, 92–4, 102,
  181, 185
music psychology/therapy 6, 84,
  87–93, 97, 101–4, 163, 170
technology modules 94–5
thematic analysis technique 87, 181
  criticality (*see* criticality)
  finding voice 87, 90, 96–100
  teaching and learning good writing
    87, 90, 100–3

Nathan, P. B. 13, 17
Nesi, H. 12, 15–18, 21–2, 33, 93–4, 94 n.3,
  103, 151, 181, 187
new media 85
new media studies 33–4
North, S. 13, 160, 164

occluded genre 99, 102
originality 18, 94, 94 nn.3–4, 103, 151,
  164, 167

Paltridge, B. 13, 15, 20
pedagogical approach of EAP 9–12, 14, 16,
  19, 23, 33, 50–2, 59, 84, 160, 166,
  178–9, 183, 186, 189
person-oriented approach 164
philology, European 173 n.2
plain English 67–8
poor student writing 14, 18, 62, 64, 66,
  70, 72, 87. *See also* good student
  writing
postgraduate (PG) 3, 15, 31, 38, 44–7, 68,
  87, 104, 135, 139, 161, 165, 167, 181
  compulsory programmes in music
    88–9, 91, 94
  English-speaking UK students 171
practice-based fine art course 135–6,
  139–40, 145, 151, 153–4
practitioner 1–5, 9–14, 16–17, 31–4, 50–2,
  61, 72, 74, 78, 85, 112–13, 116, 128,
  161, 179, 181–4
  epistemologies 186, 189
  genre knowledge 186–7
  practitioner-led research 19–24, 31
  role of 58
  textual meta-knowledge 187
  themes and insights 186–8
professional academics in EAP 9, 14, 151

professional genre 58, 91
professional identity of students 113
psychological reality 163

Quality Assurance Agency (UK),
        'Characteristics Statement' 94

Raynaud's phenomenon 124–5
referencing, academic skills 41, 96, 135,
        149
Reflective Portfolio assessment 11, 140
reflective writing 111–13, 122, 125, 181.
        See also academic reflective writing
        (ARW)
    personal 112
    reflection 51, 84, 90, 98, 111–13, 121,
        147, 178–81
        critical 91, 102, 124–5, 129
        demonstrating 119–20
        digital media studies 45–7, 184
        disciplinary 85
        levels of reflection 116–19, 122,
            125–7, 130
        scientific 124
report, research 3, 5, 13, 17, 31, 38–41,
        48–51, 61, 74, 86, 94–6, 114, 164,
        168, 170–1, 178–81, 183–5, 187–8
research method 4, 36–7, 71, 135, 170–1,
        182
    cross-disciplinary primary research
        149
    experimental research method 20
    semi-structured interview 6, 36, 61–2,
        86–7, 136, 180–2
rhetorical structure theory 188
Ross, John 163
rubrics, assessment 7, 78, 136, 138–41,
        145–6, 182
    criteria for marking written tasks 145
Russell Group university 1, 61
Ryan, M. 112, 117, 128–9

Samraj, B. 14, 167
Samson, J. 84
scholarship 2–3, 9–10, 19–20, 139. *See also*
        collaborative scholarship model
second-language writing in ESP 32
semi-structured interview method 6, 36,
        61–2, 86–7, 136, 180–2

Sharpling, G. 11, 21, 76, 78
signposting 47, 96–8
smooth read ideology 60, 64, 76
social competence 184
social-constructivist approach 86
social genre 12
social science 5–6, 16–17, 34–5, 49, 52, 83,
        86, 90, 159–60, 165, 170, 182
sociolinguistics 160, 170–1
soft discipline 58, 159–62, 164. *See also*
        hard discipline
stance 43, 66, 70, 85, 99, 104, 167
St. John, M. J. 10
straightforward formatting 148
Street, B. 57, 78, 88, 100, 165
Street, B. V. 13–14
structure 11, 17, 22, 47, 78, 80, 96, 100–1,
        113, 138, 171
    genre 32–3, 50
    industry-standard (assignment) 40
    and style (surface features) 97–9
    systematic 13
student writers/writing 7, 24, 57, 136, 138,
        160, 185
    ability 24, 49, 68–70, 78, 91, 152
    artistic practice 7, 140, 148, 151, 153
    ARW 112–14, 120, 123–7, 129–31
    dissertations in fine art (*see* fine art,
        dissertations in)
    excerpts from 141, 144–5, 150, 166,
        169
    feedback for (*see* feedback)
    in linguistics 165–6, 168
    Reader Engagement Framework 138
    studio practice 135–7, 140, 142,
        147–55
    themes and insights 183–6
style, writing 8, 43–4, 67, 85, 97–100, 102,
        141–2, 144–5, 149, 152, 160, 165,
        170, 185
    and content 25
    direct 142, 144, 155
    simpler 69
    textual 166
subject specialists/lecturers 1–7, 12, 18,
        23–5, 31, 33, 35–42, 44–52, 74, 131,
        155. *See also* content specialists/
        tutors
    assessment rubrics 145

in fine art 139, 147–53, 155
on language 67, 150
semi-structured interviews of 61–2, 64–5
simplicity in writing 67–9
on terminology 72
traditional dissertation genre 147–8
Swales, J. 12–13, 179, 187–8

tacit knowledge 57
Tardy, C. 138, 144
Tardy, C. M. 14, 17–18, 21
Teaching Excellence Framework 11
terminology 4, 9, 60, 69, 71–2, 77, 114, 159, 162, 172, 175, 180, 185
textual competence 185, 187
thematic analysis technique in music 87, 181
    criticality 87, 90–6
    finding voice 87, 90, 96–100
    teaching and learning good writing 87, 90, 100–3
theoretical-descriptive linguistic writing 159, 161, 164, 166–8, 170–5, 182

traditional assessment genres 58, 136
traditional dissertation genre 61, 147, 151, 153
Tribble, C. 13–14, 17, 37
Turner, J. 13, 59–60, 66
    smooth read ideology 64, 76

UK EAP 10–11
undergraduate (UG) 8, 11, 15, 31, 43, 84–8, 91, 112, 159, 161, 167–8, 185
usage-based linguistics 163

Wingate, U. 10–14, 17, 22–3, 90
    argumentation 104
    formal schemata 96
    structure and style (surface features) 97–8
writing genres 6, 32, 83, 85–6, 88, 90, 92, 96, 103, 137, 152, 154
'Writing-PAD'-Writing 137–8

year-round teaching 1

Printed in Great Britain
by Amazon

51319760R00117